# THE POTATO YEAR

*365 ways of cooking potatoes*

LUCY MADDEN

Published by Milu Press, 1997

ISBN 0-9525348-0-0



Printed by R & S Printers, Monaghan, Ireland

SOLANUM
TUBEROSUM

# ACKNOWLEDGMENTS

There are so many people who have helped with the production of this book to whom I truly owe thanks. I've discovered that the potato is a great leveller and the very mention of this book has struck a responsive culinary chord in all sorts of gatherings while I have been collecting and collating potato recipes.

Heartfelt thanks are due to An Bord Glas for the help and patience they have shown over the years of putting this book together. I'd also like to thank my daughter Amelia Raben for her work on the manuscript, Peter Bland for his illustrations, Mike O'Toole for his photography and exceptional patience, Brenda Dermody, Pat Scott, the Smyth family of Monaghan, Roberta Reeners and of course my husband Johnny for stoically eating his way through numerous potato dishes, sacrificing his waistline in the process.

Where possible specific credits appear through the book but I would like gratefully to acknowledge and thank the following for their kind permission to reprint copyright material:- Cambridge University Press for extracts from 'The History and Social Influence of the Potato' by Redcliffe Salaman, published 1949; the Estate of James Joyce for a quote from 'The Dead'; Peters, Fraser and Dunlop Group Ltd. for 'Giving Potatoes' by Adrian Mitchell from 'Nothingmas Day', published 1984, and for a line from 'Blazing Fruit' by Roger McGough, published 1991; Faber and Faber for an excerpt from 'Seeing Things' by Seamus Heaney, published 1991, Jill Norman for the lines from 'An Omelette and a Glass of Wine' by Elizabeth David, published 1989; Curtis Brown for an extract from 'Some Experiences of an Irish R.M.' by E.OE. Somerville and Martin Ross, published 1899; the trustees of the Estate of Patrick Kavanagh, c/o Peter Fallon, Literary Agent, Loughcrew, Oldcastle, Co. Meath, Ireland for extracts from 'Tarry Flynn', published 1948, and 'A Soul for Sale',1947; Sophie Grigson for an extract from 'Jane Grigson's Fruit Book', published 1991; Michael Joseph Ltd. for extracts from 'The Ladies of Llangollen, a Study in Romantic Friendship' by Elizabeth Mavor, published 1971; Elizabeth

Lambert Ortiz for extracts from 'The Book of Latin American Cookery', published 1969 and Professor Kevin Whelan of the Royal Irish Academy for material from the Thomas Davis Lecture series.

Unfortunately I have not been able to credit some of the original writers of the recipes since some of these I have been unable to trace. Many of the recipes in this book were sent to me, hand-written but relayed from books and magazines over the years by friends and often the original sources of the recipes were lost. For omissions I am sorry.

# INTRODUCTION

This book is the result of a long love affair with the world's favourite vegetable. It was not love at first sight. Potatoes are history made manifest, but their charms are not obvious ones. The poor modest potato, the most democratic of vegetables, seen everywhere yet so often misunderstood and unappreciated.

I only have to think of the potatoes of my youth in the 1950s in London - soggy, and often discoloured nonentities that shared plates with meat and greens. English cuisine had managed to adopt pasta (how else Macaroni Cheese?), but where were the gratins, the potages, the soufflées and salads that the French had created for the potato? I once came across a dish called 'Pommes à l'Anglaise' in a French cookery book to discover with shame that the potatoes were boiled and served 'as a garnish for boiled fish'. Marie Antoinette had worn potato flowers in her hair; it was impossible to imagine any of our Queens similarly coiffured. Even our ubiquitous chip had been invented in France.

It was then, with high expectations that I came 20 years ago to live in Ireland, the land of the potato. Perhaps here I would discover ways of cooking potatoes that would make palatable something that was intrinsically dull. And true, traditional Irish food had evolved delightful dishes out of potatoes. I knew because I had read about them but where were the dishes of yesterday, the Boxty, Champ and Colcannon, the potato breads and cakes but between the pages of a book? Certainly they were not to be found in public places, and rarely in private houses.

How, then, was it that the Incas had deemed this vegetable so worthy of respect that they were prepared to kill each other in order to nourish it? In their art they celebrated the potato with the bizarre and often monstrous clay potato pots moulded into human forms that were often mutilated, sometimes sexually explicit. Elaborate rites and festivals surrounded the growing and harvesting of the plant.

Brought to Europe by a Spaniard from its place of origin in the High Andes, the potato has found its way all round the world. It is not just the most consumed vegetable in Europe and the United States, but it is grown widely in the Far East and Africa.

Since the days of Shakespeare and Ben Johnson the potato has been lauded in literature and heralded in song. Artists (albeit a few) painted it. Poems are written in praise of it. A whole folklore has grown up around the plant.

Here too, is a vegetable whose contribution to world events is far more than just a food source but one that can truly be said to have changed the course of history. In Ireland it played its most consequential role. The potato flourished in the damp, peaty soils of Ireland and eliminated the old enemy, hunger, for generations of peasants afflicted by chronic poverty.

The writing of this book coincided with the 150th anniversary of the Great Potato Famine of 1845-46, that calamitous failure of the potato crop which reduced the population of Ireland by some $2^1/_2$ million. Even today the effects of that catastrophe are incalculable, yet it is undeniable that the resulting diaspora into the United States has had a profound effect on the last 150 years of that country as well as Ireland and England.

The potato, then, has become a part of our civilisation. An invaluable food source, yes, but also a part of our culture, our folklore and our social fabric.

But what of our tables? My own interest in cooking potatoes evolved from the restoration of a large and neglected Victorian walled garden where I made my first attempts at growing potatoes. At the same time we began here in County Monaghan to run my husband's old family home as a hotel. Visitors from all over the world brought new information and ideas about potatoes. I learned that they are cooked in pine resin in Virginia, U.S.A and deep fried in beer batter in Australia. The Chinese make nests of them, the Japanese eat them with a peanut sauce. From the Continent I discovered the cream laden and garlic spiked gratins, little pancakes flavoured with cinnamon and honey, the Latkes of Jewish cookery, the joy and infinite variety of potato soups, salads pungent with oils, garlic and herbs. Why on earth had so many of us just been boiling them for so many years?

But attitudes to potatoes were changing, in the late 1970s and 1980s gourmets began to take them more seriously, but the relationship was a troubled one. There was the underlying suspicion that potatoes were not in spirit with the whole *nouvelle cuisine* movement - too fattening, too common? - and when they did appear it was almost fancifully in miniature on a moon-shaped plate shared with other vegetable artwork.

Then, miraculously, in the early 1990s, potatoes became fashionable. Restaurants in the world's smartest capitals began to feature them with pride. Food writers wrote about them. The gardening columns were devoted to the different varieties and ways of growing them. We could eat them again. Potatoes were 'in'.

In this book I have collected together some of the ways of cooking potatoes that my family and I have loved best. A few recipes I have included for their curiosity value. The idea of producing a book in calendar form came to me having heard friends complain that the very over-availability of choice numbs the mind. How to single out one dish with so much from which to pick? Thus it is that each day in this book has a different suggestion using ingredients that are available at that time of year. One of the charms of the potato is its changing form throughout the year. How different is the sturdy generosity, the firm-textured masculinity of the winter crop to the delicate, more ephemeral delights of the summer's offerings.

As far as quantities in this book are concerned, the recipes, will serve 4 average appetites, unless otherwise stated. But what is average? What is an adequate portion to one person is another's appetiser.

Potatoes are indeed treasures of the earth. So yes, a love letter to the potato is well in order - lovely potatoes, how versatile, how prolific, how pleasurable and inspirational you are. What other food can provide such epicurean delights when, fresh from the soil, steamed in its own skin and unadorned by artifice, can also lend itself to an infinite variety of disguises and culinary uses?

I ask you, what plant is as nutritional, as adaptable to different conditions in growing or cooking or is just as utterly beautiful as the potato?

# CHOOSING AND COOKING POTATOES

There are two main schools of potato eaters; those who prefer the waxy variety and those who prefer the floury kind. The latter group predominates, particularly in Ireland.

In potato cookery both schools are accommodated. Floury potatoes are best for baking, mashing and chipping while the waxy varieties are more suitable for sautéeing and salads. Which kind you prefer for boiling and steaming is a matter for personal preference and to some extent, nationality. Only in Ireland have I met the bursting, dry mouthful of perfection that is Kerr's Pinks or Golden Wonder. The English prefer their potatoes wetter and waxier. This soapiness is disdained in Ireland.

It is the dry matter that is the key to taste and quality in potatoes. An Bord Glas, the Horticultural Board in Ireland carried out research into this recently and Golden Wonder was found to have the highest dry matter content and Cara the lowest. For Vitamin C, Kerr's Pink had the highest mean and Record and Pentland Dell the lowest. For 'flouriness' Golden Wonder and Kerr's Pink did best with Cara found to be the 'soapiest'.

But 'horses for courses' and every potato variety will have its devotee. Even the "I'm a meat and potato man" will have his own particular favourite. Potato buyers are becoming very discerning. At a large supermarket in Dublin recently I found thirteen different varieties on sale. The days are past when greengrocers asked 'Reds or Whites?' and one was given a bagful of earth that hid all sorts of unpleasantnesses.

If you are going to grow potatoes buy fresh, certified seed potatoes every year rather than saving them from last year's crop which increases the risk of virus disease. Buying unusual seed varieties is becoming easier and if unusual varieties are what you want, you may have to grow them for yourself because unfortunately some of the 'connoisseur' kinds are commercially not viable - the curvaceous and excellent Pink Fir Apple, for example, is difficult to harvest because of its small knobbly shape and is susceptible to disease. Potato growing, however, is a joy and nothing compares to the pleasure of pushing back the earth in early summer to reveal the little waiting tubers. More than this, though, it is vital that the home growers help to keep alive the old and more exotic varieties that the commercial growers can't - or won't - produce.

It is not given to many people in this world to be able to go to the garden when potatoes are needed. Most of us must depend on what is supplied locally, and what is supplied locally will largely depend on demand, so by demanding different kinds the news will filter back to the growers.

There are just a few rules to remember with potatoes. Don't refrigerate them, they become sweet. Since the nutrients lie under the skin, only peel if necessary. Peeled potatoes turn brown through oxygenation, so cook them at once or keep them for a few hours, if necessary, in cold water. Potatoes should be clean and free of disease and never greened by exposure to the light. Do not eat green potatoes. Buy new potatoes in very small quantities since they don't store well. Don't keep cooked potatoes for re-use longer than 24 hours.

I prefer to steam potatoes rather than boil them, although this means sacrificing the potato water which can be used for stocks and sauces. When cooking potatoes for puréeing, I cut them into small even-sized pieces which speeds up the process and ensures that the potatoes cook evenly. The recipes in this book do not mention which variety is most suitable to which dish because often those varieties are not available. When a recipe calls for a new potato, I have said so. 'New' potatoes are not necessarily special varieties as all types of potato can be bought as 'new' early enough in their season. Potatoes divide into 'earlies' and 'maincrop'; here is a list of some of the better known types of potato available in Ireland and the uses to which they can be put.

# POTATO VARIETIES

## BOILED OR STEAMED

Earlies: Home Guard, British Queen, Wilja, Balmoral, Pink Fir Apple
Maincrop: Kerr's Pink, Golden Wonder, King Edward, Cara, Maris Piper, Rooster, Cultra, Pimpernel

## JACKET BAKED

Cara, Desiree, King Edward, Maris Piper, Pentland Dell, Rooster, Pimpernel, Golden Wonder, Romano, Kerr's Pink, Balmoral, Cultra, Pentland Squire

## PURÉED

Golden Wonder, Maris Piper, Kerr's Pink, King Edward, Pimpernel, Pentland Dell

## DEEP FRIED

Earlies: Home Guard, British Queen, Wilja, Ulster Sceptre
Maincrop: Desiree, Golden Wonder, King Edward, Kerr's Pink, Record, Pentland Dell, Cara

## SALAD

Earlies: Most early potatoes such as Wilja, La Ratte, Belle de Fontenay and Pink Fir Apple.
Maincrop: Rooster, Cultra, Desiree and Golden Wonder

## ROASTING

Cara, Desiree, Golden Wonder, Rooster, King Edward, Maris Piper

NEW YEAR'S DAY

# DUBLIN CODDLE

A complete meal, said to have been much favoured by Dean Swift. The basic ingredients are the potatoes, sausages and bacon but you can improvise with what you have to hand. Sometimes I add root vegetables such as parsnips or turnips and always a handful of fresh herbs. Some might regard any departure from the traditional ingredients as sacrilege.

1 1/2 lb (700g) potatoes, peeled and quartered
1 lb (450 g) thick sausages, cut in half
3/4 lb (350 g) gammon or bacon
2 large onions
Parsley
Sea salt and freshly ground black pepper

Trim any fat from the gammon and place in a large saucepan with the onions. Cover with water and bring to the boil and simmer for 20 minutes. Add the sausages and the potatoes. Add the seasonings (I always include a couple of bay leaves).

Cook until the potatoes are soft, but not disintegrating. Sprinkle with chopped parsley.

*An Anthology of the Potato, a book of poetry by Robert McKay, was published in Dublin in 1916.*

## 2 JANUARY
## ST BERCHTOLD'S DAY, SWITZERLAND
# ROSTI

This recipe has been given to me by a Swiss friend who assures me that in Switzerland the reputation of a restaurant can rise or fall on its skills with Rosti.

You will need a grater with large holes and a frying pan. In the old days, each Swiss housewife would keep a heavy cast-iron pan solely for making Rosti and omelettes and would wipe it clean with salt. A large non-stick frying pan will serve, but a lid is an essential.

The ingredients are 3 lb (1.4kg) of potatoes, peeled and cooked the day before they are to be eaten. A waxy type of potato is preferable and they should be left slightly underdone.

Grate the potatoes. In the pan heat plenty of butter (or you can use oil, or oil and butter, or lard), add the potatoes, cover with the lid and cook for 2 minutes.

Remove the lid, sprinkle with salt and 1 or 2 tablespoons of water. Cover with the lid again.

Cook for another 2 minutes, remove the lid and gently turn over the cake. Continue this 2 minute rhythm of turning over the Rosti until the potatoes are well fried. Then press the potatoes down and slightly away from the edge of the pan shaping them into a flat 'cake'. Turn up the heat and let a brown crust develop. Add fresh butter around the sides.

Cover the Rosti with a warmed plate and invert the pan onto the plate to serve so that the brown crust is uppermost.

*"The scrofulous are common in Switzerland, where the people support themselves above all on potatoes. I am persuaded, myself, that the scrofulous troubles which prevail in our Cantons are entirely the result of this harmful dietary and the absence of exercise."*

*Daniel Langhaus, a Swiss physician, writing in 1768.*

3 JANUARY
FEAST OF SAINT GENEVIÈVE,
PATRON SAINT OF PARIS

# POTATOES À LA PARISIENNE

These are normally served as a garnish. We like them so well, we cannot be so restrained with them. Obviously, amounts here will depend on your appetite for these little golden balls. Meat jelly is a prerequisite of a well-stocked kitchen. It is obtained by pouring, into a small jar, the fats and meat juices left in a roasting tin after the cooked meat has been removed. This is then put into the fridge to solidify. The cold fats are then removed, leaving the intensely flavoured meat juices at the bottom.

Large potatoes
Butter
A little concentrated meat jelly
Chopped parsley

Using a round vegetable scooping spoon, cut out perfect little balls from the potatoes. What is left can be used for soup.

Heat the butter in a large sauté pan and cook the potato balls until golden all over. Add the meat jelly and sprinkle with the parsley. Eat at once.

*In 1771, the potato was regarded with such suspicion that the French government asked the Medical Faculty of Paris to investigate it. Their opinion was that it was a most beneficial and healthy food.*

4 JANUARY
WASSAIL EVE

# POTATO AND CHERVIL SOUP

As long as the winter is not too severe, chervil seems to survive outside from the previous summer's sowing; as an insurance, I keep a patch of it for over-wintering in the greenhouse.

1lb (450 g) potatoes, peeled and roughly quartered
2 fat bunches of chervil
$^1/_4$ pint (150 ml) cream
Salt and freshly ground black pepper

Cut the stalks off the chervil leaves, tie in a bunch and chop the leaves. Put the potatoes into a pan with the stalks, half the chopped leaves, the seasoning and enough water to cover. Bring to the boil and simmer until the potatoes are very soft. Remove the stalks and liquidize.

Reheat the soup gently, add the cream and more black pepper, taking care not to let the soup boil. Lastly, add the remaining chopped chervil leaves.

*"Let the sky raine potatoes."*
*Falstaff in* ***The Merry Wives of Windsor.***

5 JANUARY

# SNOW POTATOES

We have inherited a very old potato press which is seemingly indestructible. If you don't have a potato press (they can be obtained at good kitchen shops) a strong sieve will do the job well. Only floury potatoes are suitable for this dish.

$1^1/_2$ lb (700 g) potatoes
Butter to taste

Boil the potatoes with very little water until soft. Strain and make sure they are as dry as possible. Put them through the potato press or sieve onto a warmed serving plate. Have the butter ready heated and pour over the potatoes. Eat at once. Butter amounts will depend on your personal preferences.

*" 'My belief is ,' said Tracey savagely, 'that music's a fashion, and as delusive a growth as Cobbett's potatoes, which will go back to the deadly nightshade, just as music will go back to the tom-tom.' "*

*From* ***Sandra Belloni*** *by George Meredith, 1864.*

## 6 JANUARY
## TWELFTH NIGHT
# POTATO PIZZA

Tonight Befana, the good fairy of Italian children, comes to fill their stockings with toys and sweets. The ubiquitous pizza, beloved of children everywhere, is, I think, enhanced by the addition of potato. This makes a fairly substantial dish that will feed 4-6 people.

6 oz (175 g) potatoes, boiled and puréed
1lb (450 g) plain flour
1 sachet of Fast-Action yeast
6 fl oz (175 ml) water saved from cooking potatoes
1 teaspoon salt
4 fl oz (100 ml) olive oil
2 tins tomatoes, drained and chopped
8 oz (225 g) mozzarella cheese, sliced
1 tin anchovies, each fillet halved
Dried oregano or basil

If you have a food processor, life in the kitchen is simple. Put the flour, yeast, water, salt, potatoes, and olive oil into the bowl and mix until the dough is silky and elastic. Without a food processor, the mixing will have to be done by hand and takes longer, adding the liquid ingredients to the dry ones and working until the dough is pliable.

With Fast-Action yeast, only one proving is necessary. Press the dough out onto a greased tin, cover with a clean cloth and leave in a warm place to rise. This should take an hour or two.

Arrange the tomatoes, cheese and anchovies on the pizza base. Sprinkle with the herbs and leave for a further 15 minutes. Put in a hot oven(gas mark 8/450°/230°C) and bake for 20 minutes. Eat as soon as it leaves the oven.

*"This swelling bursting vegetable flesh always devising new forms and yet so chaste. I love a potato because it speaks to me."*

*From **The Tin Drum** by Gunter Grass, 1959.*

## 7 JANUARY

# OHIO PUDDING

Although this is like a suet pudding, it contains no fat at all and is most welcome on a cold winter day. Grate the vegetables very finely or there will not be enough moisture to bind the ingredients together.

4 oz (110 g) finely grated raw potato, peeled
4 oz (110 g) plain flour
1 level teaspoon baking powder
1/2 level teaspoon salt
1/2 level teaspoon bicarbonate of soda
4 oz (110 g) granulated sugar
4 oz (110 g) finely grated raw carrot
6 oz (175 g) seedless raisins

Sift the flour, baking powder, salt and bicarbonate of soda. Add the sugar, then the potato, carrots and raisins.

Put into a well-greased pudding basin, cover with greaseproof paper well tied with string or, better still, a pudding cloth, and steam for 2 hours.

*"All the evidence, including, as we shall see, the personal testimony of Clusius, is that Peru was the native home of the potato."*

*From **The History and Social Influence of the Potato** by Redcliffe Salaman, 1949.*

8 JANUARY

# SKY AND EARTH

The combination of potatoes and apples is a harmonious one; in Germany the two are puréed together, sprinkled with breadcrumbs and, traditionally, served with pickled blood sausage. Here the apples and potatoes are kept separate.

2 lb (900 g) potatoes, peeled
2 large cooking apples (or 3-4 pears)
$^1/_4$ pint (150 ml) warm milk
4oz (110 g) butter
Sea salt and freshly ground black pepper
2 oz (50 g) sugar
1 tablespoon oil
1 medium onion, sliced
1 lb (450 g) sausages

Cook the potatoes in a little water until tender. Meanwhile remove the core from the apples, peel them and cut in half. Cook gently with 2 oz (50 g) of the butter, the sugar and a little water, until they are just soft and retain their shape. The water will evaporate leaving a buttery sauce.

Drain the potatoes and make a purée with the warm milk and 2oz (50 g) of the butter. Season. Heat the oil and fry the onion. Remove from the pan and keep warm. Fry the sausages. On a warmed serving dish, first put the potato purée, cover with the onion and surround with the sausages and warm apples.

*"Mashed potatoes cannot hurt you darling*
*Mashed potatoes mean no harm*
*I have bought you mashed potatoes*
*From my mashed potato farm."*

*From* ***Giving Potatoes*** *by Adrian Mitchell.*

# 9 JANUARY
# CHOCOLATE AND HAZELNUT REFRIGERATOR CAKE

This is a rich dense cake. The recipe was given to me by *An Bord Glas*, Ireland's Horticultural Development Board.

4 oz (110 g) cold mashed potato
2 oz (50 g) hazelnuts
4 oz (110 g) plain chocolate
4 oz (110 g) butter
1 egg
1 oz (25 g) sugar
1 teaspoon instant coffee
1 teaspoon vanilla essence
2 oz (50 g) glacé cherries
4 oz (110 g) crushed biscuit crumbs

Roast the hazelnuts for a few minutes, remove the skins by rubbing in a clean cloth and chop roughly.

Melt the chocolate in a basin over a pan of hot water. As soon as it is melted, remove from the heat. Melt the butter.

Beat the egg with the sugar, coffee and vanilla essence. Stir in the butter and the chocolate, then the hazelnuts and glacé cherries and finally the potatoes and crushed biscuits. Press into a small, greased loaf tin and put in the refrigerator for at least 2 hours. Turn out and serve in thin slices.

*"Potatoes...the inestimable gift to the numerous class of the needy, which was to have the greatest influence on Man, his liberty and happiness."*

*From* ***Tableau de Paris, Volume IV, 1782-88,*** *by Mercier, dramatist and critic.*

10 JANUARY

# LETTUCE AND POTATO SOUP WITH SALMON QUENELLES

This is a beautiful soup; a coming together of foods that have a natural affinity for each other. This amount will serve 6 people.

4 medium potatoes, peeled and cut into matchsticks
2 heads of lettuce, cleaned and cut into strips
1 shallot, finely chopped
2 oz (50 g) butter
$2^1/_2$ pints (1.4 litres) chicken stock
15 fl oz (400 ml) cream

For the quenelles:
11 oz (310 g) salmon
1 egg white
10 fl oz (275 ml) cream

For the quenelles, put the salmon flesh (it must be totally free of bone and skin) into a food processor with the egg white and half the cream and whisk until the mixture is very smooth. Pass through a sieve and put into the fridge for at least an hour. 10 minutes before you cook the quenelles, stir in the rest of the cream.

Blanch the cut potatoes in salted water for 3-5 minutes until just tender. Drain and refresh in cold water and put aside.

Cook the lettuce with the shallots in the melted butter, keeping back about a quarter as decoration. Allow to cook very gently for about 5 minutes and then cover with the stock and the cream. Bring to the boil and then simmer for a half-hour. Put the broth through a sieve or food processor but don't over-process - the soup is more visually appealing if still flecked with green.

Make the quenelles by poaching little teaspoonfuls of the salmon mixture in boiling salted water - they will take minutes to cook and will float to the surface when ready. Take them out with a slotted spoon and serve in the soup with the matchstick potatoes and decorated with the remaining thin strips of lettuce.

*"If beef's the King of Meat,*
*Potato's the Queen of the Garden World..."*
*Old Irish Saying.*

## 11 JANUARY

# HAZELNUT POTATO CROQUETTES

Almonds can be used here, instead of hazelnuts, but I think less successfully.

1 lb (450 g) potatoes
4 oz (110g) hazelnuts
2 small egg yolks
Sea salt and freshly ground pepper
1 oz (25 g) butter
A little hot milk

Roast the hazelnuts for a few minutes in a very hot oven. Rub the skins off the hazelnuts in a clean tea towel. Chop them finely. Peel and boil the potatoes, dry and purée. Add the egg yolks, seasonings, butter and milk and then form into little cylinder shapes.

Roll in the nuts and fry in clarified butter or, best of all, hazelnut oil.

*"We being on land, the people came down to us to the water side with shew of great curtesie, bringing to us potatoes, rootes, and two very fat sheep."*

*Sir Francis Drake, writing in his journal off the coast of Chile in November 1577.*

## 12 JANUARY

# ALICE B. TOKLAS POTATOES

This is very self-indulgent and wonderful. It must have been served to Picasso and Hemingway who were regular guests of Alice B. Toklas and her companion Gertrude Stein in pre-war Paris. The recipe is as she wrote it.

"Bake four large potatoes, peel them and put through the food mill. While the potatoes are still hot, add two cups of butter and one teaspoon of salt. Undoubtedly 1 lb of butter is extravagant but try it once."

*The Potato Museum in Washington D.C. was run by Tom and Meredith Hughes. It was from here that they hosted a 'Potato Eaters' Night' once a week and each guest had to bring a potato dish, anything from starters to desserts.*

## 13 JANUARY

## CANUTE'S DAY, SWEDEN

# JANSSON'S TEMPTATION

This is a famous Swedish dish, but not one for slimmers. Theories conflict about its origin. One account has the eponymous Jansson, one Erik Jansson, a deeply religious man who was forbidden any enjoyment by his church. He succumbed, however, to one temptation and his name was thus immortalised. Another version attributes the dish to a Swedish opera singer called Adolf Janzen, a socially ambitious fellow who liked to give his sophisticated friends food with a peasant origin.

$1^1/_2$ lb (700 g) potatoes, peeled and finely sliced
2 large onions, peeled and finely sliced
2 tins anchovy fillets
$^3/_4$ pint (400 ml) cream
Freshly ground black pepper
A little butter

You will need a gratin dish and some foil. Layer the potatoes and the onions with the anchovies in the dish, peppering as you go. Finish with potatoes on the top layer.

Pour over $^1/_2$ the cream and a little of the anchovy oil. Dot with a little butter if you like. Cover with the foil and cook in a hot oven for 20 minutes. Then pour in the rest of the cream and turn the heat down low. The potatoes will take another hour to cook. Remove the foil for the last 10 minutes.

*"I have fine potatoes,*
*Ripe potatoes!*
*Will your Lordship please to taste a fine potato?*
*'Twill advance your wither'd state.*
*Fill your honour full of noble itches."*

*From* ***The Loyal Subject*** *by John Fletcher, 1617.*

## 14 JANUARY

# POTATO, FISH AND LEEK SALAD

Perhaps smoked fish, such as haddock, is best for this warm salad, but I have made it with baby squid cooked in garlic, and also monkfish or little pieces of salmon seasoned with lemon juice. Lamb's lettuce can occasionally be bought, but I grow it in the garden (it seeds itself) and eat it as a salad during the winter months.

1 lb (450 g) waxy potatoes, peeled
1 lb (450 g) leeks, as small as possible and cleaned
1 lb (450 g) fish, fresh or smoked
2 shallots
2 tablespoons of lemon juice
6 tablespoons of hazelnut oil
Sea salt and freshly ground black pepper
A large handful of lamb's lettuce

Cut the potatoes and leeks into inch-size pieces, and steam. Keep warm. Cut the fish in little pieces, then steam. This will take a few minutes. Mix the very finely chopped shallots with the lemon juice, oil and seasoning.

Put the vegetables and fish on individual plates with a few leaves of lamb's lettuce. Heat the dressing and pour over. Eat at once.

*"The very general use which is made of Potatos (sic) in these Kingdoms as food for man, is a convincing proof that the prejudices of a nation, with regard to diet, are by no means unconquerable..."*

*Adam Smith, writing in 1773.*

## 15 JANUARY

# POTATO JAM

It must be admitted, no-one is going to reach over pots of apricot or raspberry jam or fresh strawberry conserve to get at a pot of potato jam but no doubt, like everything else,it has its devotees.

2 lb 12 oz ( 1.250 kg) potatoes
4 oz (110 g) mixed glacé fruit
2 tablespoons rum
2 lb 4 oz (1 kg) sugar
1 sachet of vanilla sugar (available at good grocers)
1 tablespoon orange flower water

Soak the glacé fruit for two hours in the rum. Peel the potatoes and cook until tender in water. Drain, reserving about $^1/_2$ pint (275 ml) of the cooking water and purée the potatoes. Make a syrup with the water and the sugar. Add the purée and cook over a gentle heat for about 30 minutes until the jam becomes transparent.

Remove from the heat and add the fruit, rum and orange flower water and put into clean pots. The jam should keep up to 3 months in the fridge.

*"It all started yesterday evening*
*as I was helping the potatoes*
*off with their jackets..."*

*From **Blazing Fruit** by Roger McGough, 1991.*

16 JANUARY

# POTATO BREAD ROLLS

Eat these buttery little rolls warm from the oven with honey for breakfast or with cheese and soup for lunch.

7 oz (200 g) warm, mashed potatoes
$^1/_2$ pint (275 ml) milk
1 lb 6 oz (625 g) plain flour
2 teaspoons salt
2 teaspoons sugar
1 sachet Quick-Action yeast
8 oz (225 g) butter, melted
Beaten egg
Poppy seeds (optional)

If you have a food processor, the preparation of these rolls is simple - all the hard work is done by the machine.

Scald the milk, allow it to cool until lukewarm. Sift the flour and salt into the potato, stir in the sugar and then sprinkle with the yeast.

Pour in the lukewarm milk and the melted butter and stir or process until the dough is formed. Knead until silky and elastic, then put into a clean bowl, cover with cling film or a cloth and leave in a warm place to rise until the mixture has nearly tripled in volume.

Knock back the dough and with floured hands make into about 16 little rolls. Place on a greased baking sheet, leave to rise for another half hour, then paint with the beaten egg and the poppy seeds and bake at gas mark 6/400°F/200°C for about 15-20 minutes until lightly browned.

*Bringing a shipload of potatoes back to Queen Elizabeth, Sir Francis Drake was faced with an outbreak of scurvy on his ship. His wise Captain-at Arms fed the sailors on raw potatoes, and so saved their lives.*

17 JANUARY

# CREAM OF POTATO SOUP WITH SCALLOPS

Scallops are not easy to find, but their delicate sea flavour makes a search worthwhile. They are expensive, but served in a soup can add an extravagant touch to more homely food.

3/4 lb (350 g) potatoes, peeled and diced
1 oz (25 g) butter
1 medium onion, finely chopped
1 1/2 pints (900 ml) good chicken or vegetable stock
Sea salt and freshly ground black pepper
4 scallops
1 pint (570 ml) milk
1 egg yolk
2-3 tablespoons cream
Chopped parsley

Melt the butter in a pan and add the onion and the potatoes. Cook until transparent and then add the stock and seasonings, bring to the boil and cook gently until the vegetables are tender. Liquidize and put back into a clean pan.

Take off the red coral part of the cleaned scallops and slice. Heat the milk and poach the white part of the scallops for 4 minutes. Remove from the milk and slice very thinly.

Beat the egg, add the hot milk and the cream. Mix with the potato purée and heat, but take care not to boil. Add the scallops, including the red coral, allow to heat again and serve with chopped parsley.

*A research laboratory in Ohio is using sophisticated laser technology to peel potatoes. Said the project manager; "You just see a little puff of vapour and there is a naked potato."*

## 18 JANUARY

# POMMES ANNA

This is one of my favourite ways of cooking potatoes. It was invented at the Café Anglais in Paris. The cooking method enhances the potato flavour so the result will be as good as the quality of the ingredients. The cookery writer Marcel Boulestin suggested that the best utensil for cooking Pommes Anna is a wide copper pan with a well-fitting lid. Lacking this, I use a wide, shallow ovenproof dish.

1½ lb (700 g) potatoes, peeled and thinly sliced
3-4 oz (75-100 g) butter
Sea salt and freshly ground black pepper

Wash the potato slices in cold water, dry well and season with salt and pepper. Butter your dish generously and then put the potato slices in circles so that they overlap each other, basting with butter as you go. Cover with a lid and bake in the oven (gas mark 6/400°F/200°C) for about 45 minutes or until the potatoes are well browned outside and soft inside.

Traditionally, the potatoes are turned out onto the lid and returned to the oven for a minute more.

*Carlos Ochos was a 'potato hunter' in the 1970s who, at considerable personal risk, undertook to trek all over South America gathering as many potato varieties as possible before they were lost to disease, development or desertification. About 1% of the world's potato varieties are now named after him.*

19 JANUARY

# CRAINQUEBILLE POTATOES

The joy of this dish is that it is - almost - a meal in itself. Tomatoes are somewhat tasteless at this time of year so are better cooked.

$1\frac{1}{2}$ lb (700g) potatoes, peeled and quartered
2 large onions, chopped
$\frac{1}{2}$ pint (275 ml) good chicken stock
2-3 oz (50-75 g) butter
Bouquet garni
Clove of garlic
4 large tomatoes
Salt and freshly ground black pepper
Breadcrumbs

Cook the onions slowly in the butter. Add the potatoes to the onions. Add enough stock to cover the potatoes (you may need a little extra). Put in the bouquet garni and the chopped garlic and cover the top with sliced tomatoes. Season well.

Bring to the boil and transfer at once to a hot oven (gas mark 7/425°F/220°C) for 15 minutes. Lower the heat to gas mark 4/350°F/180°C until the potatoes are tender. Then sprinkle with breadcrumbs and brown under the grill.

*In Scotland, in the 18th century, Presbyterian clergy declared the potato unsafe to eat because it was not mentioned in the Bible.*

## 20 JANUARY

# POTATO SODA BREAD

Like most soda bread, this is best eaten on the day of baking. It is a moist, crunchy bread that is lovely warm with jam or with a bowl of vegetable soup for lunch.

6 oz (175 g) potato, cooked and sieved
12 oz (350 g) wholemeal flour
4 oz (110 g) pinhead oatmeal
2 teaspoons bicarbonate of soda
2 teaspoons salt
Generous oz (25 g) butter or margarine
$^{3}/_{4}$ pint (425 ml) buttermilk

Combine the flour, pinhead oatmeal, bicarbonate of soda (sieved) and salt in a large bowl. Rub in the butter or margarine and still using your fingertips, mix in the potato.

Stir in the buttermilk - the mixture will seem wet but put it into a 2 lb (900 g) loaf tin that has been well greased. Bake in the oven at gas mark 7/425°F/220°C for about 15 minutes and then turn down the heat to gas mark 5/375°F/190°C for a further 20 minutes or so until the loaf sounds hollow when tapped on the bottom.

*"About the middle of the nineteenth century they (potatoes) were generally incorporated into the loaf with the object, not of saving flour, but of improving the flavour, moisture and keeping quality of the bread. The practice, still common, was a generation back almost universal amongst those who made their bread at home, as well as in the village bakeries."*

*From* ***The History and Social Influence of the Potato*** *by Redcliffe Salaman, 1949.*

21 JANUARY

# PIGEON AND VENISON PIE

This pie has potato in both the pastry and the filling. The presence of potato in pastry has the effect of lightening it, yet binding it together, thus making handling easier.

For the pastry:
2 oz (50 g) mashed potato
2½ oz (65 g) self-raising flour
½ teaspoon salt
6 oz (175 g) butter

For the filling:
2 plump pigeons
3 onions, 2 of which are diced
1 carrot
Piece of celery
Bouquet garni
A few cloves
3 tablespoons sunflower oil
12 oz (350 g) venison, cut into bite-size pieces
Flour for dusting

Prepare the pastry by mixing the flour, potato and salt and rubbing in the butter. Bind with a few drops of cold water and put in the fridge for at least an hour.

With a sharp knife, cut out the breasts of the pigeon and divide each into 4 pieces. Put the carcasses into a stock pot with an onion, the carrot, piece of celery, bouquet garni and the cloves. Cover with water, bring to the boil and simmer for 45 minutes. Then drain and reserve the liquid - there should be about ¾ pint (reduce it if necessary).

Fry the diced onions gently in the sunflower oil until translucent. Remove from the pan. Dust the venison pieces and pigeon breasts with the flour. Put into the pan. Raise the heat and brown the pieces of game. Return the onions to the pan, put in the pigeon stock and stir round until the sauce is smooth. Bring to the boil, cover and simmer for a half hour.

Put into a flan dish and allow to cool. Cover with the pastry and cook at gas mark 6/400°F/200°C for 30 minutes or until the pastry is golden.

*In her **High Spots on the Andes**, Mrs Clarence Woods speaks of visiting a Potato Fair in La Paz where 89 different species of potatoes were exhibited.*

## 22 JANUARY

# COCONUT MACAROON BARS

This recipe was given to me by the Berkeley Court Hotel in Dublin.

3 oz (75 g) mashed potatoes
5 oz (150 g) cooking chocolate
12 oz (350 g) icing sugar
3 oz (75 g) dessicated coconut

Place half the chocolate in a bowl over a pan of hot water. Grease a shallow baking tin (8 x 6 inches) and coat the base with half the melted chocolate. Leave aside to set.

Gradually work the icing sugar and coconut into the cold potato. Beat for 3-4 minutes. Press this mixture into the tin and flatten with a palette knife. Melt the remaining half of the chocolate and pour over the mixture. Once the chocolate has set, cut into little squares.

*For a long time after its introduction into Europe, the potato was considered with suspicion. This was because it is a solanaceous plant like belladonna and henbane and it was from these that the Borgias used to make their poisons.*

23 JANUARY

# HASH BROWNS WITH RED PEPPER SAUCE

Hash Browns is the name Americans give to fried leftover potatoes. There are many interpretations of this, but the result should be golden and very crispy. The potatoes for this dish are best parboiled some hours before you wish to cook them to avoid falling apart in the pan. A wide, heavy pan is essential.

2 lb (900 g) cooked cold potatoes, diced in thick chunks
4 tablespoons vegetable or olive oil
$^1/_2$ lb (225 g) bacon, diced
1 medium onion, finely chopped

For the sauce:
2 large red peppers
5 fl oz (150 ml) chicken stock
3 fl oz (75 ml) tomato juice
Sea salt and freshly ground black pepper

Heat the oil until very hot and put in the potatoes, bacon and onion which will immediately form a crust. Cook over a fairly high heat, turning from time to time so the potatoes become golden on all sides.

To prepare the sauce, place the red peppers under a blistering grill so that the skins just begin to blacken. Put in a plastic bag for 5 minutes, then wash off the skins. Cut up the peppers and discard the seeds. Put in a food processor with the stock and purée. Add tomato juice to get a saucelike consistency and season. Warm up in a pan and serve with the potatoes.

*The writers Somerville and Ross stated that there were two important things in Irish life - potatoes and hounds.*

24 JANUARY

# POTATO DUMPLINGS

Vary the flavour of these little dumplings by adding 2-3 oz (50-75 g) grated cheese or a little chopped garlic. Experiment with different herbs available - for example, rosemary or chervil. Eat the dumplings with a spicy tomato sauce or add them to a cooked casserole or serve in a well-flavoured consommé.

1 lb (450 g) potatoes, peeled
3 oz (75 g) flour
1 whole egg
1 egg yolk
Sea salt and freshly ground black pepper
Fresh chopped parsley

Steam or bake the potatoes and when cooked put through a sieve. Mix with the flour, egg and yolk and season. Add the parsley. Roll into small balls and flatten out into cylinders.

Poach in boiling salted water for about 5 minutes.

*The Smithsonian Museum of Natural History in Washington D.C. put on an exhibition in 1992 called 'Seeds of Change' that focused on plants - among them the potato - that altered life in the New and Old World after the arrival of Columbus in America.*

25 JANUARY

# POTATOES WITH KALE AND BACON

Kale is an integral part of an Irish garden in winter and spring. Eat the young leaves after the plant has been subjected to frost.

4 large potatoes, peeled and diced
8 oz (225 g) bacon, cut in little strips
2 oz (50 g) butter
1 clove garlic, chopped
1/2 pint (275 ml) chicken stock
1 lb (450 g) kale, chopped
1 tablespoon red wine vinegar
Sea salt and freshly ground black pepper
Parsley

Sauté the bacon quickly until crisp. Remove from pan and keep warm. Add the butter and garlic to the same pan and then pour over the stock and the kale from which you have removed any coarse stems.

Add the potatoes and cook uncovered until the potatoes are tender and all the liquid has been absorbed (it may be necessary to add a little more stock during the cooking process). Stir in the vinegar and season to taste. Serve in a warmed dish sprinkled with the bacon and the parsley.

*The Latin name for potatoes is Solanum tuberosum.*

## 26 JANUARY
## AUSTRALIA DAY (WATTLE DAY)
# CHIPS IN BEER BATTER

I am told that these are sold in the fish and chip shops in Sydney. They are not for those with delicate appetites. They are improved by pepping up with a sprinkling of vinegar.

Large potatoes, cleaned and cut about 1/8 inch thick

For the batter:
4 oz (110 g) plain flour
Pinch of salt
2 tablespoons sunflower oil

$^1/_4$ pint (150 ml) of warm ale
Flour for dusting
1 white of egg
Oil for deep frying

To prepare the batter, sift the flour and salt into a basin and mix with the oil and ale until very smooth. Allow to stand in a cool place for 1 hour.

Wash the potato slices and dry well. Dust with flour.

Whip the egg white until stiff and fold into the batter. Coat the potato slices with the batter and deep fry until golden. Drain and eat at once.

*In 1843, Lord Melbourne, who gave his name to Melbourne, Australia, allotted areas of his Derbyshire land for market gardening. This became known as Lord Melbourne's Potato Land.*

27 JANUARY

# BAKED EGG AND POTATO CASSEROLE

Very simple, and easily assembled, this casserole makes a good supper dish.

$1^1/_2$ lb (700 g) potatoes, cleaned and diced
2 tablespoons butter
2 tablespoons oil
1 medium onion, chopped
Sea salt and freshly ground black pepper
4 eggs
4 tablespoons grated Gruyère cheese
4 tablespoons cream

Heat the butter and the oil. Sauté the potatoes until they start changing colour. Add the onion and continue cooking until the potatoes are tender. Season and transfer to an ovenproof dish.

Break the eggs into little hollows in the potatoes and cover with the cheese and the cream. Bake in the oven (gas mark 5/375°F/190°C) for about 10 minutes or until the eggs are cooked. Eat at once.

*Flamboyant French chef and food writer Alexis Soyer set up soup kitchens in the 1846 famine in Dublin, feeding 26,000 people daily at barely half the usual cost. The nutritional value of these soups caused much controversy.*

## 28 JANUARY

# FRANKLIN'S POTATOES

The mingling of breadsauce with potato purée may seem curious, but it works; it is, of course, especially good with a plump roast chicken.

1 1/2 lb (700 g) potatoes, peeled
1 medium onion
A few cloves
1/2 pint milk (275ml)
A bay leaf
2 tablespoons fresh white breadcrumbs
A little nutmeg
Sea salt and freshly ground black pepper
2 oz (50 g) butter

Boil the potatoes and while they are cooking, prepare the bread sauce. Peel the onion and stick a few cloves into it. Put with the milk and the bay leaf, bring to the boil and simmer very gently for about 5 minutes. Remove the onion, add the breadcrumbs and transfer the sauce to a double boiler or *bain-marie* and cook over barely simmering water for about 20 minutes.

When the potatoes are cooked, dry them well and make a purée. Stir in the bread sauce, and finally the butter.

*In his **The English Hus-wife**, published 1615, Gervase Markham gave an account of a pie that comprised best pastry filled with artichoke bottoms, thickly sliced boiled potatoes with a topping of candied eringo-roots mixed with very thick slices of dates. The pie also contained beef marrow, spices, currants and raisins. After baking, the pie was filled with white wine, rosewater, cinnamon and vinegar.*

29 JANUARY

# CARAMELISED SWEET AND SOUR POTATOES, CARROTS AND GREEN PEPPER

Use a firm-fleshed potato here, such as Rooster. This amount serves 4-6 as a side dish, and it is also excellent vegetarian food.

1 $^1/_2$ lb (700 g) potatoes
2 oz (50 g) butter
2 tablespoons brown sugar
1 teaspoon ginger
$^1/_2$ level teaspoon chilli powder
Sea salt and freshly ground black pepper
2 carrots, cut in large splinters
1 green pepper, de-seeded and cut in little strips
Juice of 1 orange
1 tablespoon vinegar

Steam the potatoes, then peel and cut into quarters lengthways. Heat the butter in a wide pan and add the sugar, ginger, chilli powder and seasonings. Allow to cook for a few moments and then add the potatoes, seeing that they are well coated with the spices. Continue to cook on a high heat, stirring all the time, until the potatoes are caramelised. Remove from the pan and keep warm.

Add the carrots and the green pepper and fry for 5 minutes. Add the orange and the vinegar and cook till the liquid is reduced by half. Return the potatoes to the pan and stir gently until evenly mixed.

*"Potatoes and Jerusalem artichokes are roots of less note than any I have yet mentioned, but as they are not without their admirers so I shall not pass by their cultivation."*
*From **New Improvements in Planting and Gardening**, by R. Bradley, 1717.*

30 JANUARY

# BODGE

This is a relative of cottage pie, and a rather attractive one at that.

2 lb (900 g) potatoes, peeled and boiled
1 lb (450 g) onions, chopped
1 lb (450 g) minced beef
2 cans chopped tomatoes
2 tablespoons tomato purée
Sprig of thyme and chopped parsley
1 oz (25 g) butter
1 oz (25 g) flour
Bay leaf
3/4 pint (400 ml) milk
4 oz (110 g) cheese
Sea salt and freshly ground black pepper

While the potatoes are cooking, cook the onions in a little oil until transparent, add the minced beef and brown. Put in the tomatoes, tomato purée and seasoning. Cook for several minutes.

Prepare a sauce with the butter, flour and milk, flavouring with the bayleaf, and finally the cheese. When the potatoes are soft, drain well and make a purée.

Put half the meat at the bottom of a casserole dish, half the tomato sauce, half the cheese sauce and then repeat. Cover with the potato purée (dot with more butter if required) and put in a hot oven (gas mark 7/425°F/220°C) to brown.

*"You wouldn't love a man with a potato-nose."*
*From **Asphodel** by Elizabeth Braddon, c. 1870.*

31 JANUARY

# POTATO GRIDDLES

A substantial supper dish. Serve with a salad of whatever you have to hand.

12 oz (350 g) potato
1 small onion, grated
4 oz (110 g) salami, cut in small dice
4 tablespoon self-raising flour
2 beaten eggs
Sea salt and freshly ground black pepper
Oil for frying
Chopped parsley

Peel and grate the potatoes. Squeeze out excess moisture in a clean towel. Mix the potatoes, onion, salami, flour and eggs and beat until well amalgamated.

Heat the oil and drop spoonfuls of the mixture into the pan. Fry for about 8 minutes, turning once. Drain on kitchen paper and sprinkle with parsley.

***England's Happiness increased, or a Sure and Easie Remedy against all succeeding Dear Years; by a Plantation of the Roots called Potatoes.***

*Book Title, 1664.*

# LEMON PIE

This pie has a good lemony flavour and a slightly sponge-like consistency. Serve it straight from the oven with cream.

3 oz (75 g) cooked potatoes, puréed
6 oz (175 g) shortcrust pastry
2 oz (50 g) butter
2 oz (50 g) caster sugar
Grated rind of 1 lemon
1 whole egg and 1 yolk, beaten

Line a 6-inch flan tin with the pastry and bake blind at gas mark 7/425°F/220°C for 10 minutes.

Cream the butter and sugar until light and fluffy and then stir in the potatoes, lemon rind and eggs. Blend well. Pour into the pastry case and bake at gas mark 4/350°F/180°C for 30 minutes.

*The Irish language evolved many different words to describe types, sizes and conditions of potatoes. These include Steodaire (small worthless potato), Gruan prata (lumpy potato), Ceaist phratai (batch of potatoes roasted in ashes), Caochan (eyeless potato), Muireog (potato head), Bruitin (mashed potatoes), Gataire (potatoes roasted in embers, as a treat)...and many others.*

2 FEBRUARY

# BAKED POTATO WITH CHEESE AND EGG YOLKS

Potatoes cooked in their skins keep their nutrients best. Baked potatoes are improved by brushing with oil and salt before you cook them. Or heat the oil gently with a few chopped cloves of garlic before coating the potatoes prior to cooking them.

4 large potatoes
4 oz (110 g) Cheddar cheese
2 egg yolks
Sea salt and freshly ground black pepper

Bake the potatoes in their jackets for 1 hour in a hot oven. Remove from the oven and, when cool enough to handle, cut in half and scoop out the middle. With a fork mash the potato with the cheese, egg yolks and seasoning. Put the mixture back into the skins and return to the oven for 10-15 minutes until browned.

*A rare variety of French potato - Bonnotte de Noirmoutier - which almost died out in the 1960s was sold at the Drouot auction house in Paris for £387 a kilo in 1996. Grown on a bed of seaweed, the growing cycle begins on 2 February and ends exactly 90 days later. The slightest bruising causes self-mashing.*

3 FEBRUARY

# ROAST POTATOES

There are some basic rules to be followed to achieve perfection in this method of cooking; perfection being crisp on the outside, soft inside. Always use a floury potato. The results will only be as good as the ingredients and the fat is crucial so use a highly-saturated fat - best is perhaps beef though rendered chicken, goose or duck fats are good too, as is olive oil, groundnut or sunflower oil. Deep-fried potatoes passed off in hotels as roast potatoes are an abomination.

There is a division among cooks about whether to parboil. I prefer to boil peeled potatoes in salted water for about 5 minutes and then shake them roughly in a colander to break up the surface. Some people scour the potatoes with a fork. You can dust with a little flour if you like. Sprinkle with sea salt.

Never cook the potatoes round a joint of meat as this can make them soggy (and pan juices should be kept for the gravy). The fat must be hot when you put in the potatoes and they need to be roasted for a minimum of an hour in a hot oven - gas mark 7/425°F/220°C. When you put the potatoes into the fat roll them around so that the surfaces are covered. Turn them once or twice during the cooking.

Roast potatoes are lovely on their own. They don't necessarily have to share the plate with meat.

*"The English at the rates the Irish do, can't live...give them potatoes they'll boyle and roast/ And stroke up their mustachoes."*

*Anonymous play written in 1675.*

4 FEBRUARY

# POTATO SPONGE CAKE WITH WALNUTS

This is a light cake, made without butter, and best eaten warm from the oven.

11 oz (310 g) potatoes, cooked and purēed
6 eggs
7 oz (200 g) caster sugar
Grated rind of a lemon
3 oz (75 g) flour
1/2 teaspoon cinnamon
2 oz (50 g) walnuts, broken into little pieces

While the puréed potatoes are cooling, start to prepare the cake. Separate the eggs, beat the yolks with the sugar until the consistency is silky. Add the lemon rind, the flour, the cinnamon and lastly the potatoes. Add the walnuts to the mixture. Whip the egg whites until stiff and fold them in gently.

Have ready a cake tin, well oiled and lined with greaseproof paper. I use a narrow (4x12 inch) bread tin. Bake in the centre of a moderate oven (gas mark 4/350°F/180°C) for about an hour. If the top of the cake gets too brown, turn the heat down halfway through cooking.

*Potatoes were the first edible plant to be grown in Europe from tubers and not from seed.*

## 5 FEBRUARY
## RUNEBERG'S DAY, FINLAND
# SWEET POTATO CASSEROLE

What a curious recipe this is. It originates in Finland, yet I have come across a similar dish in the north of England. In both recipes the starch in the potato is allowed to sweeten over a number of hours. With the English recipe this was done during the cooking period - 4 hours - but with the Finnish dish the potato is cooked and then left at room temperature for the sweet taste to develop. When to eat it? As a pudding, apparently or, as we prefer it, with a few apple slices added and then served with roast pork.

1 lb (450 g) potatoes
1 heaped tablespoon flour
1 teaspoon salt
1/2 pint (275 ml) warmed milk
1 oz (25 g) butter
1 large eating apple, peeled and sliced (optional)

Clean the potatoes but do not peel. Boil or steam them and when very dry, purée. Mix in the flour and then leave at room temperature for at least 4 hours.

Taste the mixture and if it is not sweet enough you may add a little sugar. Stir in the salt, milk and butter (and the apple if using) and put into a greased casserole dish. Bake for 1-2 hours at gas mark 2/300°F/150°C.

*"They used to make a kind of bread with potatoes called 'Stampy'. They would grate the potatoes on a tin grater, and then squeeze them into a tub of water. The Stampy was made on a breadtree, which was a kind of sloping board put before the fire to hold bread. Stampy was only usually made for Christmas or November night, unless you had a good supply of potatoes, when you might make it once a week."*

*From **'The Tailor and Ansty'** by Eric Cross, 1942.*

## 6 FEBRUARY

# POTATO BREAD

I have adapted this from a recipe published in *The Bread Book* by Audrey Ellison. This differs from most bread recipes that contain potatoes because here the potato is added raw.

8 oz (225 g) raw potato, peeled
3/4 pint (400 ml) milk
1 sachet Quick-Action dried yeast
2 lb (900 g) plain flour
2 teaspoons salt
1 egg, beaten
3 tablespoons buttermilk

Bring the milk to the boil. Grate the potato and add it to the milk. Leave until lukewarm.

Add the dried yeast to the sieved flour and salt and stir in the potato/milk mixture. Add the egg and buttermilk and knead well. Put in a covered bowl in a warm place to rise for 2-2 1/2 hours. Knead again and divide between 3 well-greased bread tins. Leave to rise again for about 40 minutes and then bake at gas mark 4/350°F/180°C for 45 minutes.

*"...lovers of toast and butter will be much pleased with this kind of bread. The potato is not added here with a view to economy, but to increase the lightness of the bread, in which state it will imbibe the butter with more freedom..."*

*From* ***Receipts in Modern Cookery; with a Medical Commentary***
*by Dr. A. Hunter, 1805.*

## 7 FEBRUARY

# WOOLTON PIE

This was named after Lord Woolton, who became British Minister for Food in April 1940. It was a hotchpotch, as many wartime dishes must have been, of what you could glean at the time. Basically, it was diced cooked root vegetables in a white sauce or gravy and topped with cooked sliced potato that was browned under a grill. Undeniably, it has its place in our cuisine today.

Lord Woolton's 'Potato Plan' urged people to grow potatoes instead of relying on imported grain; potatoes had to "go into action on the Food Front...you can save shipping by eating potatoes instead of bread. The potatoes are here; they are a healthy food. Let your patriotism direct your appetite."

A food columnist in a wartime issue of Woman magazine wrote: "What a joy it is to concoct a delicious little meal knowing that it has not made the smallest inroad on your rations!" Even Christmas cakes included the ubiquitous potato (grated raw). A dish known as Portable Potato Piglets (baked potatoes stuffed with a tiny amount of sausage meat) attained some popularity but perhaps this has less appeal to contemporary palates.

A proposal for using potato judiciously came in the form of a suggestion that margarine for sandwiches "could be extended by melting it and mixing it with an equal quantity of mashed potato." Let us say no more about that.

*"Those who have the will to win*
*Cook potatoes in their skin*
*Knowing that the sight of peelings*
*Deeply hurts Lord Woolton's feelings."*
*Jingle issued by the Ministry of Food.*

## 8 FEBRUARY

# CHIPS

Some confusion exists about the name of these potatoes. What we call 'chips', in America are known as 'French fries'; what the Americans refer to as 'chips', we call 'crisps'. Staggering choices face 'crisp' lovers today; they come flavoured with Cajun, Italian or barbecue spices, vinegar, jalapeno peppers (almost incendiary), yoghourt and green onion, bagel pastrami, punjab puri, salsa and chocolate coated. Even hedgehog-flavoured crisps have their admirers.

The best chips in Europe are found in private houses where they can be prepared with love and attention.

For really top-class 'fish and chips' peel your chips and slice into chip sizes. Leave for at least half an hour in cold water to remove excess starch. We have an old metal 'chipper' that produces even-sized chips in seconds. The Belgians favour smaller chips like matchsticks. Families who love chips would do well to invest in an electric deep fryer. Occasional chip fanciers can get away with a good high-sided frying pan.

For really crisp chips, cook them twice. Using a chip basket, half cook in fat at a temperature of 360°F/185°C. Drain, then deep fry again at 390°F/195°C to brown.

Drain on kitchen paper and eat immediately.

*George Crum, the chef at Moon's Lake House in Saratoga Springs, N.Y. is said to have devised 'Saratoga Chips' in 1853 to placate a cantankerous customer who complained that the fried potatoes were too thick. The first crisp to arrive in Britain was in 1920, made by a Frank Smith in his garage in Cricklewood, North London. He added the blue twist wrapper of salt.*

## 9 FEBRUARY

# GRATIN SAINT HUBERT

Saint Hubert is the patron saint of hunting.

$1\,^1/_2$ lb (700 g) potatoes, peeled and grated
3 oz (75 g) Gruyère cheese, grated
1 large slice ham, cut into little strips
$^1/_2$ pint (275 ml) milk
Sea salt and freshly ground black pepper
$1^1/_2$ oz ( 40 g) butter
$^1/_4$ pint (150 ml) cream

Wash the grated potato in cold water and then dry well using a clean cloth. Butter a gratin dish and layer the potatoes with the cheese and the ham and any butter left over. Pour over the milk, already seasoned and cook in a medium oven (gas mark 5/375°F/190°C) for 45 minutes to an hour. Add the cream and increase the heat (gas mark 7/ 425°F/ 220°C) until the surface is browned in 5-10 minutes.

*John Gerard, in his Catalogue, published 1596, provides one of the first recorded mentions of the potato. Grown in his garden in Holborn, he called the plant Papus Orbiculatus. In the second edition, he calls them 'Bastard Potatoes.'*

## 10 FEBRUARY

# FAÇON SAVOYARDE

This rather curious dish originates from the Savoy region in France and constitutes a sort of sweet pudding. The sweetness is imparted by the raisins. It's a heavy, sustaining winter food best eaten at lunchtime with a salad.

1 1/2 lb (700 g) potatoes, peeled and grated
2 1/2 oz (60 g) raisins
2 eggs, beaten
12 fl oz (325 ml) milk
1 heaped tablespoon flour
1 oz (25 g) butter, cut into little knobs
Salt and pepper
Nutmeg

Soak the raisins in water for about 3 hours. Squeeze out any excess moisture from the grated potatoes in a clean tea towel. Put the potatoes in a bowl, add the raisins, eggs, milk, flour, the butter and the seasonings.

Put into an ovenproof dish (it's unnecessary to grease the dish) and cook at gas mark 8/450°F/230°C for 45 minutes and then turn down the heat to gas mark 5/375°F/190°C for a further 15 minutes.

*"This plant, called cartoufle, bears fruits of the same name resembling truffles and so called by some. It came to the Dauphine from Switzerland not long since."*

*From* ***Théâtre d'Agriculture et mesange des champs*** *by Olivier de Serres, 1600.*

11 FEBRUARY

# SALADE FRANÇILLON

This luxurious salad is for the seriously rich. Also known as Japanese salad, it was all the rage among fashionable Parisians in the late 19th century. It was first described in *Françillon*, a play by Alexandre Dumas *fils*, although it is not known if it was his invention.

2 lb (900 g) very small new potatoes
4 pints (2.3 litres) mussels
1 pint (570 ml) champagne
2 shallots, finely chopped
2 pints (1.1 litres) meat stock
5 fl oz (150 ml) olive oil
2 fl oz (50 ml) white wine vinegar

Sea salt and freshly ground black pepper
2 tablespoons parsley, finely chopped
2 tablespoons chives, finely chopped
2 oz (50 g) black truffles, thinly sliced

Scrub the mussels, rinsing them several times in cold water and remove the beards. Put them in a wide pan with half the champagne and the shallots. Cover the pan and cook over a high heat until the shells open. Discard any unopened mussels. When cool, remove the mussels from the shells.

Boil the potatoes in the stock until tender. Drain them and slice thinly. Marinade in the remaining champagne for a half-hour.

Make a dressing with the oil, vinegar and seasoning. Combine the mussels and the potatoes and add the dressing very gently so as to avoid breaking the potatoes.

Serve in a crystal glass bowl, decorated with the herbs and sliced truffles.

*In **Larousse Gastronomique**, the encyclopaedia of classic French cookery, it is suggested that Salade Françillon be served in the shape of a 'calotte de savant' (wise man's skull cap).*

12 FEBRUARY

# POTATOES WITH CARROTS AND SESAME SEEDS

Cook these potatoes in a wok or a wide, preferably non-stick, pan. Carrots are one of the few vegetables that can be as good old as young; the sweet earth-taste of the long-matured carrot has as distinct a flavour as the fledgling fingertips of the young vegetable.

1 1/2 lb (700 g) potatoes, cleaned and cut into little dice
1/2 lb (225 g) carrots, cut in julienne strips
6 tablespoons sesame oil
2 oz (50 g) sesame seeds
Sea salt
A large pinch of cayenne pepper
1 tablespoon lemon juice

Heat the oil in a large frying pan and when very hot, put in the potatoes (only peeled if necessary). Lower the heat and allow to cook for about 5-10 minutes, moving around the pan so the potatoes brown on all sides and are just tender. Add the carrots and cook for a further 3 minutes, again turning the contents of the pan. Add the sesame seeds and cook for another few minutes until the potatoes are cooked.

Add the salt, cayenne pepper and lemon juice. Stir and fry for another 3 to 4 minutes.

*"Tuesday 12th February. 9. My head aches. Mem. not eat another boil'd potato in haste..."*
*From* ***A Year with the Ladies of Llangollen*** *by Elizabeth Mavor, 1971.*

## 13 FEBRUARY
# POTATO KISSES

This is the time of year for romance, so why not make a box of these and send them to your sweetheart?

1 medium-size potato
1 teaspoon vanilla extract
1 oz (25 g) butter
8 oz (225 g) icing sugar
4 oz (110 g) powdered milk
Melted chocolate

Peel and boil the potato gently. Mash it with a fork and add the vanilla and the butter. Add the sugar and the powdered milk, mixing well.

Chill in the refrigerator until you can knead it into small shapes - kisses and hearts. Dip in chocolate and allow to cool.

*"Nevertheless they are flatulent, and therefore some use them for exciting Venus."*
*Clusius, writing in 1601.*

### 14 FEBRUARY
### ST VALENTINE'S DAY

# BRAENDENDE KAERLIGHED
# (Burning Love)

Here is a Dutch recipe most suitable for St Valentine's Day. Hearty food for the hot-blooded.

2 lb (900 g) potatoes, peeled
2 large onions, chopped
6 medium tomatoes, chopped
3 oz (75 g) butter
A little oil for frying
Sea salt and freshly ground black pepper
1 lb (450 g) streaky bacon

Boil the potatoes until tender. Meanwhile, cook the onions and tomatoes in a little oil until they are almost a purée.

Purée the potatoes, add the butter and milk and pile onto a serving dish in a pyramid. Surround with the tomato mixture and top with grilled bacon.

*"Potatoes are cheaper...now is the time to fall in love."*
*Song by Eddie Cantor.*

15 FEBRUARY

# ROASTED ROOT SOUP

This is a soup to make when you have a few root vegetables left after a weekend, but not enough of each to cook on their own. You can adjust to what is at hand.

2 large potatoes
1 large onion
1 turnip
1 bulb fennel
1 parsnip
2 large carrots
2 stalks celery
1 head garlic
1-2 tablespoons butter
2 pints (1.1 litre) vegetable stock
$^1/_4$ pint (150 ml) red wine
Bouquet garni
1 tablespoon Dijon mustard
2 tablespoons tomato paste
1 tablespoon soy sauce
Juice of $^1/_2$ lemon
Sea salt and freshly ground black pepper
8 oz (225 g) cooked kidney beans

Peel and cut up all the vegetables into dice. Spread them over a wide baking dish, dot with the butter and add about $^1/_2$ pint of the stock. Put in a hot oven (about gas mark 7/425°F/220°C) for about 20 minutes, shaking the dish to see that the vegetables don't stick.

Pour over the wine and, with a wooden spoon, scrape the bottom of the pan to remove all the browned pieces of vegetable, then put everything into a clean saucepan. Cover with the remaining stock. Bring to the boil and while you are doing this, in a separate bowl, mix the mustard, tomato paste, soy sauce and lemon juice. Add to the soup and when boiled, simmer for about 15 minutes.

Season to taste and serve with the warmed-up kidney beans.

*To think 'bad potatoes' of something means to attach very little importance to it.*

## 16 FEBRUARY

# POTATOES STUFFED WITH ANCHOVIES

A tin or two of anchovies is a most useful ingredient in a well-stocked larder.

4 large potatoes, boiled and peeled if necessary
4 oz (110 g) mozzarella cheese, thinly sliced
1 tin anchovies, drained and cut in little slivers
4 dessertspoons olive oil
1 oz (25 g) butter

Drain the potatoes and leave to cool. Take a slice off across the top of the potato, hollow out the middle with a spoon leaving a space about the size of a dessertspoon. Mash the hollowed-out potato with a fork and incorporate a dessertspoon of olive oil.

In the hollow in the potatoes, put the cheese, a little anchovy and then more mozzarella. Close the potato with the mashed potato. Flatten the surface so as to make a lid. Put the potatoes in an ovenproof dish, put a little pat of butter on each and put in a hot oven for 10 minutes.

*"Potatoes are good for none but swine, and those they won't fatten."*
*Sir Archibald Grant, writing in 1757.*

## 17 FEBRUARY

# POTATOES À LA CREME, AU GRATIN

This is a recipe from Francatelli's *Modern Cook*, published in 1865. Its laborious methods and extravagant presentation do not seem in the spirit of these times but the book is a real joy. Charles Elmé Francatelli was chief cook to Queen Victoria. His recipes include

Ornamental Borders of Potato-Paste, Scollops of Sheep's Tongues and Calf's Brains. The following recipe is altogether more manageable in a modern context.

"Cut some boiled potatoes in slices, about an inch in diameter, prepare...a large ragout spoonful of Béchamel or Veloute sauce, into a stewpan with four ounces of grated Parmesan cheese, two ounces of fresh butter, the yolks of four eggs, a small piece of glaze, some lemon-juice, nutmeg, pepper and salt; stir this preparation over a stove-fire, until it be well mixed, without boiling. Stick some neatly cut pointed croutons of fried bread round the bottom of the dish, in the form of a coronet; place a close circular row of potatoes and mixture until the dish is complete. Smooth the top over with some of the sauce, shake some fried breadcrumbs and grated Parmesan cheese over the surface, so as to entirely cover it; put the potatoes in the oven for about twenty minutes, to be warmed through and serve."

*Francatelli invented a potato soup for Queen Victoria which consisted of a potato broth poured onto French beans, asparagus heads and little quenelles of potato.*

## 18 FEBRUARY

# POTATO, SAUSAGE AND TOMATO PIE

The appeal of this dish depends on the quality of the sausages. Beef sausages will not do. Very patient cooks can make their own with garlic and herbs and unusual flavourings. Butchers' pork sausages will do quite well for this dish, though. It is a favourite with children.

2 lb (900 g) potatoes, peeled and cooked
1 lb (450 g) sausages
2 fl oz (50 ml) milk
1 tin tomatoes
1 oz (25 g ) butter

Purée the potatoes. Add the milk. Season. Brown the sausages very quickly in hot oil and if they are very thick, cut them in pieces.

Put half the potato on the bottom of an ovenproof dish and then half the tomatoes. Season again. Lay the sausages on this, cover with the rest of the tomatoes and finish with the rest of the potatoes. Dot with little pieces of butter and bake in a moderate oven for about 45 minutes or until browned.

*Marilyn Monroe dipped potato chips in champagne in the film* ***The Seven Year Itch.***

## 19 FEBRUARY

# BAY POTATOES

Dried bay leaves should not be kept too long as they lose their flavour.

2 lb (900 g) potatoes
4-6 bay leaves
1 pint (570 ml) chicken , vegetable or game stock
Sea salt and freshly ground black pepper

Clean the potatoes well and only peel them if necessary. Cut into even-size pieces, put into a pan with the bay leaves and cover with the stock. Bring to the boil and cook gently with the lid on until the potatoes are almost ready, then remove the lid and finish cooking. The stock will reduce and become syrupy. Remove the bay leaves before serving.

*"If there is a vegetable which is taken for granted it is the humble potato; it is expected twice a day and received twice a day in that spirit of resignation to one's fate that is characteristic of the Christian husband."*

*Marcel Boulestin, 1932.*

20 FEBRUARY

# WARM POTATO SALAD WITH LAMB'S LETTUCE

Lamb's lettuce, often called corn salad, is at its most abundant now.

2 lb (900 g) potatoes, peeled
2 handfuls of corn salad
1 teaspoon Dijon mustard
$^{1}/_{2}$ glass white wine
2 tablespoons white wine vinegar
5 tablespoons olive oil
Sea salt and freshly ground black pepper

Steam the potatoes. Cut in pieces if very large. Mix the mustard, wine, oil, vinegar and seasonings. Put the corn salad and then the warm potatoes on a plate. Pour over the dressing and eat immediately.

*In days when salt was expensive, children were told to point their potatoes at the salt cellar before eating them. A meagre diet was known as dining on 'potatoes and point'.*

21 FEBRUARY

# SPICED MASHED POTATOES

The turmeric in this dish gives it a deep golden glow. The resulting purée compliments cold meats and salads.

1 $^{1}/_{2}$ lb (700 g) potatoes, peeled and cooked
2 tablespoons oil

6 cardamom pods
½ green pepper, cut in small dice
½ inch piece fresh ginger, finely chopped
1 teaspoon salt
1 teaspoon turmeric
Juice of a lemon
1 oz (25 g) dessicated coconut

Make a purée with the potatoes and keep warm. Open the cardamom pods and remove the black seeds. Heat the oil and fry the seeds for a few moments, then add the pepper, the ginger, the salt and the turmeric and fry over a low heat for 5 minutes.

Add the potatoes, the lemon juice and lastly the dessicated coconut. Beat with a wooden spoon to a light consistency before serving.

*"The universally adored and ever popular potato, produced at the earliest period of the dinner, was eaten with everything right up to the sweets."*

*From the* ***Memoirs of Captain Gronow****, 1861.*

22 FEBRUARY

# ROSEMARY POTATOES

No garden should be without a bush of rosemary, with its calm year-long beauty, and its fragrant green spikes. Old lore has it that you should not buy rosemary, but wait to be given it by a friend.

2 lb (900 g) potatoes, peeled and cut into even sizes
4 tablespoons olive oil
2 oz (50 g) butter
Sea salt
3 sprigs rosemary
2 garlic cloves, finely chopped

Brown the potato pieces in the oil and butter and put them in the oven with the salt, rosemary and garlic cloves.

They will cook in a hot oven (gas mark 7/425°F/220°C) in about 45 minutes. Serve with roast meat or eat on their own.

*"Turnips and Potatoes etc, that grow almost on the top and surface of the earth are better than other roots and more familiar to our natures than such as grow deeper in the ground, because they participate more of the influences both of the air and sun than the others."*

*From* ***The Way to Health*** *by Thomas Tyron, 1683.*

## 23 FEBRUARY

# PAN HAGGERTY

Pan Haggerty comes from the north of England and straight out of a farmhouse kitchen, I feel. The traditional fat for frying this was probably lard or dripping.

1 1/2 lb (700 g) potatoes, peeled and sliced as thin as possible
1 oz (25 g) butter
1 tablespoon sunflower oil
6 oz (175 g) cheese, grated
1 large onion, sliced
Sea salt and freshly ground black pepper

Melt the fats in a wide frying pan and swirl around to cover the base. Line the pan with half the potatoes. Combine the grated cheese, sliced onion and seasoning and put in the pan. Arrange the remaining potatoes on top.

Cover the pan with a plate and cook over a low heat for about 40 minutes or until the potatoes are tender. Brown the top of the dish under a hot grill. Serve very hot.

*"Father is rather vulgar, my dear. The word Papa gives a pretty form to the lips. Papa, potatoes, poultry, prunes and prism are all very good words for the lips..."*

*From* ***Little Dorrit*** *by Charles Dickens, 1855.*

24 FEBRUARY

# QUENELLES OF POTATOES

Versatility is the word here. These little quenelles are excellent in soups or stews, as an accompaniment for meat or just on their own, with perhaps a dusting of cheese.

4 large potatoes
2 oz (50 g) butter
$^1/_4$ pint (150 ml) double cream
Grated nutmeg
Sea salt and freshly ground black pepper
2 egg yolks
1 egg white, whipped to a stiff froth

Bake the potatoes until tender. Scoop out the the centres and rub through a sieve. Put the sieved potato into a pan with the butter, cream and seasonings. Stir over a brisk heat until the mixture amalgamates and does not stick to the pan.

Remove from the heat, cool a little and then add the egg yolks and the whipped egg white. Shape into the size you want and poach for 5 minutes or so in boiling water with a little salt added. Drain and serve.

*"...They had only recently done away with the cubicles, too, in which you could have your chop, prime chump, with a floury potato, without seeing your neighbours, like a gentleman."*
*From* ***The Forsyte Saga*** *by John Galsworthy, 1922.*

25 FEBRUARY

# GRATIN WITH SWEET POTATOES AND COCONUT

The sweet potato (*Ipomoea batatas*) is not a member of the Solanum family, therefore not a potato at all, although after its introduction into Europe via Spain in the early 16th century, there was confusion about the two tubers. The sweet potato, however, can be cooked in most of the same ways that apply to our potato. The botanist George Washington Carver is said to have invented 500 uses for the sweet potato. Here the two are cooked together.

12 oz (350 g) potatoes, peeled and thinly sliced
12 oz (350 g) sweet potatoes, peeled and thinly sliced
3 oz (75 g) boiling water
3 oz (75 g) creamed coconut
2 oz (50 g) butter
5 fl oz (150 ml) cream
Sea salt and freshly ground black pepper
A little nutmeg

Pour the boiling water over the creamed coconut and stir until smooth. Grease a wide ovenproof dish with half the butter and put the potatoes in layers with the coconut, the cream and the seasoning.

Dot with the remaining butter and cover with greaseproof paper. Cook at gas mark 7/425°F/220°C or until the vegetables are tender.

*An obelisk on the land of the now-ruined Killua Castle in Co. Westmeath commemorates the planting of the first potato in Ireland. This was built by the Chapman family, cousins of Sir Walter Raleigh, in 1810.*

26 FEBRUARY

# EMPTY LARDER DINNER

This is a time of year when nothing much grows in the garden; it's a time when stocks run low and often the Mother Hubbard syndrome catches us all out. This is a dinner to meet such an emergency.

1-2 lb (450-900 g) potatoes, peeled and sliced
2 onions, thinly sliced
1 oz (25 g) butter
Sea salt and freshly ground black pepper
Milk
Handful of grated cheese
Handful of chopped parsley

Put the potatoes and the onions into a pan with the butter. Just cover with equal quantities of milk and water.

Put on the lid and simmer gently until the potatoes begin to break up. Throw in the cheese and chopped parsley and serve very hot, with slices of freshly made toast.

*"How often, when faced with that moon-shaped saucer containing, at the most, three mouthfuls of 'select vegetables', placed beside the dinner plate with its floral arrangement of sauces and a sad sliver of meat or fish hiding in the centre, how often have you longed to call out, 'Bring me a bowl of potatoes'."*

*The journalist Patrick O'Connor.*

27 FEBRUARY

# POTATO WITH SCRAMBLED EGGS AND CAVIAR

The colours of this are wonderful. It is a painting on a plate and makes a seductive first course.

2 large or 4 medium potatoes
8 eggs
Sea salt and freshly ground black pepper
1 oz (25 g) butter
5 oz (150 g) jar red caviar

Bake the potatoes and remove the pulp. This can be reserved for soup. Scramble the eggs with the seasoning and butter (adding, if you feel extravagant, a few shrimps or little ribbons of smoked salmon) and divide between the potato shells. Put a spoonful of red caviar on each potato.

*"You say potatoes...and I say potahtoes..."*
*Cole Porter.*

## 28 FEBRUARY

# POTATO ROCK CAKES

These are surprisingly good. The presence of potato in baking seems to have a lightening effect, contrary to what one might suppose.

2 oz (50 g) mashed potatoes
2 oz (50 g) margarine
2 oz (50 g) flour
2 oz (50 g) sultanas
2 oz (50 g) sugar
1 teaspoon baking powder
A little candied peel
1 egg, beaten

Rub the fat into the flour, mix with the other ingredients and finally the beaten egg. Drop in dessertspoonfuls onto a greased baking tin. Bake in a hot oven (gas mark 7/425°F/220°C) for 15-20 minutes.

*Antoine-Auguste Parmentier was a French pharmacist who first became acquainted with potatoes when a prisoner of the Germans during the Seven Years' War. On his return home he hosted all-potato dinners at which he entertained the nobility of Europe. One of his guests was Benjamin Franklin, who later introduced the plant to Thomas Jefferson, who then grew potatoes in his garden at Monticello.*

## 29 FEBRUARY
## LEAP YEAR DAY

# SAUSAGE AND POTATO ROLLS

These are mouth-watering, light and popular with children. Use good quality sausages that are not too salty.

8 oz (225 g) potatoes, cooked and puréed
1 oz (25 g) flour
2 egg yolks
1 oz (25 g) butter, melted
8 sausages
Sea salt
1 egg white

When the puréed potatoes are cool, mix with the flour, egg yolks and melted butter. Divide into 8 portions and press out into squares.

Have the sausages quickly browned in hot oil and cooled. Place one on each potato square and fold over to form a roll.

Place on an oiled baking tray, brush with the egg white and bake in a moderate oven (gas mark 5/375°F/190°C) for about 10-15 minutes, or until browned.

*"Potato roots are now so common amongst us , that even the husbandman buys them to please his wife. They nourish mightily...engendering much flesh, blood and seed but withal increasing wind and lust."*

*From* ***Health Improvement*** *by Thomas Moffett, c.1595.*

ST DAVID'S DAY

# LEEKS AND POTATOES WITH WELSH RAREBIT

This is a good lunch dish. I've taken liberties with traditional fare by marrying the time-honoured Welsh rarebit with the Swiss way of serving potatoes accompanied by melted Raclette cheese and by including leeks. You may be lucky enough to get some little new potatoes (probably imported) but if not, an old variety will do.

2 lb (900 g) potatoes, cleaned
6-8 leeks, as small as possible
8 oz (225 g) dry, well-matured Cheddar cheese, grated
2 oz (50 g) butter
$^{1}/_{4}$ pint (150 ml) brown ale
Salt and cayenne pepper

Steam the potatoes. Prepare the leeks by cutting off almost all the green part and steam them until just tender.

Put the cheese into a pan with the butter, ale and seasonings. Stir over a gentle heat until well melted (but do not allow to get too hot) and when the mixture is smooth and creamy, pour over the potatoes and leeks.

*"A person in 1805 heard an old man, who, had he been living would have been 104 years old, say that when a boy he had seen a couple of potatoes brought to his father's house in Llanbedrig and that the man who brought them told the people present that they were eatable. Some present bit them and finding them nauseous threw them away. This was the first root of that kind seen in Lleyn."*

*From* ***Tours in Wales*** *by Richard Fenton, 1804-13.*

## 2 MARCH

# BOXTY - Bacstai

Boxty, in a variety of forms, is a traditional Irish food associated most with the northern counties of Cavan and Donegal. It was usual to make boxty on Hallowe'en and All Saints' Day. The ingredients include raw as well as cooked potatoes. For a long time it was the staple food of the poor and people were ashamed to admit eating it but now it is made commercially and exported to America. It may have been invented as a way of dealing with 'watery' potatoes because a watery potato is an anathema to an Irishman. Boxty can be cooked in a number of ways - fried, boiled or baked in an oven, as in this recipe.

8 oz (450 g) raw potatoes, peeled
8 oz (450 g) freshly mashed cooked potato
8 oz (450 g) self-raising flour
1 teaspoon baking powder
Salt
1 oz (25 g) melted butter or bacon fat
2-3 fl oz (50-75 ml) milk

Grate the raw potatoes in a piece of clean muslin or cloth over a bowl. Wring out the potatoes with vigour and retain the potato liquid.

Put the raw and cooked potatoes together. When the starch has fallen to the bottom of the liquid (this will take minutes) pour off the water and add the starch to the potatoes. Add the flour, baking powder, salt, melted butter and milk. Mix well, then add enough milk to make the boxty into a soft dough.

On a floured surface, knead the dough and then shape into four round cakes. Mark each with a cross and put on a greased baking sheet. Bake at gas mark 3/325°F/170°C for about 30-40 minutes. Eat fresh from the oven with butter.

*"Boxty on the griddle*
*Boxty in the pan*
*If you don't eat Boxty*
*You'll never get a man."*
*Old Irish Rhyme.*

## 3 MARCH

# BOXTY PANCAKES

The word boxty is thought to come from the word *bochty* or *bocht* meaning poor. When milk and salt are added is sometimes referred to as 'dippity'. Here the boxty comes in the form of pancakes.

8 oz (225g) peeled raw potatoes
8 oz (225 g) freshly cooked mashed potatoes
3 oz (75 g) flour
1/2 level teaspoon baking powder
1/2 teaspoon salt
1 egg
Approx 5 fl oz (150 ml) milk

Grate the raw potatoes and wring out in a clean cloth. Combine with all the other ingredients, adding the milk last until the whole is of a dropping consistency. Drop in spoonfuls onto a hot griddle and eat very hot with lots of butter.

*"Butter on the one side*
*Gravy on the other*
*Sure them that gave me Boxty*
*Were better than my mother."*

*Old Irish rhyme.*

## 4 MARCH

# TATIE HASH

In the northern counties of England this was a favourite dish for Ash Wednesday. 'Taates' is a Lancashire dialect term for potatoes. 'Taates' have found their way into many 'yellowbelly' (a native of Lincolnshire) recipes over the years.

1$^1/_2$ lb (700 g) potatoes, scrubbed and thinly sliced
8 oz (225 g) lamb, cut into small pieces
6 oz (175 g) black pudding, thinly sliced
1 large onion, thinly sliced
1 leek, sliced
1 heaped teaspoon thyme leaves
1$^1/_2$ pints (900 ml) good meat stock

Layer the first 5 ingredients in a pie dish, sprinkling with the thyme as you go.

Pour over the stock, cover the pie and cook at gas mark 6/400°F/200°C for 1 hour. Remove the lid and cook uncovered for a further 45 minutes.

*'Lobscouse' was a highly flavoured dish of potatoes, onions and meat that became so associated with the seamen of the Lancashire ports that in time sailors were nicknamed 'Lobscousers'.*

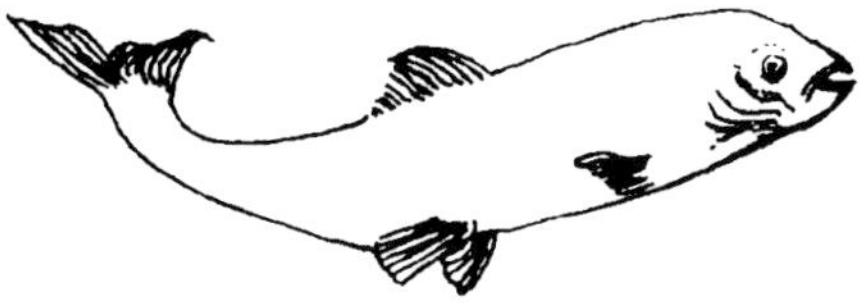

5 MARCH

# SCALLOP AND MONKFISH POTATO PIE

Fish pies are always welcome and this recipe uses an unusual combination of fish, although if scallops and monkfish are not available, you will have to substitute whatever is and vary your cooking time accordingly.

1 1/2 lb (700 g) potatoes, peeled, cooked and puréed
4 scallops
3/4 lb (350 g) monkfish tails (off the bone)
A bay leaf
1/2 pint (275 ml) milk
Sea salt and freshly ground black pepper
2 tablespoons butter
1 tablespoon flour
1/2 lb (225 g) mushrooms, sliced
2 tablespoons sherry
A little butter

While the potatoes are cooking, clean the monkfish and cut in pieces. Do the same with the scallops, reserving the red coral.

Simmer the fish (except for the coral) in milk, flavoured with the bay leaf for about 10 minutes or until cooked (the scallops will take less time). Strain, keeping the liquid.

Heat the butter, stir in the flour and the milk to make a sauce. Season, add the mushrooms and simmer for 10 minutes, making sure the sauce doesn't stick. Add the sherry and finally the fish. Cover with potatoes and dot with butter and bake in the oven at gas mark 6/400°F/200°C for 15-20 minutes.

*A Colorado grower wrote a 120-page epic in rhyme to the potato and its origins.*

## 6 MARCH

# POTATO AND PASTA WITH HERBS

A truly lovely dish that uses herbs available at this time of year.

1 lb (450g) potatoes, peeled and cut in bite-size pieces
10 oz (275 ml) small pasta shapes
6 fresh sage leaves
2 teaspoonfuls fresh rosemary leaves
Chopped parsley and chervil
10 peppercorns
6 juniper berries
Sea salt and freshly ground black pepper
2 tablespoons olive oil
2 oz (50 g) butter

Boil the potato pieces for 10 minutes or until just tender. Cook the pasta until *al dente* and while these are cooking prepare the following paste: pound the herbs in a pestle and mortar and season. Stir in the olive oil and add the butter. When the potatoes and pasta are cooked, drain and stir into the herb sauce.

*"In 1917 it was only because we had a good stock of potatoes in hand, that we survived the critical U-Boat peril."*

*From* ***Land at War****, British Government publication, 1944.*

## 7 MARCH

# POTATO, RED ONION AND CHEESE FLAN

Use a mature farmhouse Cheddar for this flan. It needs a robust flavour which will not come from an insipid cheese.

4 medium potatoes, peeled
3 oz (75 g) plain flour
3 oz (75 g) wholewheat flour
4 oz (110 g) butter
1 oz (25 g) lard
2 medium red onions, sliced
4 oz (110 g) grated Cheddar cheese
3 eggs
8 fl oz (225 ml) cream
2 fl oz (50 ml) milk
Sea salt and freshly ground black pepper

First make up the pastry by combining the flours and rubbing in 3 oz (75 g) of the butter and the lard until the mixture is crumbly. Add about 3 tablespoons cold water and mix until the pastry forms a dough that leaves the bowl clean. Put in a polythene bag and chill for a half hour in the fridge, then remove and line an 8-inch pie dish.

Boil or steam the potatoes until tender. Melt the remaining butter and allow the onions to cook gently, without browning, for 5 minutes.

Slice the potatoes and layer the flan case with the onions and cheese. Beat the eggs with the cream and milk and season. Pour into the flan case, and bake at gas mark 5/375°F/190°C for about 30-35 minutes.

*Potato losses from weevil damage in the Andean countries are estimated at $17 million a year. The International Potato Centre in Lima, Peru is currently working on natural methods to eliminate potato pests by developing biological pesticides, friendly fungi, pest-devouring bacteria and aphrodisiac traps.*

## 8 MARCH

# EGG AND POTATO PÂTÉ

It is essential that you make this with freshly puréed potatoes. You can add a lump of softened butter to the final result.

1 lb (450 g) potatoes, peeled and boiled
4 eggs, hard-boiled
1 tablespoon sesame oil
1 tablespoon chopped parsley
Sea salt and freshly ground black pepper

Remove the shells from the hard-boiled eggs. With a fork, mash the potatoes and eggs while still warm, add the oil, seasoning and parsley.

Mould into a little round and serve with a green salad arranged around it. Offer hot toast as well.

*The Norwegians used to make whiskey from potatoes. They believed it was not ready for drinking until it had made a round trip by ship to Australia. The labels had to establish the veracity of the claim.*

9 MARCH

# POTATO AND CHICKEN STOVIES

Stovies came from the French *étouffée,* which means stewing in an enclosed vessel.

2 lb (900 g) potatoes, peeled and sliced thickly
1 chicken
4 oz (110 g) butter
2 leeks, cleaned and sliced
1 onion
3 tablespoons dry white wine
1/2 pint (275 ml) stock
Sea salt and freshly ground black pepper

Cut up the chicken into pieces (reserving the carcass for stock). Alternatively you could use whole chicken breasts, but these will take less time to cook.

In a wide, thick pan with a lid heat the butter and sauté the chicken until lightly browned. Add the potatoes and leeks, cover with the wine and stock and seasonings. Cook very gently for a quarter of an hour or so until the chicken and potatoes are cooked.

*"Now, incredible as it may seem, suddenly, lately, potatoes, which were never even 'society gossip' have become 'news'."*

*Marcel Boulestin, 1932.*

## 10 MARCH

# LENTEN PIE

Originally this pie was served with puff pastry, presumably to elevate its rather prosaic status. I have substituted filo pastry which cooks more quickly so is added to the pie halfway through the cooking process. Not usually a recommended method with filo pastry as it can make it soggy, but it seems to work here.

12 oz (350 g) potatoes, peeled and thinly sliced
2 eggs, hard-boiled and sliced
8 oz (225 g) onions, thinly sliced
8 oz (225 g) cooking apples, peeled, cored and thinly sliced
1 teaspoon salt
$^{1}/_{2}$ teaspoon paprika
2 oz (50 g) butter
$^{1}/_{4}$ pint (150 ml) chicken or vegetable stock
4 sheets filo pastry

Parboil or steam the potatoes for about 10 minutes until just tender. Drain.

Layer the potatoes in a 9-inch pie dish with the eggs. onions and the apples, seasoning as you go. Cut the butter in little pats and put on top. Pour over the stock, cover with damp greaseproof paper and cook at gas mark 6/400°F/200°C for 25 minutes.

Brush each sheet of filo pastry with melted butter. Take the pie dish from the oven and remove the greaseproof paper. Paint the rim of the dish with melted butter and arrange the filo pastry as artistically as you can, folding up the edges so there is no necessity to trim. Filo pastry is very adaptable and there is no need to cover the whole pie surface.

Put back in the oven for another 15-20 minutes until golden.

*At the end of the 18th century, Count Rumford reported a soup that was brewed in Epping Workhouse that consisted in part of 28 lb potatoes, 4 lb pickled pork, 6 stones of shins and legs, 6 lb skibling (meat waste) and 20 lb of Scotch oatmeal.*

## 11 MARCH

# BOURBONNAIS PIE

The Bourbonnais was an ancient province of France renowned for its hearty and copious cuisine. This potato pie makes a robust meal for about 6 people. Its charm lies partly in the whole onions that are hidden among the potato layers.

2 lb (900 g) potatoes, peeled and thinly sliced
10 oz (275 g) plain flour
5 oz (150 g) butter
6 small to medium onions , peeled
Sea salt and freshly ground black pepper
1 egg yolk
6 fl oz (175 ml) cream

Make pastry with the flour and butter, adding a little cold water if necessary for binding the dough together. Chill in the fridge in a polythene bag for a half hour.

Line the bottom and sides of a deep ovenproof dish with pastry, reserving enough to cover the top.

Put the sliced potatoes into the dish, seasoning the layers and then push the peeled but uncut onions down among the potatoes. Cover with the pastry lid and make sure that the pie is quite sealed. Paint with the beaten egg yolk and cook at gas mark 4/350°F/180°C for 1 hour 30 minutes. If the pastry becomes too brown, cover it with a loose layer of silver foil.

Remove from the oven and with a sharp knife, remove the circle of pastry on top. Pour in the warmed cream and put back the pastry lid before serving.

*Juice extracted from raw potatoes has been used for centuries to nourish, heal and protect the skin. It has also been used as a cure for eczema.*

## 12 MARCH

# POTATO AND CHOCOLATE CAKE

So many chocolate cakes seem dry. This recipe makes a lovely, moist cake. Serve filled with whipped cream.

4 oz (110 g) potato, peeled and cooked
2 tablespoons double cream
2 1/2 oz (65 g) butter or margarine
7 oz (200 g) caster sugar
2 oz (50 g) plain chocolate
1/2 teaspoon bicarbonate of soda
3 eggs, separated
4 oz (110 g) plain flour
Pinch of salt
1 teaspoon baking powder
2 fl oz (50 ml) milk
1 tablespoon rum

Purée the potatoes. Add the cream and place in a bowl over a pan of hot water.

Beat the butter and the sugar. Melt the chocolate and stir it in. Add the potatoes. Dissolve the bicarbonate of soda in a little water and add to the mixture. Beat in the egg yolks.

Sift together the flour, salt and baking powder. Fold into the mixture alternately with the milk and rum. Whip the egg whites until stiff, stir in a spoonful and then fold in the rest. Divide the mixture between two prepared cake tins and bake for approximately half an hour at gas mark 5/375°F/190°C.

*It has been said that the Quechua Indians of South America had a thousand words in their language to describe the potato.*

13 MARCH

# POTATO CHOUX CASES

It might seem strange that the addition of potato improves choux pastry but I believe it to be so. The pastry may not keep so long, though. Eaten at once, these little balls of pastry are exquisite.

7 oz (200 g) potato, peeled, cooked and sieved
5 oz (150 g) butter
4 fl oz (110 ml) cold water
6 tablespoons flour
2 small eggs, plus 1 egg yolk
Pinch of salt

Put the butter and water in a saucepan, melt the butter and bring to the boil. Add the sifted flour and beat until the mixture leaves the side of the pan.

If you have a food processor, simply put the mixture into the bowl, add the eggs, one by one and then salt and potato. Process until the dough is very smooth. (At this stage it will come to no harm if left for a few hours, covered, in the fridge.)

Put into a forcing bag and pipe the mixture onto a greased baking tin. Brush the remaining beaten egg yolk on the little cases and bake for about a half-hour at gas mark 6/400°F/200°C. Then lower the temperature to gas mark 4/350°F/180°C for a further 10 minutes to dry them out. The cases should be a pale gold colour and feel very light.

Treat them as *vol-au-vent* cases, and fill with savoury mixtures or you can use them as eclairs, filled with cream and covered with chocolate or coffee icing.

*"I met in this town (Limerick), a certain reverend doctor, inventor of a new method of growing potatoes. This consists in cutting out, in spring, the shoots or eyes and planting them. It appears that the result is just as good as if the potatoes were cut up and planted, and with this benefit, that the tubers furnishing the shoots are still available as food - for pigs at any rate."*

*A Frenchman, de Latocnaye, writing about a journey through Ireland in 1796-97.*

14 MARCH

# SALAD OF POTATO CAKES WITH CHIVES

Like many excellent ways of cooking potatoes, this comes from Germany. These flat crisp discs are excellent on their own or as an accompaniment to meat dishes. They can be used, too, to make an excellent first course. By taking any salad leaves available in early spring from the garden - over-wintered spinach beet, sorrel, lamb's lettuce, radicchio - and turning them in a pungent dressing of lemon juice and a nut oil, and then using two potato pancakes per person to make a kind of sandwich of the salad, something very beautiful can be created on the plate. Don't make it like a set piece; allow the arrangement to be free. Decorate with little pieces of chervil.

1 lb (450 g) potatoes, peeled and grated
2 shallots, finely chopped
3 egg yolks, beaten
2 tablespoons chopped chives
Sea salt and freshly ground black pepper
Peanut oil for frying
Salad leaves
Lemon juice
Walnut or hazelnut oil

Wash the grated potato and dry well. Mix with the shallots, the egg yolks, the chives and the seasoning. In a wide frying pan heat the peanut oil and, taking little handfuls of the potato mixture, press down to form flat circles in the hot oil. Fry until brown on both sides.

Meanwhile have the salad leaves well washed and tossed in enough lemon juice and oil to flavour them well. When the potato is cooked, serve as suggested above.

*'Erdappelgrutze' were potato noodles made by the peasants of northern Germany at the end of the 18th century. The pulp was pressed through a mill and dried. The noodles were sometimes used in breadmaking. The idea was resuscitated by the Nazis.*

15 MARCH

# POTATO, CHEESE AND GARLIC BREAD

Use a well-matured Cheddar for this excellent loaf. It is at its best eaten warm at lunchtime with a strong flavoured pâté or cheese.

12 oz (350 g) potatoes
2 cloves garlic
2 teaspoons salt
12 oz (350 g) self-raising flour
2 teaspoons mustard powder
4 oz (110 g) Cheddar cheese, grated
1 egg
5 tablespoons milk

Crush the garlic with the salt. Mix the flour, mustard, garlic/salt mixture and the cheese.

Coarsely grate the peeled potatoes and add to the dry ingredients. Fold in the beaten egg and milk and knead to a smooth dough.

Shape into a round on a well-greased tin tray and cut into 4 wedges. Bake at gas mark 5/375°F/190°C for 45-50 minutes until golden.

*Up to a 1,000,000 people are estimated to have died as a result of the Irish Potato Famine in 1845-46. It also resulted in the emigration of up to 1½ million people from the island.*

16 MARCH

# PERUVIAN POTATOES

The cuisine of South America includes numerous ways of cooking potatoes. In Brazil we were served a repulsive dish of cold puréed potato, gluey with mayonnaise. We were unlucky on that occasion. The enormous range of peppers and spices, the fruits and vegetables, the marriage of native Indian cooking with influences of the Old World have created most distinctive and distinguished dishes. I have adapted this dish from a Peruvian recipe. Originally it was served in little rolls but is more manageable cooked as a large flat cake that will serve 6 people.

1 1/2 lb (700 g) potatoes, peeled
1 large egg, beaten
2 tablespoons oil
1 medium onion, chopped
1 clove garlic, chopped
8 oz (225 g) minced meat
2 large tomatoes, seeded and chopped
1/2 teaspoon chilli pepper, very finely chopped
2 oz (50 g) seedless raisins
A pinch of cumin
6 black olives
Seasoning to taste
4 hard-boiled eggs
A little flour
Oil for frying

Boil and purée the potatoes. Stir in the beaten egg. In the oil cook gently the onion and garlic for a few minutes and then add the minced meat. Cook for a few minutes more and then add the tomato, chilli pepper, raisins, cumin and olives. Season and move around over a gentle heat until the meat is cooked.

With floured hands take half of the potato purée and form a flat pancake, put the meat mixture onto this and cover with the sliced hard-boiled eggs. Cover with the rest of the potato. Heat a little oil in the bottom of a wide frying pan and slide the pancake into this. Fry on both sides until browned.

*In **The Potato of Romance and of Reality**, 1925, W.E. Safford says that the pottery found in early Peruvian tombs indicates that a variety of potato was in use about 200 AD , if not earlier.*

## 17 MARCH
## ST PATRICK'S DAY
# CHAMP

Champ is a traditional Irish dish that is served piled high and usually eaten with a spoon. A well is made in the centre of the potato and melted butter poured into the hole. Other names for this dish are 'thump' or 'stelk'. The Irish food writer, Theodora Fitzgibbon suggests that the name 'champ' originates in the northern counties and the dish includes nettle tops or chives. She gives the name 'cally', 'poundies' or 'pandy' for the traditional mixture of mashed potatoes with onion, milk and seasoning. It is very delicious and you will need at least 2 lb of potatoes for 4 people. A similar dish, Red Champ, made with mashed beetroot and garnished with beetroot is said to have originated in the Scottish borders.

2 lb (900 g) potatoes, peeled and boiled
Salt
Small bunch of scallions (spring onions) or 1 medium onion, chopped
$^1/_2$ pint (275 ml) milk or cream
A lot of butter, melted

Make a purée with the potatoes and the salt. Put the scallions or onion into the milk, bring to the boil and simmer for 5 minutes. Add to the potatoes. The result should be very soft and smooth.

*"George told me. 'Me grand-uncle was in Monaghan gaol for a debt of eleven shillings. Me granny bought him his dinner of champ every day. Twenty one and a half Irish miles to Monaghan, she'd have the champ warm enough to melt the butter'."*

*From **The Green Fool** by Patrick Kavanagh, 1938.*

18 MARCH

# MARIA O'FARRELL'S POTATOES WITH CREAM AND PARMESAN

This is absolute gluttony.

2 lb (900 g) potatoes, peeled
8 oz (225 g) butter
$^1/_2$ pint (275 ml) cream
4 oz (110 g) Parmesan cheese

Melt the butter in a large earthenware pot and add the potatoes. Leave them on a high heat until the butter is bubbling and then turn down to a gentle heat. Cook the potatoes for 30 minutes or so and then turn (they should be brown underneath).

Cook on for a further 30 minutes or so until the potatoes are cooked through. Just before serving, add the cream and Parmesan cheese, gently amalgamating the ingredients.

*The process of crisp-making converts £1 worth of potatoes into £13 worth of crisps.*

## 19 MARCH

# SWEETCORN POTATOES

Sweetcorn has many charms, one being that it is available from a freezer or a tin and doesn't suffer too much from being kept in either.

1 1/2 lb (700 g) potatoes, peeled and boiled
Sea salt and freshly ground black pepper
1 large tin or 8 oz frozen sweetcorn (or fresh)
Butter

Prepare a purée of potato. Season. In a pan gently heat the sweetcorn and just before serving, add it to the potatoes with a generous knob of butter.

*" 'Excellent,' James Bond said to the barman, 'But if you can get a vodka made with grain instead of potatoes, you will find it still better.' "*

*From* ***Casino Royale*** *by Ian Fleming, 1953.*

## 20 MARCH

# HASSELBACK POTATOES

These are known in our house as 'Judy' potatoes after the sister-in-law who introduced them into our lives. What a good turn she did us. Quantities here are impossible to give because it depends on the size of the potatoes. You will need the same amount as if you were serving roast potatoes.

Potatoes
Butter
Good chicken stock
Sea salt and freshly ground black pepper

If the potatoes are large, cut in half. Cut a slice off the side of the peeled potatoes so that they have a flat base. With a sharp knife make a series of cuts vertically down into half the potato so that it resembles a crown. Make sure you don't cut the potato right through.

Place the potatoes in a well-buttered baking dish, put a little dab of butter on each potato and then season. Pour the stock over the potatoes so that it is roughly $^{1}/_{4}$ inch covering on the bottom of the dish.

Put into a hot oven (gas mark 7/425°F/220°C) and cook as for roast potatoes, but baste frequently, and by the time the stock is all absorbed (45 minutes to an hour, depending on size), you will have perfect golden potatoes.

*In 1771, Parmentier listed vegetables that could be used in times of food shortages. These included acorns, horse-chestnuts, roots of bryony, iris, gladioli, couch-grass and...potatoes.*

## 21 MARCH

# CARAMELISED POTATOES

This is a traditional Danish way of cooking potatoes and usually made with very small new potatoes. If you can't get these, you can use old potatoes, but cut them into small even-sized pieces. I cook these in a heavy, flat-bottomed wok.

1$^{1}/_{2}$ lb (700 g) potatoes
1 oz (25 g) sugar
2 oz (50 g) butter, preferably unsalted
Sea salt

Wash the potatoes well. Do not peel. Melt the sugar gently until it just turns brown and then stir in the butter. Add the potatoes and cook very gently over a lowish heat, turning the potatoes frequently so they are coated with the caramel. Sprinkle with sea salt and serve.

*"It (the potato) is favourable to population; for it has been observed that in the western parts of Ireland where it is almost the only diet of the labouring poor, it is no unusual thing to see six, seven, eight, ten and sometimes more children, the issue of one couple, starting almost naked out of a miserable cabin, upon the approach of an accidental traveller."*

*From* **The Practical Farmer or The Complete English Traveller** *by David Henry, 1771.*

## 22 MARCH

# POTATOES AURORE

A good supper dish. To speed the cooking time of baked potatoes, try standing them in very hot water for 5 minutes before putting them in the oven.

4 large potatoes, cleaned
A little double cream
4 hard-boiled eggs
4 oz (110 g) bacon, diced
Sea salt and freshly ground black pepper
Nutmeg

Bake the potatoes and put the pulp into a bowl. Stir in the cream, then add the whites of the hard-boiled egg, finely chopped. Have ready fried the pieces of bacon and add. Season and put back into the potato shells.

Before serving, sprinkle with the chopped egg yolks.

*"I have tried to make it clear how these people eating their potatoes under the lamplight, have dug the earth with those very hands they put in the dish , and so it speaks of manual labour, and how they have honestly earned their food."*

*Vincent Van Gogh, in a letter to his brother, speaking of his painting* **The Potato Eaters.**

23 MARCH

# POTATO AND CHEESE TORTILLA

This makes a lovely supper dish with a mixed salad.

1½ lb (700 g) potatoes, peeled and boiled
2 oz (50 g) butter
2 small egg yolks
3 oz (75 g) plain flour
2 teaspoons mustard
1 tablespoon Worcestershire sauce
4 oz (110 g) strong cheese, grated
Sea salt and freshly ground black pepper
1½ teaspoons dried yeast
4 tablespoons tepid milk

Make a purée of the potatoes and add the butter, egg yolks, flour, mustard, Worcestershire sauce, cheese and the seasonings.

Sprinkle the yeast on the milk and leave for 10 minutes. Beat into the potato mixture and leave in a warm place for 30 minutes.

In a large pan put a little hot oil and press the dough into this, cooking over a moderate heat for about 6 minutes. Turn with care, and cook for a further 6 minutes. Both sides should present a crusty, light golden surface.

*Under such headlines as 'Spuddy Stupid', scorn was poured on an installation made by Argentinian artist Victor Grippo and exhibited at the Ikon Gallery in Birmingham. His installation included potatoes wired up to a voltmeter to reveal them as potential sources of energy.*

24 MARCH

# COLUMBIAN POTATOES

A very good vegetarian dish, this is a reworking of the Latin American fondness for potatoes with chillies and cheese.

1 1/2 lb (700 g) small new potatoes, cleaned
1 tablespoon butter
2 scallions, sliced
1 green pepper, sliced
1/2 red chilli pepper, minced or chopped finely
2 large beef tomatoes, skinned and sliced
6 oz (175 g) mozzarella cheese, diced
1 egg, beaten

Steam the cleaned potatoes and while this is in progress, melt the butter and sauté the scallions and pepper for a few minutes. Add the tomatoes and simmer gently for 10 minutes. Over a low heat, add the cheese and as soon as it is melted, take off the heat and stir in the egg. Serve with potatoes.

*During the Gold Rush of 1898, because so many of the prospectors were suffering from scurvy, potatoes were exchanged with gold on a weight-for-weight basis. The tubers' high vitamin C content helped to alleviate the disease.*

25 MARCH

# POTATOES PIZZAIOLA

This is a student favourite in a house in Dublin where my daughter lived. Ingredients can be adapted to what is affordable and it can nourish large quantities.

$1^1/_2$ lb (700 g) potatoes, washed and thinly sliced
2 tablespoons sunflower or olive oil
2 fat cloves garlic, chopped
1 red pepper, thinly sliced
Sea salt and freshly ground black pepper
$^1/_2$ pint (275 ml) tomato juice
A few fresh tomatoes, skinned and sliced
4-6 oz (110-175 g) mozzarella cheese, very thinly sliced

Heat the oil and sauté the garlic and potato very slowly until the potatoes start to turn transparent. Add the red pepper, the seasonings, the tomato juice and the tomatoes and simmer over a low heat until the potatoes are soft, stirring now and then.

Take off the heat, cover with the cheese and allow it to melt before you serve.

*"And now for supper, the round board being spread:*
*The van a dish of coddled onions led;*
*I' th' Body was a salted tail of sammon*
*And in the Rear some rank Potatoes came in."*
*From* ***Songs and Poems of Love and Drollery*** *by Thomas Weaver, 1654.*

26 MARCH

# POTATOES AND CHEESE GRIDDLE SCONES

Cook these on a griddle or in a non-stick frying pan. Excellent with bacon, sausages or just a salad.

12 oz (350 g) potatoes, peeled, cooked and puréed
2 oz (50 g) fromage frais
2 oz (50 g) Cheddar cheese, grated
$^1/_2$ oz (15 g) softened butter
1 clove garlic, finely chopped
Sea salt
Flour

When the potato purée has cooled mix it with the fromage frais, cheese, butter, garlic and salt to taste and turn out onto a floured surface. With floured hands pat to about 1 inch thick. Cut into little rounds with a cutter.

Cook on a heated griddle or pan for about 5 minutes each side or until well browned.

*"The man who has not anything to boast of but his illustrious ancestors is like the potato - the only good thing belonging to him is underground."*

*Sir Thomas Overbury, 1613.*

27 MARCH

# CHOCOLATE, POTATO AND PECAN CAKE

This is an old-fashioned, dense cake with an unusual and elusive taste. It's the sort of cake that calls out to be dunked in strong coffee halfway through a cold morning.

7 oz (200 g) potatoes, peeled, cooked and sieved
6 oz (175 g) margarine
8 oz (225 g) sugar
4 eggs
12 oz (350 g) plain flour, sifted
1 tablespoon baking powder
1 teaspoon salt
1 teaspoon cinnamon
1 teaspoon cloves
1 teaspoon allspice
1/2 teaspoon grated nutmeg
1/4 pint (150 ml) milk
3 tablespoons black treacle
1 1/2 oz (40 g) plain chocolate, grated
1 teaspoon vanilla essence
4 oz (110 g) chopped pecans

This cake can be made almost entirely in a food processor. Cream the margarine and sugar and add the potato. Add the eggs, one at a time and then the flour, baking powder, salt and spices.

Add the milk and treacle and then the grated chocolate and vanilla. Lastly stir in the nuts. Turn into a well-greased 10-inch ring mould.

Bake at gas mark 7/425°F/220°C for about half an hour and then turn the oven down to gas mark 4/350°F/180°C. The cake should be cooked after 1-1¼ hours. Leave for 10 minutes before turning out.

*Good Friday is known as 'Spud Day' in Birmingham because it is the only day the Devil goes to church and thus a good day for planting potatoes and parsley. In Galway, is was considered unlucky to plant potatoes on a 'Cross day': this was any day that was a '4th day' after Christmas, counting with Christmas as the first day. In Kerry a piece of cypress wood was stuck into the potato ridge on planting day. When harvesting occurred, a branch of the same was burnt.*

## 28 MARCH
# BEIGNETS

The obligation to serve potatoes with every meal is a shackle from which a wise cook frees herself. These little beignets served as a dessert could be a concession to those, usually of the male sex, who feel that a meal without potatoes is not eating at all.

2 lb (900 g) potatoes
Grated skin of half an orange
1 tablespoon Grand Marnier
11 oz (310 g) flour
2½ oz (60 g) butter
1½ oz (40 g) sugar
3 egg yolks
Salt
Icing sugar
A little marmalade

Cook the potatoes in their skins and when cool, peel and put the pulp through a sieve. Mix the orange skin with the Grand Marnier.

Add the flour, butter, sugar, egg yolks and salt to the potato and work the preparation over a gentle heat for 5 minutes. Add the orange mixture.

Leave the mixture to get cold and then press out with floured hands until it is about half an inch thick. Cut into little shapes and deep fry in hot oil. Drain and eat at once with a little warmed marmalade as a sauce.

*A 'skeehogue' is a shallow wicker basket into which cooked potatoes were put. This allowed the water to drain out.*

29 MARCH

# POTATO WITH SEMOLINA

Rather a curious recipe this, but not without charm. It was given to me by a French friend who serves spoonfuls of the semolina/potato combination with a purée of pears and a few pieces of black pudding. It's not something one would want to eat in large quantities, or even too often, but it makes for a change.

1 lb (450 g) potatoes
$^{1}/_{2}$ pint (275 ml) warm milk
6 oz (175 g) semolina
2 oz (50 g) butter
Salt
Fresh fruit purée

Boil or steam the potatoes in their skins, peel them and make a purée with the warm milk. Stir in the semolina and the butter. Cook gently for 5 minutes over a low heat.

With a tablespoon dipped in warm melted butter, take out spoonfuls of the mixture to form egg shapes and put them onto a warm plate. Serve with the fruit purée.

*The 'Irish Apple' was a variety of potato in use as early as 1770 and was renowned for its dryness after boiling. It did not survive the coming of the blight - the fungus Phytophthora infestans in 1845.*

30 MARCH

# POTATO AND SAUSAGE SOUP

For this sustaining soup, you can use whatever smoked sausage most appeals to you. Frankfurters are a good addition.

4 medium potatoes, peeled and diced
1 oz (25 g) butter
1 medium onion, chopped
3 stalks celery, thinly sliced
2 carrots, thinly sliced
Bouquet garni
2 tablespoons wine vinegar
1 pint (570 ml) beef stock
1 pint (570 ml) water
1/2 small head cabbage, thinly sliced
8 oz (225 g) smoked sausage

Melt the butter in a large pan. Add the onion, carrot and celery and sauté until transparent. Add the bouquet garni, vinegar, stock and water. Bring to the boil, add the cubed potatoes and cook slowly until the vegetables are soft. After 15 minutes cooking time, put in the cabbage.

Before you serve, add the smoked sausage, cut in small pieces.

*The U.S. Department of Agriculture has made an absorbent powder out of potatoes for use in nappies.*

31 MARCH

# POTATOES WITH CELERY

I have eaten a similar dish to this cooked with peas instead of celery - a substitution that might find more favour with children.

1 lb (450 g) potatoes, scrubbed
1 head of celery, cleaned and cut into pieces
1 small onion, diced
2 oz (50 g) butter
1 tablespoon flour
$^1/_2$ pint (275 ml) ham stock
$^1/_2$ pint (275 ml) milk
2 tablespoons cheese, grated
2 tablespoons breadcrumbs

Boil the potatoes in salted water and steam the celery pieces. As soon as the potatoes are tender, cut into slices.

Sauté the onion in the melted butter for a few minutes, stir in the flour and then add the stock and milk to make a smooth sauce. Put the potatoes and celery in a casserole dish, pour over the sauce, sprinkle with the cheese and breadcrumbs and cook in a hot oven, gas mark 7/425°F/220°C for 10 minutes, or until the top is browned.

*It is said that the potato was accidentally introduced into England from Ireland, as a result of a shipwreck off the Lancashire coast.*

APRIL FOOL'S DAY

# HALF-BAKED POTATO

You can experiment with different flavourings for these potatoes with various herbs and spices.

4 large potatoes
4 tablespoons oil
2 teaspoons cumin or caraway seeds
Sea salt

Scrub potatoes and cut in half. Lay face down in a baking tin and pour oil and sprinkle seeds and salt over them.

Bake in a hot oven (gas mark 7/425°F/220°C) until soft inside - about half an hour.

*"Here's taters hot, my little chaps,*
*Now just lay out a copper*
*I'm known up and down the Strand*
*You'll not find any hotter."*

*Baked Potato Seller in* ***London Cries****, 1813.*

2 APRIL

# A WARM SALAD WITH CREAM AND DILL

Dill sown early in a greenhouse should be producing leaves by now. Dill appears with great reluctance if sown outside in my garden and runs to seed at the first chance.

$1^1/_2$ lb (700 g) potatoes, old or new
3 shallots, finely chopped
1 tablespoon of butter
6 fl oz (175 ml) cream
2 tablespoons dill leaves, chopped
Sea salt and freshly ground black pepper
4 handfuls mixed salad leaves

Boil or steam the cleaned potatoes until tender. Cook the shallots in the melted butter until translucent, then stir in the cream and the dill. Bring to the boil and season. Put the salad leaves on plates, place the potatoes on top and pour over the warm dressing. Eat immediately.

*"...the other day she call'd in here, and saw Lady Mount Cashell eating plain boil'd Potatoes for her luncheon in the middle of the day. She then heard for the first time that that was the principal Food of the Irish, and immediately resolv'd on giving Lady Mount Cashell a breakfast in compliment to her country. We went there and literally found nothing but Potatoes dress'd in Fifty different fashions. I thought the repast would never have been at an end, such was the torture she had put her fancy to in devising methods to diversify the cookery."*
*From* ***An Irish Peer on the Continent****, 1801-1803; a narrative of the tour of Stephen, 2nd Earl Mount Cashell as related by Catherine Wilmot, published 1924.*

3 APRIL

# CRÊPES PARMENTIER

Half pancake, half potato cake, these are good served as part of a brunch. Don't attempt to make them too large, for example, 4 inches in diameter is best.

8 oz (225 g) potato, peeled, cooked and puréed
1 teaspoon salt
1/2 pint (275 ml) milk, warmed
2 large eggs, beaten
1 tablespoon cream
2 oz (50 g) clarified butter

Make a batter with the potato, salt, milk, eggs and lastly the cream and leave to stand for 1 hour.

Add enough cold water (approximately 2-4 fl oz/50-110 ml) to give the batter the consistency of thin cream. Heat the butter in a wide frying pan and cook the crêpes for about 1 minute on each side or until browned.

*Marilyn Monroe once posed as 'Miss Idaho Potato'.*

## 4 APRIL

# BAKED POTATOES WITH GARLIC AND NUT SAUCE

The coming together of such wonderful and wholesome ingredients can only result in perfection. Since discovering Karate Chop Potatoes in Lyndsey Bareham's excellent *In Praise of the Potato*, I couldn't imagine dealing with them in any other way. After baking, the potato is put into a clean cloth and dealt a quick chop with the hand. The skin will burst open and reveal a floury 'smile' on the top of the potato. Over-enthusiam results in disintegration.

4 large potatoes, washed
2 oz (50 g) walnuts
2 oz (50 g) unblanched almonds
2 large cloves garlic
6 tablespoons of sunflower or olive oil
1 tablespoon lemon juice
Sea salt and freshly ground black pepper

Bake the potatoes. If you have a food processor, this sauce is easily made, otherwise you should use a pestle and mortar. Put 6 tablespoons of just boiled water into the processor bowl and, while in motion, add the nuts and garlic. Once they are mixed add the oil in a thin constant stream. Lastly, add the lemon juice and seasoning.

Eat with the freshly baked potatoes.

*Until 1770 three plants were called 'potato'; these were the yam, the sweet potato and the white potato - this last was known as the 'Irish potato' in America as early as 1635.*

## 5 APRIL

# PEASANT POTATOES

The acidic flavour of the sorrel adds a piquancy to the potatoes in this dish. This is a good accompaniment to white meats.

1lb (450 g) potatoes, peeled and thinly sliced
2 oz (50 g) butter
Large handful of sorrel leaves
1 large clove garlic, chopped
1 tablespoon chopped chervil
Approx. 1/2 pint (275 ml) good stock

Melt the butter in a wide, heavy pan and put in the sorrel leaves, stripped of any coarse stalk. Allow the leaves to wilt briefly. Put in the potatoes. Add the garlic and chervil. Pour over just enough stock to cover the potatoes.

Bring to the boil, cover the pan and then simmer for 10 minutes. Remove the cover and allow to cook until the potatoes are soft and the liquid is reduced to a thick sauce.

*Thomas Jefferson is credited with introducing French Fries to Americans. When he had them served at a dinner at the White House he was criticised for "putting on airs by serving novelties".*

6 APRIL

# BAKED POTATOES WITH JUNIPER BUTTER SAUCE

The sweet, pungent taste of crushed juniper berries has an affinity with venison, pork and chicken. It is also the prevailing flavour in gin. Served as a sauce with baked potatoes, its aromatic properties can be appreciated.

4 large potatoes
8 oz (225 g) butter
1 small onion, finely chopped
Juice of 1/2 lemon
A clove of garlic
1 teaspoon juniper berries
Sea salt and black peppercorns

Scrub the potatoes and bake until tender. Cook the onion until transparent in the butter. Add the lemon juice. In a pestle and mortar pound the garlic, juniper berries, salt and peppercorns. Add to the onions and butter and take off the heat.

When the potatoes are cooked, put them in a clean cloth and gently press to break open the skin. Heat the butter sauce and pour into the top of each potato.

*The now rare 'Lumper' potato was said to have 'tears in his eyes' for the Irish who died in the potato famine.*

## 7 APRIL

# WARM POTATO SALAD WITH DANDELION LEAVES

New potatoes are available in the shops now. This salad is popular in France. You can gather little dandelion leaves along the hedgerow and a very pleasurable activity it is too. A patch of dandelions is better covered with an upside down pot for a week or so to blanch the leaves. The French call dandelions *pissenlits,* presumably because they were thought to cause bed-wetting.

1 lb (450 g) new potatoes
4 oz (110 g) smoked bacon, cut in little pieces
2 tablespoons olive, hazelnut or sesame oil
4 tablespoons wine vinegar
Sea salt and freshly ground black pepper
A few spring onions
A handful of freshly picked dandelion leaves

Steam the potatoes and when cool enough to handle, push off the skins and quarter. Meanwhile, have the bacon pieces quickly fried.

Make a dressing with oil and vinegar and seasonings and turn the warm potatoes in this. Sprinkle with the bacon and put with the spring onions and the dandelion leaves.

*"Will your Ladyship have a potato pie? 'Tis a good stirring dish for an old lady after a Long Lent."*

*From* ***Love's Cure or the Martial Maid*** *by John Fletcher, 1623.*

8 APRIL

# PUMPERNICKEL BREAD

Pumpernickel bread is made from rye flour. Its keeping properties are excellent; in fact it should be kept for 2 days after baking before it is cut.

4 oz (110 g) potatoes, peeled, cooked and purėed
1 lb (450 g) wholewheat flour
4 oz (110 g) rye flour
2 teaspoons salt
1 packet Quick-Action dried yeast
1 dessertspoon molasses
$^3/_4$ pint (400 ml) warm water
1 tablespoon caraway seed

Mix the wholewheat and rye flours with the salt and add the dried yeast. Dissolve the molasses in the warm water and mix with the flours to make a dough. Add the potatoes - at this stage the dough will be sticky and a little extra flour may be needed. Knead in a food processor or by hand on a floured surface.

Put in a clean bowl, cover and leave for about 2 hours for the dough to double in volume. Knock it back, divide between 2 small greased bread tins, cover with oiled polythene and leave to prove again for another 1-$1^1/_2$ hours.

Sprinkle with the caraway seed and bake at gas mark 5/375°F/190°C for an hour.

*Marlene Dietrich once wrote: "Potatoes; I love them. I eat them." When she was pursued by an aggressive autograph hunter in a restaurant, she signed the book and then took a forkful of pommes purėed and mashed it between the leaves of his book.*

## 9 APRIL

# SLIMMER'S CHIPS

This must seem like a contradiction but the fat here is kept to an absolute minimum. Peel and boil or steam whole potatoes. When just tender, cool and then cut into chip slices.

With a pastry brush, put a few little dabs of oil on the chips and cook under a hot grill, turning frequently, while they brown. Not the real McCoy, but not a bad substitute for the figure conscious.

*Paul Henry's painting **The Potato Diggers** currently hangs in the National Gallery in Dublin and portrays the women of Connemara digging potatoes.*

## 10 APRIL

# POTATO CHUTNEY

The visual appeal of potato chutney would have to be rated low, but setting that aside, it makes a robust and piquant accompaniment to cold meats. Unlike most chutneys, it should be eaten within 24 hours.

1 lb (450 g) floury potatoes, peeled and boiled
1 medium onion, very finely chopped
1 teaspoon fresh ginger, grated
2 tablespoons wine vinegar
1 clove garlic
Sea salt and freshly ground black pepper
1/2 red or green chilli, skinned and chopped into little pieces
2 oz (50 g) raisins
1 tablespoon chopped chives

When the potatoes are boiled, dry well and mash lightly with a fork. While still warm, add the onion, ginger, vinegar, the garlic crushed in the salt, the chilli pepper, raisins and the chives and the raisins. Allow to get cold before you eat.

*The 'King Edward' variety of potato was originally raised by a gardener in Northumberland who christened it the 'Fellside Hero'. The name was changed before the potato was launched on the market.*

## 11 APRIL

# COD, SALMON AND POTATO IN CREAM SAUCE

Here is a lovely dish of the utmost simplicity that takes about 15 minutes to prepare - if the potatoes are small enough they take no more than 10 minutes to steam.

2 lb (900 g) very small new potatoes, cleaned
3 oz (75 g) butter
6 fl oz (175 ml) cream
12 oz (350 g) fresh cod, cut into pieces approx. 1x2 inches
12 oz (350 g) fresh salmon fillet, cut into pieces approx. 1x2 inches
Sea salt and freshly ground black pepper
Parsley or chervil, chopped

Put the potatoes on to steam and, when they are almost tender, put the butter and cream in a large heavy frying pan over a moderate heat and let the butter melt. Add the fish pieces and cook for about 3 minutes during which time the fish will become opaque. On no account let the liquid boil - the whole process must be very gentle. Add the potatoes and seasoning and cook for another 3 minutes or so. Season, sprinkle with parsley or chervil and serve at once.

*"For the thousandth time, why, why, why I ask, do we, the English, the pioneers of European potato cultivation, now grow such uninteresting potatoes...?"*

*From **An Omelette and a Glass of Wine** by Elizabeth David, 1984.*

12 APRIL

# POTATO SKINS ROASTED WITH GARLIC

Another excuse for eating garlic, if such a thing were needed. If you don't like garlic, these skins could be eaten with a dip made of sour cream and chives, or avocado, or smoked fish or melted cheese.

For each person you will need the peelings of 4-5 large potatoes. Keep the potatoes for another dish. See that the peelings are very clean and dry and then pour over a good quality olive oil, turning them over so that each piece of peel has contact with the oil, but isn't drowned. Season well with sea salt and black pepper.

Put into an ovenproof dish and then for each person add a head of garlic, left unpeeled, and then pushed down among the peelings.

Roast in a hot oven (gas mark 7/425°F/220°C) for 30-40 minutes or until the skins are golden brown. Each person is then given a plate of potato skins arranged around a head of garlic.

The warm garlic, sucked out from its skin, acts as a sauce for the crisp peelings. Sprinkle with salt again. The only way to eat these potatoes is with the fingers.

*"Here's Cucumbers, Spinnage and French Beans*
*Come buy my nice Sallery.*
*Here's Parsnips and fine Leeks*
*Come buy my Potatoes too."*

***A Roxburghe Ballad**, c.1700.*

13 APRIL

# POTATOES WITH CREAM

Potatoes and cream are natural partners; not for the dieter, perhaps, but for the very hungry and hard-worked, most sustaining and quite delicious. This recipe is, perhaps, better cooked with new potatoes but is good, too, with old ones.

1½ lb (700 g) potatoes
Sea salt and freshly ground black pepper
A little nutmeg
¼ pint (150 ml) milk
A generous ½ pint (275 ml) cream

Steam or boil the potatoes in their skins. When they are cooked but firm, peel them and cut into slices. Sprinkle with salt, pepper and nutmeg.

Put in a clean pan and cover with milk and cream, reserving a little cream. Bring to the boil and reduce until the cream is thickened. Away from the heat stir in the additional cream and serve.

*In 1937, Captain D.J. Jones, in his steamer Marie Llewellyn that was loaded with potatoes, tried to run General Franco's blockade off the Spanish coast. He was prevented by a British warship and became known as 'Potato' Jones.*

### 14 APRIL
### PAN-AMERICAN DAY
# POTATOES WITH EGGS AND CHORIZO

Or - *Huevos con Papas y Chorizo*...a very hearty Mexican breakfast. Perfect for brunch.

2 large potatoes, peeled and diced
1 lb (450 g) chorizo sausage
1 large onion, chopped
4 eggs
1 avocado, sliced
A little parsley, chopped

Put the sausages into a large wide pan and cook, mashing them at the same time with a fork so that some fat is released. Add the potatoes and onion. Cover and cook over a medium heat until the potatoes are tender. This will take about 15 minutes.

Take off the lid, make 4 indentations in the potatoes and break an egg into each. Cover and cook until the eggs are set in about 5 minutes. Serve with the avocado and parsley.

*"It has been asserted by the highest authorities that the woman who can cook a potato to perfection can cook anything."*

*From **Potato Cookery 300 Ways** by C. Herman Seen, 1907.*

15 APRIL

# LAYERED POTATOES AND MUSHROOMS WITH TWO CHEESES

Fresh ricotta has a bland taste that comes into its own cooked in conjunction with more defined flavours.

1 lb (450 g) potatoes, cleaned and very thinly sliced
2 oz (50 g) butter
8 oz (225 g) mushrooms, sliced
2 cloves garlic, chopped
6 oz (175 g) ricotta cheese
3 oz (75 g) Parmesan cheese, grated
Sea salt and freshly ground black pepper

Reserve the potatoes in cold salted water. Melt the butter and sauté the mushrooms with the garlic until just turning colour. Do not overcook. Drain the mushrooms, reserving the liquid.

With a fork, mash the two cheeses together. Drain the potatoes and dry them well. Butter a 9-inch pie dish and put a layer of potatoes at the bottom, then half the mushrooms. Spoon over some of the mushroom liquid and then spread the cheese mixture on top. Follow with another layer of mushrooms and lastly the potatoes. Season as you go and finish by pouring any remains of the mushroom liquid over the whole.

Cover with wet greaseproof paper and bake at gas mark 7/425°F/220°C for 45 minutes.

*"A harvest dinner was given by a landlord to his tenantry...Great was the work of destruction going on upon huge mounds of beef, joints of pork and mutton, pyramids of greens and potatoes, enormous puddings, pies of Brobdingnag dimensions, jugs of beer and jars of teetotal temperance cordial. One man had a plate before him which was piled high with contributions from every dish on the table, a large slice of plum pudding resting very amicably beside a goodly segment of corned beef, flanked with greens. Still he seemed not quite satisfied - there was evidently something wanting to complete his happiness. He had not potatoes."*

*From Letters from the Coast of Clare,* **Dublin University Magazine**.

16 APRIL

# POTATOES IN SPICED YOGHOURT

Yoghourt is easily made with a Thermos flask and a thermometer. A tablespoon of yoghourt stirred into a pint of milk that has been brought to blood heat, left overnight in the Thermos, makes perfect yoghourt.

1 lb (450 g) potatoes, cleaned
2 tablespoons oil
1/2 teaspoon finely chopped fresh ginger
1/2 teaspoon cinnamon
1/2 teaspoon ground cardamom
Pinch of powdered cloves
2 bay leaves
Sea salt and freshly ground black pepper
1/2 pint (275 ml) unsweetened yoghourt

Boil or steam the cleaned potatoes (peel if old ones are used) until tender. Keep warm while you prepare the rest.

Heat the oil in a wide pan and put in all the spices. Cook for a few moments and then add the potatoes. Put a lid on the pan and shake it so that the potatoes are covered with the spices. Finally add the yoghourt and sprinkle with salt before serving.

*"The leaves of Potato are manifestly hot and dry in the beginning of the second Degree, as manifestly appear by the Taste. But the Roots are temperate in respect to heat or cold, dryness and moisture: They Astringe, are moderately Duiretick, Stomatick, Chylisick, Analeptick, and Spermatogenetick. They nourish the whole body, restore in Consumptions, and provoke Lust."*

*From* ***The English Herbal*** *by William Salmon, 1710.*

17 APRIL

# WARM SALAD OF POTATOES, QUAIL'S EGGS AND ROASTED PEPPERS

The only problem with this salad is that the ingredients must be warm when they come together and the preparation of the eggs and the peppers must be done at the last minute.

1½ lb (700 g) very small new potatoes
1 teaspoon sugar
8 tablespoons olive oil
3 tablespoons wine vinegar
Sea salt and freshly ground black pepper
4 tablespoons chopped herbs - parsley, chives etc.
2 red peppers
12 quail's eggs
1 tin anchovies, drained and cut in tiny strips
A few capers

Clean and steam the potatoes. Meanwhile, prepare the dressing by mixing the sugar with the oil and vinegar and season to taste. Stir in half the herbs.

Put the peppers in a very hot oven (gas mark 8/450°F/230°C) for 5 minutes or so until the skins are charred and loose. Wash briefly under a cold tap rubbing off the skins and removing the seeds. Cut into little strips.

Put the eggs into cold water, bring to the boil and simmer for 30 seconds. Drain and as soon as you can handle them, peel.

When the potatoes are tender, drain and bring together with the peppers and the eggs. Pour over the dressing and move the ingredients around in this. Add the anchovies and the capers, sprinkle with the rest of the herbs and serve.

*The first published account of the potato is in* ***La Cronica Del Peru*** *by Piedro de Cieca, printed in Seville in 1553. The plant is described and illustrated by an engraving.*

18 APRIL

# POTATOES IN BUTTER

This is for butter lovers. The results depend on your generosity with the butter. Quantities will depend on appetite; enormous quantities of these are consumed in our house. Take new, cleaned potatoes, no bigger than a golf ball and put in a fat lump of butter melted in an ovenproof dish on the top of an oven. As soon as the butter starts to sizzle, and the potatoes are covered, put into a hot oven for 20-30 minutes until they are tender and golden skinned. Sprinkle only with sea salt.

*"I'll give you a song, 'tis a true Irish strain*
*Our cruiscins and glasses my boy let us drain.*
*Our voices in chorus now manfully lend*
*And sing the potato's the Irishman's friend*
*With my Ballinamona oro, a laughing potato for me!*

*'Tis the root of all roots and that everyone knows*
*And best of all places in Ireland it grows*
*So grateful of care it repays well our toil*
*And like a true Paddy is fond of the soil*
*With my Ballinamona oro, a mealy potato for me.*
*Tis said that from Quito to Europe it came,*
*To Spain first imported, pappa its name*
*Not amiss, for well bedded or early or late*
*With my Ballinamona oro, a lumping potato for me.*

*Prata na hEireann, the Irish potato*
*It's progeny various would puzzle a saint,*
*Pink, purple, and white, red, russet and black*
*But all the same hue, with no coat on their back.*
*With my Ballinamona oro, the land of potatoes for me."*

***Prata na hEireann (The Irish Potato) 19th century ballad.***

19 APRIL
PRIMROSE DAY

# POTATOES IN MEAT JUICES

When you have cooked a roast of meat, and tipped off the excess fat into a bowl, if it is left to harden in a cold place, you will find that a small amount of concentrated meat jelly will have gathered at the bottom. It is the addition of this to gravies and meat sauces that intensifies the taste. An onion put in the roasting tin when the meat is cooking, increases the flavour and colour of the gravy too.

1 lb (450 g) potatoes, peeled and quartered
2 tablespoons sunflower oil
3/4 pint (400 ml) good meat gravy

Put the potatoes in a sauté pan with the oil. Let them brown quickly and then pour over the gravy. Cover with a lid and transfer to the oven, approximately gas mark 6/400°F/200°C for 45 minutes until the potatoes are tender.

*The Scots use a large potato for the head of a scarecrow and call it a 'Potato Bogle'.*

20 APRIL

# CHIP BUTTY

I know nothing about potato sandwiches, so had to turn to a friend who tells me that he lived off them many years ago while a student at Trinity, Dublin. The secret, he tells me, is 2 fresh slices of 'white pan' bread, thickly smeared with butter, and on one piece a decent coating of HP sauce. The hot chips are then placed on this (he liked to put them in a pattern) and then the second slice is pressed down on top. The sandwich is then cut in half but not, he stresses, as triangles. Any attempt at gentrification would be out of keeping with the whole tradition of chip butties.

In celebration of the 150th anniversary of the Royal College of Art, an *Artists' Cookbook* included a recipe by Alf Dunn that suggested sprinkling the chips with garlic salt. While the chips are cooking, cut slices of granary bread and spread thickly with butter. Drain the chips and fill the sandwiches, sprinkling them with salt and vinegar. A good sandwich should be more chips than bread and should ooze butter when bitten. Serve with a glass of beer.

*In 1983 the Ukranian Academy of Science claimed to have successfully tested a generator that used a potato as a source of electricity. The researchers said that a single potato would provide electricity for nearly a month.*

## 21 APRIL
# POTATO GNOCCHI

Be sure to see that the potatoes are very dry before you purée them.

1 lb (450 g) potatoes
2 oz (50 g) butter
1 egg and 1 egg yolk
2 1/2 oz (60 g) flour
Salt and pepper
A little nutmeg
Butter

Peel and boil the potatoes, drain and sieve. Add the butter, egg and yolk, flour and seasonings. Divide the mixture into little balls and flatten slightly.

Poach gently in boiling salted water. They should be cooked in 5 minutes and will rise to the surface. Take them out with a slotted spoon, drain. You can eat them straight away or put in a gratin dish with some butter and heat in the oven (gas mark 6/400°F/200°C) for 15 minutes.

*The Prussian name for the War of the Bavarian Succession (1778-1779) was 'The Potato War', largely because the operations revolved around the acquisition or denial of the potato supplies to the enemy.*

22 APRIL

# CINNAMON POTATO BUNS

This is one of my favourite potato recipes. The result is a cross between an Eccles cake and a croissant. Perfect for brunch parties (the quantities given make about 2 dozen buns), hot from the oven, and for committed gluttons, a slit made in the centre and fresh butter put inside. Sometimes I use half the dough for buns, and make a loaf of bread with the other half (it freezes well) cooked in the normal way for bread.

8 oz (225 g) potatoes, cooked and puréed
4 oz (110 g) butter
3½ oz (90 g) sugar
½ pint (275 ml) milk
2 teaspoons salt
2 eggs
2½ lb (1 kg 125 g) flour
1 packet Quick-Action yeast

The dough is quickly made in a food processor. I doubt if I should have the patience to make it without one. Place the butter, sugar, salt, milk and potatoes in the bowl and mix well. Add the beaten eggs, the flour and the yeast and enough tepid water to make a pliable dough. Place in an airtight container in a warm place overnight.

Filling:
4 oz (100 g) butter
4 oz (110 g) granulated sugar
1 teaspoon cinnamon
4 oz (100 g) raisins
4 oz (110 g) light brown sugar
4 oz (110 g) chopped walnuts

Divide the dough into two parts. Roll each part out into a thin rectangle about ¼ inch thick. Mix the sugar and cinnamon and sprinkle over the dough. Add the raisins, brown sugar and nuts. Drizzle the butter over the whole surface and roll up as for a roulade.

Cut into $^1/_2$ inch slices and place side by side in a well greased pan. Allow to rise again. Bake at gas mark 5/375°F/190°C for 20-25 minutes. Irresistible!

*To say 'small potatoes' about something means to attach very little importance to it.*

## 23 APRIL
## ST GEORGE'S DAY
# LANCASHIRE HOTPOT

The hotpots of my childhood in post-war London remain through the years as memories of "lumps of fat in washing-up water" as my brother used to call them as he tipped our platefuls out of the window. How different the refined, and more expensive, stews of today. The recipe below is not authentic Lancashire.

$1^1/_2$ lb (700 g) potatoes, peeled and thinly sliced
$1^1/_2$ lb (700 g) lean lamb, cubed
2 tablespoons olive oil
4 medium onions, sliced
1 clove garlic chopped
8 oz (225 g) mushrooms, sliced
Sea salt and freshly ground black pepper
Good meat stock
A little melted butter

Trim any fat from the lamb and brown it quickly in heated oil. Remove from the pan, add the onions and the garlic and allow to cook for a few minutes. Add the mushrooms, cook for a few more minutes, then season.

Put the lamb back into the pan and cover with a good meat or vegetable stock. Bring to the boil and put into a casserole dish.

Cover with the potatoes. Brush with the melted butter and cover with a piece of wet greaseproof paper.

Cook for $1^1/_2$ hours in a slow oven (gas mark 3/325°F/170°C). Remove the paper and cook for a further 20 minutes allowing the potatoes to brown.

*Sir Francis Drake brought the first shipload of potatoes home to Queen Elizabeth. An outbreak of scurvy among the sailors caused the feeding of the precious cargo to the crew. The raw potatoes saved their lives but the Queen received only one plant. The story goes that the cook threw away the tubers and cooked the leaves.*

## 24 APRIL

# CHOCOLATE MUESLI BISCUITS

More nutritious than most biscuits, it is impossible to detect the potato in these.

6 oz (175 g) potato, boiled and puréed, left to cool
2 oz (50 g) self-raising flour
2 oz (50g) butter
2 oz (50 g) light, soft brown sugar
6 oz (175 g) muesli
$^1/_2$ teaspoon mixed spice
1 egg
6 oz (175 g) good quality chocolate

Sift the flour into a bowl and rub in the butter. Stir in the soft brown sugar, muesli and mixed spice. Add the potato and egg, mix well and form into little balls the size of a walnut. Place on a well greased baking sheet and with a fork, press into little rounds. Cook in the centre of the oven at gas mark 5/375°F/190°C for 30 minutes. Transfer to rack and allow to cool.

Melt the chocolate in a double boiler and spread a little over each biscuit, making a swirl with a fork.

*While living at Neuenen, a district of Holland, Vincent Van Gogh painted many pictures that showed the dominant nature of potatoes in the diet and culture of the peasantry. These paintings include still life pictures of potatoes.*

25 APRIL

# POTATOES WITH LAMB'S LIVER, BACON AND AVOCADO

Here is a good combination of colours and flavours - bland and sharp, hot and cold - that elevates the old favourite 'liver and bacon' into something more sophisticated.

2 lb (900 g) potatoes, thinly sliced
2 tablespoons oil
2 large onions, thinly sliced
1 lb (450 g) lamb's liver, cut into strips
8 rashers streaky bacon, cut into strips
Sea salt and freshly ground black pepper
1 teaspoon French mustard
1 tablespoon wine vinegar
3 tablespoons olive oil
1 avocado, thinly sliced

Heat the oil in a large frying pan, add the onions and potatoes, then the liver and the bacon. Season as you go. Cover with a tight fitting lid and cook on a low heat for 20-30 minutes until the potatoes are just tender.

Meanwhile mix the mustard with salt and pepper to taste (and a little sugar if you like), add the vinegar and oil and amalgamate. Mix the avocado with the dressing. Put the avocado pieces on to the liver and potatoes just before serving.

*In 1663, the Royal Society of England took measures for the cultivation of potatoes in order to prevent famine.*

26 APRIL

# POTATO CHAHKEE

A chahkee is a vegetable curry.

1 lb (450 g) potatoes, peeled and quartered
3 oz (75 g) oil
1 medium onion, peeled & chopped
1 teaspoon ground chillies
$^{1}/_{2}$ teaspoon ground tumeric
1 garlic clove, peeled & chopped
Sea salt

Heat the oil and brown all the ingredients except the potatoes. Add the potatoes, stirring round the pan and allow to cook for about 10-15 minutes. Add $^{1}/_{2}$ pint (275 ml) water, bring to the boil and simmer until the potatoes are cooked.

*In Spain and Italy the potato is called Patata; in Finland, Peruna; in Columbia, Papa; in Romania, Cartofi; in Russia and Germany, Kartoffel and in Czechoslovakia, Brambor.*

27 APRIL

# POTATOES WITH BACON

Home-made stock is a prerequisite of a well-run kitchen. The success or failure of dishes is largely dependent on the quality of stock used.

1 lb (450 g) potatoes, peeled and sliced
6 oz (175 g) bacon, cut in small pieces
1 medium onion, sliced
1 oz (25 g) butter

1 tablespoon flour
$^3/_4$ pint (400 ml) good stock (chicken or vegetable)
Sea salt and freshly ground black pepper
Sprig of thyme
Bayleaf

Fry the bacon and the onion gently in the butter. Stir in the flour, cook for a few moments and then pour in the stock (previously heated). Season and add the thyme and bay leaf and lastly, the potatoes.

Cover the pan and cook for about $^1/_2$ hour or until the potatoes are tender.

*In 1793, Alexander Dumas reported that potatoes had been planted in the main flower beds of the Jardin des Tuileries. Potatoes were sometimes known as 'Royal Oranges' as a result of this.*

28 APRIL

# WARM SALAD OF POTATOES AND CHICKEN LIVERS

Even after a very cold winter it is possible, with judicious planting, to have salad leaves in the garden from very early spring. The following quantities will make a first course for 4 people.

$1^1/_2$ lb (700 g) new potatoes
12 oz (350 g) chicken livers
1 oz (25 g) butter
2 fl oz (50 ml) Amontillado sherry
2 tablespoons walnut or hazelnut oil
1 tablespoon sherry vinegar or red wine vinegar
Sea salt and freshly ground black pepper
Variety of salad leaves

Steam the cleaned potatoes and when cool enough to handle, slice thickly. Keep warm. Clean the chicken livers, cut each in half and fry quickly in the butter - they are only being 'sealed' and should remain pink inside. Keep warm.

Pour the sherry into the pan in which the livers were cooked and reduce by boiling to 1 tablespoon. Scrape these pan juices through a sieve into a small pan and then add the oil, vinegar and seasoning. Warm over a gentle heat.

Arrange the salad leaves on each plate. Place on the potatoes and chicken livers and splash on the dressing. Serve warm.

*"It would be a waste of time and space to dwell upon the importance of the Potato, either as an article of food or as regards its place in the garden. Of all cultivated vegetables it is in the greatest demand..."*

*From* ***The Profitable Culture of Vegetables*** *by Thos. Smith, 1919.*

29 APRIL

# POTATO WITH CHEESE, CREAM AND CHIVES

These elegant little offerings are ideal for entertaining. Chives are among the first herbs to appear in the year.

2 large potatoes, finely sliced
3 oz (75 g) Emmenthal cheese, grated
1 medium onion, very finely chopped
4 tablespoons double cream
Bunch of chives

Grease and line with greaseproof paper the base of 4 patty tins. Cut the potato slices into circles with a small fluted cutter. Layer the potatoes with the cheese, chives and onion, finishing with a layer of cheese.

Spoon a tablespoon of cream into each tin and bake at gas mark 4/350°F/180°C for 25-30 minutes.

*"In the potato, we have the scarcely innocent underground stem of one of a tribe set aside for evil."*

*John Ruskin, 1869.*

30 APRIL

# PURÉE OF POTATOES WITH CHEESE AND ALMONDS

This is rather rich and goes well with steamed fish or chicken.

$1^{1}/_{2}$ lb (700 g) potatoes, peeled
A little warm milk
$1^{1}/_{2}$ oz (40 g) butter
1 egg
2 tablespoons Parmesan cheese
2 tablespoons flaked almonds

Boil and purée the potatoes. Stir in the warmed milk, the beaten egg and the butter. Sprinkle with the cheese and finally the flaked almonds and brown under a hot grill.

*"The three most delightful things to see; a garden of white potatoes covered in blossom, a ship under sail and a woman after giving birth."*

*Irish proverb.*

# BORSCHT WITH POTATOES

Fidel Castro, speaking of the economic situation on May Day, 1992, talked about "The Battle of the Potato". Potatoes have sustained hungry people for generations. A Russian soup seems suitable for May Day. Serve with a spoonful of sour cream dusted with a little paprika.

8 oz (225 g) potatoes, cleaned
$1^1/_2$ pints (just under a litre) vegetable stock
2 tins tomato juice
1 onion
6 oz (175 g) carrots
8 oz (225 g) uncooked beetroot
6 oz (175 g) shredded cabbage
Sea salt and freshly ground black pepper
1 tablespoon lemon juice

Bring the stock and the tomato juice to the boil and add the vegetables shredded into julienne strips, together with the seasoning. Cook for about 20 minutes or until the vegetables are tender.

Add the lemon juice just before you serve.

*"The laying of the skin of a potato on May the first at a maiden's door is an expression of contempt for her."*

*From **Flore populaire** by Eugene Rolland.*

2 MAY

# NEW POTATOES WITH PERSILLADE

Persillade is a simple but magical concoction of parsley and garlic, chopped and added to dishes at the end of cooking.

$1^1/_2$ lb (700 g) new potatoes, freshly dug
A little butter
Sea salt and freshly ground black pepper
2-3 large garlic cloves, chopped very finely
Chopped parsley

Clean and parboil or steam the potatoes for 10 minutes. Sauté in the butter until coloured golden. Season and put in a warmed serving dish. Mix the garlic and the parsley and strew over the potatoes before serving.

*In 1897, in Friesland in Holland, a local schoolmaster called Meester K.L. de Vries took over the local potato breeding station and soon established a name for himself as a successful potato breeder. He liked to call some of his new potato types after his favourite pupils - one of these was a young girl called Bintje Jansma - and after her was named the result of a 1905 cross which has remained famous among tuber growers to this day.*

3 MAY

# POTATO MOUSSAKA

The potato has found its way into many previously unpotatoed classic dishes, and not to their detriment. This will feed 4-6 people.

1 lb (450 g) potatoes, peeled and thinly sliced
1 large aubergine, sliced
4 tablespoons olive oil
2 medium onions, chopped
1 lb (450 g) lean lamb, minced
2 cloves garlic
1 teaspoon cinnamon
6 tomatoes, peeled and quartered (or 14 oz (400 g) can chopped tomatoes)
1 tablespoon tomato purée
Sea salt and freshly ground black pepper
2 oz (50 g) butter
3 tablespoons flour
A pinch of nutmeg
1½ pints (900 ml) milk, warmed
2 egg yolks

First sprinkle a little salt on the aubergine and leave the slices to drain. Heat 1 tablespoon of the olive oil and sauté the onions until they are transparent, then put in the lamb and stir frequently until it begins to brown. Put in the garlic, cinnamon, tomatoes, tomato purée and the seasoning. Cook for 10 minutes or so.

Rinse the salt off the aubergine and pat dry. Fry the slices in the remaining oil and then drain on kitchen paper to remove as much of the oil as possible. Layer with the lamb in a wide ovenproof dish. Cover with the potato slices.

Melt the butter, stir in the flour and the nutmeg and lastly the warm milk. Allow it to thicken and then off the heat, season and stir in the egg yolks. Bake uncovered at gas mark 5/375°F/190°C for about 50 minutes until the top is browning.

*In his lecture 'Paddy and the Potato', Professor Kevin Whelan quoted a Kerry woman who settled in Philadelphia in the post-famine period and wrote of her adopted land: "There's the best of beef there on china is (sic) plates/mighty mutton and Cuban gin/And isn't that much better grub/than to be stuck in Ireland on the lumper spud."*

### 4 MAY
### INDEPENDENCE DAY, ISRAEL

# LATKES

Latkes are potato pancakes and are integral to Jewish cooking. With the addition of onion, they accompany savoury dishes or, as a dessert, served with sugar, cinnamon, honey and perhaps cream. The addition of baking powder helps to make the latkes light.

1½ lb (700 g) old potatoes
1 medium onion, grated
Juice of a lemon
1 egg
2 tablespoons flour
Sea salt and freshly ground black pepper
2 teaspoons baking powder
Butter for frying

Peel the potatoes and soak in water for about 2 hours. Drain them well, grate and wring them through a clean cloth to dry well. At this stage you can put them through a food processor for a few moments but it is not necessary. Put with the onion, the flour, the lemon juice, the beaten egg, the seasoning and the baking powder, mixing together well.

Melt the butter and drop in spoonfuls of the mixture, frying on both sides until brown. This amount will make about 8 latkes.

*"To make potato starch: Peel and grate several large raw potatoes into a basin of cold water and stir well. Let them steep, squeezing the pulp in your hands, then pour off the water and let it stand till the starch can be seen settled at the bottom. Pour off the water and dry out the starch."*

*From **Food in England** by Dorothy Hartley, 1954.*

## 5 MAY

# POTATO BURGERS

Children like these and it saves getting out the chip pan, that most hateful of culinary pursuits.

1 lb (450 g) potatoes
1 lb (450 g) raw minced beef
2 medium onions, finely chopped
Chopped herbs
Sea salt and freshly ground black pepper

Peel and grate the potatoes. Dry in a cloth and add to the other ingredients. Make into little burgers and fry in hot oil. They will take a little longer to cook than normal beefburgers.

*HOW TO MAKE VERY GOOD CUSTARDS OF POTATOES*

*"Take a Quart of new Milk, six or seven potatoes, boyled and very well broken, a couple of Eggs well beaten, sugar about a quarter of a pound, a little Nutmeg grated; mingle them well together, and put into a shallow pewter or earthen dish, or else into a Crust, having first put a little piece of Butter in the bottom, and so bake it in an Oven, or over some Coals; then keep it till it be almost cold, and you will have an excellent, dainty and wholesome Dish, being both very pleasant to the Palate, and very restorative and strengthening to the Body; and also so cheap, that for ten pence charge, as much may be made, as will serve two reasonable men for a Meal."*

*From **England's first potato cookery book** by John Forster, Gentleman, 1664.*

6 MAY

# INDIAN-STYLE POTATO AND CHICKEN CASSEROLE

I love meals that are cooked all in one dish, as is this casserole.

1 lb (450 g) potatoes, peeled and thickly sliced
1 chicken, cut into bite-sized pieces
4 tablespoons corn oil
4 cardamom pods
1/2 teaspoon fennel seed
1/2 teaspoon cumin seed
1/2 teaspoon fenugreek seed
Large cube of fresh ginger, peeled and finely grated
2 cloves garlic, very finely chopped
1 tablespoon ground coriander
2 teaspoons ground cumin
1/2 teaspoon ground tumeric
1/2 teaspoon cayenne
2 dessertspoons tomato paste
1 teaspoon salt

Heat the oil in a wide casserole type pot over a medium heat. Put in the cardamom pods, the fennel, cumin and fenugreek seeds and stir. Put in the ginger and garlic and allow to cook for a minute before adding the ground coriander and cumin, the cayenne and tomato paste.

Add the potatoes and chicken pieces, then just cover with about a pint (570 ml). water and salt. Cover the pot, lower the heat and simmer for about 25 minutes or until the chicken and potatoes are tender.

If you are lucky enough to have a few leaves of coriander, sprinkle with these before serving.

*Potato - pillin' (probably peelin') was rhyming Cockney slang for a shilling.*

7 MAY

# GRILLED POTATOES WITH MAÎTRE D'HOTEL BUTTER

This is really an excuse to eat *maître d'hotel* butter which seems, sadly, to have gone out of fashion. The butter is very traditional French cooking and is made by mixing 4 oz (110 g) fresh butter with 1 tablespoon chopped parsley, half a teaspoon of salt and flavoured with a little lemon juice.

4 large potatoes, cleaned, cut in half lengthways and then thickly sliced
A little melted butter or oil
*Maître d'hotel* butter

Parboil the potato slices in salted water for 4 minutes. Brush with oil or melted butter and cook under a low grill until soft.

Serve with little pats of the *maître d'hotel* butter.

*"These tubers are nourishing as well as a pleasant dish equal in wholesomeness and salubrity to the batata (sweet potato), whether they be baked in hot ashes, or boiled and eaten with oil, vinegar or pepper, or prepared in any other way by the hands of an able cook."*
*John Gerard, Botanist, writing in 1597.*

8 MAY

# POMMES À LA BASQUE

The Bayonne ham used in this recipe is a raw, smoked product and not easy to find. A good quality ham may have to do instead.

4 large potatoes, cleaned
4 large tomatoes, skinned, de-seeded, cut in small strips

1 large red pepper, de-seeded, cut in small strips
4 slices Bayonne ham
Sea salt and freshly ground black pepper
A little melted butter
Breadcrumbs

Cut the potatoes in half lengthways and scoop out the centres (reserve this for soup). Parboil the potato shells for about 10 minutes in salted water, and while you are doing this prepare the tomatoes as stated above. Do the same with the peppers only leave the skin intact and cook the pieces briefly in a little butter. Cut the ham into strips.

Oil a deep dish, fill the potato cases with the other vegetables and the ham, seasoning as you go, and pour a little melted butter over each. Cook in a moderate oven (gas mark 5/375°F/190°C) for 45 minutes or until soft. When cooked, sprinkle with the breadcrumbs and brown under a grill.

*In France in the 17th century potatoes were hardly cultivated at all and were known as 'truffe' and 'truffe rouge'.*

9 MAY

# WARM POTATO SALAD WITH ANCHOVIES AND BACON

I close a recipe book if I see the words "chill in the fridge" referring to a salad. Here is a dish for like-minded cooks.

$1^1/_2$ lb (700 g) small new potatoes, cleaned
4 rashers streaky bacon, cut into little strips
4 tablespoons olive oil
1 tablespoon white wine vinegar
1 teaspoon French mustard
Freshly ground black pepper
4 fillets anchovies, cut into little strips
Chopped chives

Put the potatoes on to boil in salted water and meanwhile fry the bacon pieces until crisp. Take off the heat.

Combine the olive oil, vinegar and mustard and season with pepper. Put the cooked potatoes (cut in half if not very small) into the frying pan with the bacon pieces, add the anchovies and the dressing and over a gentle heat move the ingredients around the pan to warm through. Add the chives and serve at once.

*In **The Vegetable Garden,** published 1904, W. Robinson listed 194 different varieties of potato. The late Donald McLean of Perthshire was cultivating more than 350 different kinds at the time of his death in 1988.*

## 10 MAY

# POTATO KUGEL

This is useful if you can combine the cooking with, say, a casserole that needs a longish time in the heat.

1 lb (450 g) potatoes, peeled
3 eggs
2 oz (50 g) plain flour
1/2 teaspoon baking powder
Sea salt and freshly ground black pepper

In a bowl, beat the eggs well. Grate the potatoes and squeeze as much of the liquid out of them as possible.

Add all the ingredients to the eggs, put into a casserole dish and bake for 45 minutes at gas mark 4/350°F/180°C or until the top is golden.

*Potato juice has long been considered an aid to beauty. Grated raw potato applied under the eyes is said to reduce puffiness.*

11 MAY

# NETTLE AND POTATO PURÉE

This is lovely in the late spring and early summer when the nettles are very young. Use only the tops and wear gloves when you pick them, of course.

8 oz (225 g) nettle tops
1 lb (450 g) potatoes, sliced
$^{3}/_{4}$ pint (400 ml) good chicken or vegetable stock
Sea salt and freshly ground black pepper
4 oz (110 g) fromage blanc

Put the washed nettles and potatoes with the stock in a saucepan. Cover and simmer until the vegetables are cooked, adding more stock if necessary.

Season and liquidize. Stir in the fromage blanc and eat at once.

*The Potato Museum in Washington D.C. supplied a variety of potato related items including potato jokes, books, posters,T-shirts, aprons and a Potato Museum 'beach cover-up'.*

12 MAY

# GOULASH OF POTATOES

Sometimes I put leeks with this dish, but they are not always available in early May.

$1^{1}/_{2}$ lb (700 g) potatoes
2 tablespoons olive oil
2 medium onions, chopped
3 cloves garlic, chopped

1 tablespoon wine vinegar
1 teaspoon caraway seed
1 tablespoon paprika
2 teaspoons tomato purée
1/2 pint (275 ml) chicken stock
Sea salt and freshly ground black pepper

Peel and parboil the potatoes for 10 minutes. Heat the olive oil in a heavy pan, add the onions and garlic and cook until transparent. Add the potatoes, caraway seed, paprika and tomato purée. Season and cover with the stock.

Cook over a low flame until the potatoes are cooked.

*The phrase 'Famous Potatoes' has been on the standard plate for cars in the state of Idaho since the 1920s. Various attempts over the years have been made to expunge the words from the plate.*

13 MAY

# NEW POTATOES WITH FROMAGE BLANC

There can be little in the gardening calendar to rival the delicious moment when you push back the earth to reveal the first crop of the year's potatoes. Straight indoors they must go for a preliminary wash in cold water and then into a steamer. They may take as little as 10 minutes, depending on the size. As soon as softness is achieved bring them to the table.

New potatoes, freshly dug and cleaned
A large bowl of fromage blanc
Chives
A plate of spring onions
Poppy seeds
Toasted sesame seeds
Toasted sunflower seeds

Serve the steamed new potatoes at once with the other ingredients offered on the side.

*"The annual emigration to the end of 1845 was 61,242 persons. Such however was the effect of the potato blight and the warning voice of the pestilence, that the number rose to 105,953 in 1846, after which the emigration seemed to partake of the nature of an epidemic and in 1847, the numbers who left the country more than doubled those in the previous year.... Emigration reached its highest point in 1851, when the numbers amounted to 249,721."*

*From* ***Census of Ireland***, *1851.*

14 MAY

# POTATO AND HERB PLAITED BREAD

Use any fresh herbs available in the garden - parsley, sage, thyme, marjoram - either mixed together or with one taste alone.

4 oz (110 g) potatoes
12 oz (350 g) plain flour
1 teaspoon salt
2 oz (50g) butter
1 heaped tablespoon fresh chopped herbs
1 sachet Quick-Action dried yeast
1/4 pint (150 ml) milk
1 egg, beaten
Poppy or sesame seeds

Peel and cook the potatoes, then purée. Stir the flour and salt into a bowl, rub in the butter and then stir in the yeast and the herbs.

Add the milk to the potatoes and, making a well in the centre of the flour mixture, add the potatoes and mix to a soft dough. Knead well, then place in a clean, oiled bowl and leave to rise until doubled in size.

Knead again, divide into three equal pieces and roll each into a long sausage shape. Put onto an oiled baking sheet and make a plait. Leave to prove again, about 20-30 minutes and then brush the loaf gently with the beaten egg. Sprinkle generously with poppy or sesame seeds and bake at gas mark 6/400°F/200°C for 25-30 minutes until golden brown.

*"Potatoes, three pounds a penny, Potatoes*
*Augh fait, there's a kind-hearted lass of green Erin*
*Unruffled in mind and for trifles not caring*
*Who, trundling her barrow, content in her state is*
*Still crying, three pounds for a penny Potatoes."*
*From* ***Cries of London****, Samuel Syntax, 1820.*

## 15 MAY

# GARLIC AND POTATO SOUP

Wild garlic, or ramsons (*Allium ursinum*), grows like a carpet through the woods around our house in Co. Monaghan, its heady scent perfuming the paths in May. The plant makes an excellent soup, and the leaves can be used as a vegetable, cooked with a little butter and stock. Here I have adapted a recipe devised by Colin Spence in *The New Vegetarian* and used ramsons for decorative purposes. If you have no access to wild garlic, use chopped chives instead.

1 lb (450 g) floury potatoes, peeled and thickly sliced
2 heads of garlic, peeled
3 tablespoons butter
1 tablespoon sunflower oil
Large pinch of saffron
Sea salt and freshly ground black pepper
1½ pints (900 ml) water
10 fl oz (275 ml) cream
A few leaves of ramsons
A few flower heads of ramsons

Put the garlic to cook very slowly in the melted butter and oil and when it is soft, add the potato slices, the saffron and the seasoning. Cook for a few more minutes and then pour over the water. Leave to simmer for a half hour and then put through a sieve or liquidizer.

Reheat in a clean pan with the cream. Serve with a few chopped leaves of ramsons and with a few white flower heads floating in the pale yellow soup.

*The wild flower (or weed, whichever you prefer) commonly known as Spurge is called Potatoes-in-the-Dish in parts of the west country of England.*

16 MAY

# LA TRUFFADO

Traditionally, the cheese to use in this simple but lovely dish is the fresh, unfermented cheese of Cantal called Tome. An alternative is Wensleydale.

1½ lb (700 g) potatoes, peeled and sliced
4 oz (110 g) bacon, cut in pieces
1 oz (25 g) butter
1 tablespoon olive oil
Sea salt and freshly ground black pepper
2 cloves garlic, chopped
8 oz (225 g) cheese, diced

Fry the bacon in the butter. Add the potatoes. Season and add the garlic and cook over a medium heat making sure the potatoes don't stick.

When the potatoes are tender (this may take 20 minutes), remove any excess oil and add the cheese. Remove from the heat almost immediately, leaving the cheese to melt; then eat.

*There are said to be some 10, 000 varieties of potato and if you had a different recipe for every day, you would only begin to run out of ideas after 4 years.*

17 MAY

# POTATO SOUFFLÉ OMELETTE

This is an absolute favourite in our house. The addition of smoked sausages is optional; they rather tend to take over the omelette. Unfortunately, there are those who believe they have not eaten unless meat can be detected in their food.

4 oz (110 g) potatoes, peeled and cubed
A little oil
2 oz (50 g) white bread, cubed
4 eggs
3 tablespoons white wine
2 oz (50 g) smoked sausage, cut in little pieces
2 tomatoes, skinned and chopped
1 oz (25 g) butter
Cheese

Cook the potatoes in the oil and butter for 10 minutes; add the bread and cook for another 5 minutes.

Separate the eggs, beat the yolks together with the wine. Whisk the egg whites until soft peaks and fold into the yolks.

Heat the butter in a clean pan, add the eggs and cook for a few minutes, then spread on the potato and bread cubes, the sausage and the tomato. Cook for a few minutes.

Sprinkle with cheese and brown under the grill until the cheese melts. Eat immediately.

*"As common a vegetable as is the potato, no two cooks are agreed in the best manner for cooking it".*

*From **A Married Lady, The Improved Housewife**, 1845.*

18 MAY

# SPICED POTATO BALLS

This recipe comes from Jury's Hotel in Dublin.

2 lb (900 g) potatoes, cooked and puréed
1/4 teaspoon salt
20 drops Tabasco sauce
1 egg yolk
2 tablespoons chopped spring onions
1 tablespoon chopped parsley
1 tablespoon chopped pimento
2 tablespoons Dijon mustard
2 oz (50 g) grated Parmesan cheese
20 cubes (1/2 inch thick) Cheddar cheese
1 egg
1 tablespoon milk
Toasted breadcrumbs
Oil for deep frying

Mix all the ingredients as far as and including the Parmesan cheese. Shape into balls around the Cheddar cheese cubes.

Dip in beaten egg, then breadcrumbs and deep fry until golden.

*In 1939, the Germans accused the British of airlifting Colorado beetles onto their potato fields to undermine the Reich.*

19 MAY

# POTATOES AND MACKEREL SALAD

Ideally, this should be made with fillets of fish straight out of the sea. This recipe comes from France, is simple and elegant, and is a change from the more usual dressings for potato salads.

2 lb (900 g) potatoes, peeled, cooked and sliced
6-8 mackerel fillets
1 large onion, finely chopped
A glass of white wine
2 large very ripe tomatoes, finely chopped
1 tablespoon tomato purée
Chopped parsley

Steam the fillets of mackerel. Put together with the cooked potato slices in a wide bowl. Mix the onion and one of the tomatoes with the tomato purée. Stir into the wine and disperse over the fish and the potatoes.

Arrange the other tomato around the edge of the salad, sprinkle with chopped parsley.

*A 'bog orange' was a slang term for a potato in the 18th century.*

20 MAY

ERICSON DAY, NORWAY

# LOMPE

The Norwegians have their own version of potato pancakes, which are not dissimilar from Irish potato cakes. Lompe are eaten with spread butter and Geitost cheese. Sometimes these little pancakes are used to wrap around meat or spoonfuls of berry conserve.

2 lb (900 g) potatoes
A little salt
4 oz (100 g) flour

Lompe must be cooked on a griddle or heavy frying pan. Peel the potatoes, cut up into pieces and boil in salted water. Drain and allow to become very dry before putting through a sieve. Mix with the flour and knead to a dough (you may need a little less or more flour depending on the potatoes - try and use less).

Roll the dough into a long sausage and cut into 10-12 inch lengths. On a floured surface with a rolling pin roll out the pancakes so that each is no more than 1/8 inch thick. Cook on the griddle, turning once.

*"Like everyone else around here, my father-in-law used to make his own aquavit, with potatoes which had been caught by the frost. He would throw in some berries as well and put the crock under the floor of the cowshed. It served a double purpose - the warmth from the stable manure encouraged the fermentation, and the smell discouraged the excise inspectors."*

*From* ***Country Cooking; Scandinavia*** *by Elizabeth Luard, writing in the* ***Sunday Telegraph Magazine****.*

21 MAY

# COLD POTATO AND CUCUMBER SOUP

One of the simplest soups imaginable. Resist the temptation to include onions or herbs. The only addition may be a spoonful of cream stirred into each plate and a few chopped chives.

1lb (450 g) potatoes, peeled and diced
1 cucumber, diced
Chicken or vegetable stock
Sea salt and freshly ground black pepper

Put the potatoes and the cucumber in a pan with enough stock to cover. Boil until the vegetables are tender. Season and liquidize or put through a sieve. Allow to cool before eating.

*The Swiss Army once had a marching song that saluted the potato. It was called 'Chanson des Pommes de Terre'.*

22 MAY

# HORS D'OEUVRE OF ANCHOVY, PEPPERS AND POTATOES

Browsing through old cook books is a productive pastime. I found this recipe in *Madame Prunier's Fish Cookery*, and altered it a little. It is a great favourite in our house.

2 large floury potatoes, peeled
1 green pepper
1 red pepper
1 yellow pepper
1 tin anchovies
2 tablespoons cider vinegar
6 tablespoons fruity olive oil
Sea salt and freshly ground black pepper

Remove the skins off the peppers by putting them in a very hot oven (gas mark 8/450°F/230°C) for about 5 minutes or until the skin blisters. Take them out of the oven and put them in a plastic bag. As soon as they have cooled down peel off the skins, and cut each pepper lengthways into 8 pieces, discarding any seeds.

Steam the potatoes. On individual plates lay out the strips of pepper - this is a very decorative dish - and place on top a few strips of anchovy fillets. Pour a little of the anchovy oil over each plate.

Mix together the vinegar, oil and seasoning. As soon as the potatoes are cooked and can be handled, grate a ring of fluffy potato around the peppers on each plate. Spoon over the dressing and serve immediately.

*Potatoes have even made their way onto the stage. Aphis Vast-tater was a giant tuber rising above a giant aphis that appeared in pantomimes in the 1840s. According to Mr. Alfred Smee, Surgeon to the Bank of England, the aphis vastator was the cause of the potato blight.*

## 23 MAY

# POTATO BHURTA

A Bhurta is an Indian word for mashes of potato and other vegetables and cold meats. The ingredients in almost every Bhurta include fine white onions, fresh green chillies and the juice of fresh lemons. I quote here from the *Indian Cookery Book*, published 1891.

"Take a medium sized Patna onion, slice thinly. Then slice or cut up two hot green chillies and squeeze over the onion and the chillies the juice of a fresh lemon, leave to soak. Take eight to ten well boiled potatoes, half a teaspoon of salt and a teaspoon of good mustard oil, bruise the potatoes down with a large silver or plated fork, adding, when they are half bruised, the onions and chillies, with as much of the lemon juice as may be palatable. Mix well."

*"The poor live on potatoes and milk, it is their regular diet, very little oat bread being used, and no flesh meat at all except on Easter Sunday and Christmas day. Their potatoes last them through the year; all winter long, only potatoes and salt."*

*The agriculturalist Arthur Young, writing in the 1770s.*

## 24 MAY

# POTATO PECAN COOKIES

Light in texture, the sweetness in these little nut cookies comes from a liberal sprinkling of icing sugar after they have been cooked.

2 oz (50 g) potato, cooked and puréed
4 oz (110 g) butter
8 oz (225 g) icing sugar
1 teaspoon vanilla essence
$^{1}/_{2}$ teaspoon salt
12 oz (350 g) plain flour
4-6 tablespoons milk
6 oz (175 g) pecan nuts, chopped

Cream the butter and 4 oz (110 g) of the icing sugar until light and fluffy. Stir in the potatoes, the vanilla, the salt and the flour and enough milk to make a soft dough. Add the nuts.

Put teaspoonfuls of the mixture onto a greased baking tray and flatten each one with a fork. Bake at gas mark 5/375°F/190°C for 20 minutes until they are just beginning to take colour. Remove from the oven and dust with the remaining icing sugar.

*"Thy name is Murphy. On the Antrim hills*
*There's cruffles and white-rocks; there's skerries, too, and dukes,*
*And kidneys - which is early; and champions and flukes -*
*Which doesn't help the farmer much to pay his bills;*
*The sort's not recommended.Then there's early rose,*
*And forty-folds, and flounders -which is bad;*
*And magnum bonums:- if good seed's to be had*
*It is the biggest pratie that the country grows,*
*And taste's not bad. Some grows best in rigs*
*And some in drills. There's sorts ye cudn't ate;*
*There's others dry and floury that's a trate*
*And weeshy kinds, that's only fit for pigs.*

*From **Ode to a Praitie** by John Stephenson.*

## 25 MAY
## INDEPENDENCE DAY, ARGENTINA
# EMPANADAS

Throughout Latin America these little turnovers or pies are to be found and their variations are infinite. In the elegant cafes of Buenos Aires, they are often served as appetisers. They can be filled with meat, fish, shellfish, whatever you have or, as here, with a mixture of minced beef and potatoes.

For the pastry:
8oz (225 g) plain flour
1 teaspoon baking powder
1/2 teaspoon salt
4 oz (110 g) butter
2 oz (50 g) lard

For the filling:
1 onion, finely chopped
1 medium potato, finely chopped
8 oz (225 g) lean mince
Sea salt and freshly ground black pepper
A little meat stock
1 egg, beaten

Make the pastry using, if you have one, a food processor; otherwise, rub in the fats to the sifted flour, baking powder and salt and mix to a stiff dough with a little cold water. Refrigerate for half an hour, then roll out and cut into 6-inch circles.

Mix the onion and potato with all the other ingredients except the egg. Put about 2 tablespoons across the centre of each circle, leaving a gap at the edge. Moisten the edges with the beaten egg and fold over to make a crescent, pressing the edges together. With the fingers press out indentations on the join. Prick all over with a fork and brush with the remaining egg. Bake for about 10 minutes at gas mark 6//400°F/200°C and then reduce the heat to gas mark 4/350°F/180°C for 30 minutes or until they are golden brown.

*In the high sierras of the Andes, elaborate ceremonies took place in the potato fields. Early records indicate that human sacrifices once played a part in these rituals.*

## 26 MAY

# BOYLAN POTATOES

Boylan potatoes are named after the amateur cook who invented them. He had never cooked potatoes before - or anything else come to that.

1 1/2 lb (700 g) new potatoes, cleaned
4-6 tablespoons freshly made mint sauce

Boil or steam the potatoes until tender. Slice and stir gently into the mint sauce.

*"And over the potato field*
*A lazy veil of woven sun*
*Dandelions growing on headlands, showing*
*Their unloved hearts to everyone."*

*From* ***Spraying the Potatoes*** *by Patrick Kavanagh.*

## 27 MAY

# POTATOES WITH PORT

This is party fare, although difficult to manage for large numbers.

2 lb (900 g) potatoes, cleaned
1 oz (25 g) butter
2 tablespoons sunflower oil
4 tablespoons port
Sea salt and freshly ground black pepper

Do not peel the potatoes. Slice them very thinly and dry them on absorbent paper.

Melt the butter and the oil in a very wide frying pan and lay the potatoes in circles in the heated fats. Fry over a moderate heat for about 8 minutes, then gently turn the cakes over and cook for a further 8 minutes.

Transfer the cakes to a baking tray and sprinkle with 3-4 tablespoons of port. Season and put into the oven at gas mark 6/400°F/200°C for a further 10 minutes or so until the cakes are browned.

*Starch was extracted from potatoes in the 19th century and used to add a finish to fine cotton goods, as well as in the manufacture of arrowroot, sago and tapioca. 100 lb of potatoes were said to yield 12 lb of starch.*

28 MAY

# POTATO, BACON AND ONION HOTPOT WITH LOVAGE

Lovage is a lovely perennial herb to grow if you have a dampish climate. The leaves taste a little like celery but the plants are visually distinguished. The stalks can be candied like angelica.

1½ lb (700 g) potatoes, peeled and sliced
4 onions, sliced
½ lb (225 g) streaky bacon, chopped
Sea salt and freshly ground black pepper
1 pint (570 ml) béchamel sauce
Lovage leaves, chopped

Layer the potatoes and onions together with the bacon in a casserole dish with the seasoning.

Pour over the béchamel sauce with a few chopped leaves of lovage and bake for an hour at gas mark 6/400°F/200°C.

*"By the late 18th century potatoes had taken over from oats and barley as a staple diet because the land had been parcelled up into small acreage, not large enough to grow a cereal crop for a family, but large enough to grow sufficient potatoes to feed them after a fashion."*

*Royal Irish Academy, 1834.*

29 MAY

# GOOSEBERRY AND POTATO COBBLER

One of the most exquisite combinations in the world of food must surely be gooseberries cooked with elderflower. The taste is reminiscent of Muscat grapes, sweet and sensuous, only possible for a couple of weeks each year and not to be missed. Here the fruit is given a crust topping. Eat with lashings of cream.

For the crust:
8 oz (225 g) potato, peeled, cooked and puréed
12 oz (350 g) self-raising flour
2 oz (50 g) butter, melted
6 fl oz (175 ml) milk

For the filling:
1 lb (450 g) gooseberries, topped and tailed
4 flowerheads of elderflower, well washed
2 oz (50 g) sugar
A little water

Sift the flour into a large bowl and stir in the potato. Add the butter and enough of the milk to make a soft dough. Turn onto a floured surface and push into a round.

Put the gooseberries into a flan dish with the elderflower and the sugar and pour in a little water. Cover with the crust, cut off any surplus dough around the side and bake at gas mark 6/400°F/200°C for about 25 minutes.

*"A correspondent informs us potato water thrown upon gooseberry and other fruit trees will effectually destroy the caterpillars."*

*From* ***A Year with the Ladies of Llangollen*** *by Elizabeth Mavor, 1971.*

30 MAY

# POTATO SALAD WITH BLACK OLIVES AND THYME

When buying olive oil, see that it is 'Virgin' or better still, 'Extra Virgin'. Money spent on good oil is never wasted.

2 lb (900 g) waxy potatoes
6 oz (175 g) black olives
4 fl oz (110 ml) olive oil
A few sprigs of fresh thyme
2 slices of lemon
Sea salt and freshly ground black pepper
Lemon juice to taste

Put the olives in a wide necked jar with the thyme, olive oil and lemon slices. Shake and leave for 3-4 days.

Clean the potatoes and steam and when cool enough to handle, push off the skins and slice. Pour over the olive oil and olives and seasonings. Add lemon juice to taste.

Garnish with a few sprigs of thyme.

*"All in all, the potato is about the world's most efficient means of converting pland, land, water and labour into a palatable and nutritious food."*

*From **Man on Earth** by John Reader, 1990.*

31 MAY

# POTATO AND ASPARAGUS SOUP

The Egyptians ate wild asparagus before the completion of the Pyramids. The Romans relished it. It has been said that when the Emperor Augustus wished to terminate some unpleasant business, he would proclaim, "Let it be done quicker than you would cook asparagus."

8 oz (225 g) potato, peeled and diced
2 large bundles of asparagus, approximately $1^1/_2$ lb (700 g)
2 oz (50 g) butter
1 medium onion, sliced
$1^1/_2$ pints (900 ml) chicken stock
Sea salt and freshly ground black pepper

Cut off the tips of the asparagus and reserve. Discard any coarse stalks.

Melt the butter in a heavy-bottomed pan and sauté the onion gently until translucent. Add the potato and the asparagus spears (but not the tips) and cook for a few minutes. Pour over the chicken stock, bring to the boil and cook until the vegetables are tender. Liquidize the soup, and strain through a sieve to remove any coarse pieces of the stem. Season and reheat in a clean pan. Put in the asparagus tips and cook for about 5 minutes until they are just tender.

*"A population whose ordinary food is wheat and beef and whose ordinary drink is porter and ale can retrench in period of scarcity and resort to cheaper kinds of food such as barley, oats, rice and potatoes. But those who are habitually and entirely fed on potatoes live upon the extreme verge of human subsistence, and when they are deprived of their accustomed food there is nothing cheaper to which they can resort...there is nothing beyond but starvation and beggary."*

*From* ***Economic History of Ireland from the Union to the Famine*** *by George O' Brien, 1921.*

# SPANISH POTATOES

The addition of lemon juice to potato may seem a little unusual at first, but it is a strangely seductive addiction and one that is popular in Spanish cookery.

$1\frac{1}{2}$ lb (700 g) potatoes, peeled and cut $\frac{1}{2}$ inch thick
2 tablespoons of olive oil
2 tablespoons flour
Sea salt and freshly ground black pepper
2 tablespoons chopped parsley
A little nutmeg
2 cloves garlic, sliced
1 tablespoon lemon juice
1 egg, beaten

Heat the olive oil, blend in the flour and cook for a few moments. Add the potatoes. Allow to cook for a few minutes, turning frequently. Season with the salt and pepper, garlic, parsley and nutmeg and just cover with water.

Bring to the boil and allow to simmer very gently. Do not allow the potatoes to break or disintegrate. When cooked, after about 20 minutes , remove from the heat and add the lemon juice and the egg. Mix carefully, turn out onto a dish, adding a little more parsley if you wish. Serve at once.

*It was probably a Spaniard, one of the Conquistadores, who was the first white man to see a potato growing. After the invasion of Peru in 1535, the Incas were found to be cultivating the plant.*

2 JUNE

# POTATO CAESAR SALAD

Caesar Salad was created by Caesar Cardini at his restaurant in Tijuana in the 1920s. He made theatre out of assembling the salad in front of guests. There were no potatoes in the salad, so this is a bastardised version of his original recipe, with potatoes replacing the croutons.

4 medium potatoes, scrubbed and diced
6-8 tablespoons sunflower oil
1 clove garlic, finely chopped
2 small cos lettuces
2 eggs
6-8 tablespoons olive oil
3 tablespoons lemon juice
1/2 teaspoon Worcestershire sauce
2 oz (50g) Parmesan, freshly grated

Heat the oil in a frying pan and add the potatoes and brown them over a high heat. Lower the heat, add the garlic and cook until the potatoes are tender. Remove, drain on kitchen paper and keep warm.

Separate the lettuce leaves and wash if necessary. Put into a large bowl. Put the eggs in boiling water for just 1 minute, then remove and scrape the barely cooked white and yolk out of the shell. Mix with the oil, lemon juice, Worcestershire sauce and seasoning.

Scatter the potatoes over the lettuce, spoon over the dressing and sprinkle with the cheese. A perfect first course.

*Legend has it that potatoes crossed the Atlantic ocean 7 times as ballast in ships before they were accepted in the American colonies.*

## 3 JUNE
# OFFENTORI

Over the past few years potato recipes have come to me from many different sources. This recipe was found at the back of a drawer in an old farmhouse here in Monaghan. The name remains a mystery - it sounds Middle Eastern but the ingredients are straight out of the Irish countryside.

$1^1/_2$ lb (700 g) potatoes, cleaned, cooked and puréed
8 oz (225 g) streaky bacon, diced
3 tablespoons cream
3 eggs, beaten
Sea salt and freshly ground black pepper

Heat a frying pan and put in half the bacon pieces. Fry over a high heat for a few minutes and then remove and drain.

Stir in the cream, eggs and seasoning into the potato purée and the cooked bacon. Put into a buttered ovenproof dish and sprinkle the remaining uncooked bacon on top. Put into a moderate oven, gas mark 5/375°F/190°C for about 15-20 minutes until the bacon is cooked. This is good served with liver or poultry.

*Food writer Jeanne Jones in the United States has written* ***Stuffed Spuds - 100 meals in a Potato*** *that includes recipes for Spud Stroganoff and Pina Colada Spud.*

## 4 JUNE
# ASPARAGUS WITH NEW POTATOES

This combines the two most delightful offerings of the summer garden.

2 lb (900 g) tiny new potatoes, cleaned
2 lb (900 g) fresh asparagus

Sea salt
Melted butter
A little lemon juice
Parsley

Cut any coarse part off the bottom of the asparagus and put aside. Clean the potatoes and boil in salted water with the ends of the asparagus - they should only take about 10 minutes.

Meanwhile have the asparagus tips tied in a bundle and steam. This should take about 5-10 minutes depending on the thickness of the stems.

When both vegetables are cooked, remove the coarse asparagus stems from the potatoes and put on a warmed serving dish. Surrounded by the asparagus tips. Pour over the melted butter with a little lemon juice added and sprinkle with a little chopped parsley.

*"Once upon a time my undrowned father*
*Walked into our yard. He had gone to spray*
*Potatoes in a field on the riverbank*
*And wouldn't bring me with him..."*

*From **Seeing Things** by Seamus Heaney, 1991.*

5 JUNE

# BAKED POTATOES WITH A GREEN SAUCE

A most healthy way of eating baked potatoes.

4 large potatoes, cleaned
2 green or red peppers
1 green chilli
Handful of parsley or coriander, chopped
8 oz (225 g) Greek yoghourt
3 tablespoons chicken stock

Bake the potatoes in the usual way and while they are cooking, prepare the following green sauce:-

Take the seeds out of the peppers and chilli and chop very finely. Add to the herbs and mix with the yoghourt and chicken stock.

When the potatoes are ready, put into a cloth and just 'burst' the tops. Put a spoonful of the sauce into each potato and serve.

*The late Dr Tarnower of the Scarsdale Diet allowed his dieters one potato a week — at Monday lunchtime, accompanied by the ubiquitous cottage cheese.*

6 JUNE

# MARINADED KIPPER FILLETS WITH POTATOES

Thanks, in large measure, to the writings of Elizabeth David, cooking in the 1960s began to emerge from the Dark Ages with a new respect accorded to the most commonplace of foods. It must have been the Mediterranean influence but there was a fashion for these small strips of fish which elevated the humble kipper to new status. Recently the food writer Frances Bissell suggested serving them on potatoes - an excellent combination and one that should revive the popularity of a fish not often thought of as *comme il faut.*

1 lb (450 g) potatoes, cleaned
1 lb (450 g) kipper fillets, cut into finger-sized pieces
1 medium onion, thinly sliced
2 cloves garlic, chopped
5 tablespoons olive oil
Juice of 1 lemon
Black pepper
Chopped parsley

The kipper fillets need to be marinated for about 24 hours before eating. Put them into a shallow china or glass dish with the onion and garlic and pour over the oil and lemon juice. Season with the pepper. During the marinating period turn the fillets once or twice.

Next day, boil or steam the potatoes and when tender, cut into thick slices. Divide between 4 serving plates while still warm, put the kipper fillets onto the potatoes and spoon on the marinade, adding a little more oil if necessary. Decorate with parsley.

*"You will sometimes read...that each person, before taking a bite, pointed the potato at a salt herring or a bit of bacon hanging in front of the chimney; but this...never occurred in real life."*

*From* ***English as we speak it in Ireland*** *by P.W. Joyce, 1910.*

## 7 JUNE

# NEW POTATOES WITH SORREL SAUCE

If I had only a restricted space in which to grow vegetables, I think sorrel would be my choice because it is almost impossible to buy, and a small area of sorrel will produce many leaves over the summer and autumn. It makes lovely soup as well as sauces, is unsurpassed in omelettes and gives sophistication to salads. With its distinct acidic taste, it is quite unlike any other vegetable.

New potatoes, cleaned
A bunch of sorrel
A little butter
Chicken stock
Cream (optional)

While the potatoes are steaming, wash the sorrel well and pull off any stringy stalk.

Melt the butter, add the sorrel and watch it wilt almost immediately. Add stock to taste, according to the thickness of sauce required. Purée (liquidize or put through a sieve), add a little cream and serve with the freshly cooked potatoes.

*"All day he sprayed the potatoes, and nothing was happening except his being. Being was enough, it was the worship of God."*

*From **Tarry Flynn** by Patrick Kavanagh, 1948.*

8 JUNE

# POTATO AND MOLASSES BUNS

A cross between a biscuit and a bun, these homely little cakes have a bittersweet flavour imparted by the molasses, a product of raw sugar cane.

8 oz (225 g) potatoes, cooked and puréed
8 oz (225 g) plain flour
1 teaspoon baking powder
1/4 teaspoon bread soda
1/2 teaspoon ground ginger
1/2 teaspoon ground cinnamon
1/2 teaspoon salt
5 tablespoons molasses
4 oz (110 g) butter or margarine
4 oz (110 g) soft brown sugar
4 oz (110 g) walnuts, chopped
Icing sugar

Sift the flour, baking powder, bread soda, ginger, cinnamon and salt and set aside in a warm place.

Over a low heat, melt the molasses, butter and brown sugar and stir until smooth. Add to the sieved ingredients and mix well. Stir in the potatoes and lastly the walnuts.

Drop in little spoonfuls onto a greased baking sheet and cook at gas mark 5/375°F/190°C for 15 minutes. When cold sprinkle with icing sugar.

*The first recorded appearance of the potato in Scotland was in 1701 in the Duchess of Buccleugh's household book which mentions a peck of potatoes, brought from Edinburgh and costing half a crown.*

9 JUNE

# POTATOES WITH EGG BUTTER

A Finnish friend gave us this recipe. It needs no accompaniment at all.

2 lb (900 g) new potatoes
8 oz (225 g) butter
2 hard boiled eggs, chopped

Steam the cleaned potatoes, and while doing this soften the butter so that it has a cream-like consistency.

Add the eggs and serve with the potatoes.

*A company in Idaho called Saturn Labs has marketed a line in 'liquid powders' made from potato starch. The powders, one for the feet and one for the body, go on like lotions with no 'irritating cloud dust' according to the write-up in* ***Runner's World*** *magazine.*

10 JUNE

# POTATOES WITH BASIL AND PARMESAN

A patch of basil is a must in every garden. There are many exotic kinds of this loveliest of herbs available today. Besides the better-known Sweet or Bush basil, there are red-stemmed Horapha plants from Thailand, Green Ruffles with fringed leaves and the purple-leaved Dark Opal.

$1^1/_2$ lb (700 g) new potatoes, cleaned
2-4 oz (50-110 g) butter
A little bouquet of basil
Parmesan

Cut the potatoes, if large, into even sizes. Melt the butter and cook the potatoes, keeping the pan covered and not allowing them to brown.

Coarsely chop the basil and strew the potatoes when tender with the herb and the cheese. Eat at once.

*It has been suggested by historians that the reason for the greater popularity of the potato in Ireland than in England was perhaps because the plant grew underground and was therefore less vulnerable to marauding armies.*

11 JUNE

# POTATO SALAD WITH GINGER AND HORSERADISH

Growing horseradish is no trouble - rather, the difficulty comes in eradicating it from the garden. I dig it up in the late summer, don goggles and grate it into a glass jar. Cover it with good quality vinegar and keep all year until you need it, when you just have to add fresh cream to make horseradish sauce of very high quality. (The goggles are needed in the grating because the root can have a shocking effect on the eyes).

2 lb (900 g) new potatoes, cleaned
Grated horseradish
1/2 pint (275 ml) soured cream
1/4 pint (150 ml) mayonnaise
Sea salt and freshly ground black pepper
1 inch piece fresh ginger, peeled and sliced

Steam the potatoes and while they are cooking mix together the soured cream and the horseradish. Add the mayonnaise and the seasoning to taste.

Lastly, stir in the ginger. As soon as the potatoes are cooked, pour over the sauce and allow to cool before serving.

*"Having to endure 'Famous Potatoes' on the licence plate," fumed Herme Sterger, a Republican representative for Idaho, " is like putting a moustache on the Mona Lisa."*

12 JUNE

# POTATO SALAD WITH MINT AND ORANGE

Spearmint, applemint and peppermint - these are the 3 kinds of mint commonly cultivated and they all share the same aromatic taste of menthol. I prefer the sweet and mellow taste of applemint.

1 1/2 lb (700 g) small new potatoes, cleaned and steamed
2 teaspoons grated orange rind
6 tablespoons olive oil
1 1/2 tablespoons white wine vinegar
2 tablespoons fresh orange juice
2 tablespoons chopped mint
Sea salt and freshly ground black pepper

Combine all the other ingredients and add them to the potatoes while still warm. Cool and bring to the table.

*On sale in the United States are 'Gourmet Greeting Cards' which feature pictures of sour-cream and cheese-topped baked potatoes. Each card contains 6 potato recipes.*

## 13 JUNE

# NEW POTATOES AND PEAS

Anyone privileged enough to grow their own potatoes scarcely needs to look further this month since a basket full of freshly dug potatoes can be so easily combined with another ingredient to produce a meal of great simplicity that ranks in the gourmet class.

2 lb (900 g) small new potatoes, washed
2 oz (50 g) streaky bacon, cut in little pieces
8 oz (225 g) peas, preferably fresh
1/4 pint (150 ml) cream
Fresh herbs, mint, parsley or chervil, chopped
Sea salt and freshly ground black pepper

Steam the washed potatoes until just tender. Meanwhile fry the bacon until crisp. Cook the peas in the cream until just tender and put together with the potatoes. Put in a serving dish, sprinkle with the bacon, fresh herbs and the seasoning.

*In the late 1980s the chef/patron of Ménage à Trois won the Mouton Menu competition with a dish that included tuna with red pepper purée and potato sauce.*

## 14 JUNE

### UNITED STATES FLAG DAY

# VICHYSSOISE SOUP

This internationally known (but not universally admired, see over) soup was invented by chef Louis Diat of the Ritz Carlton Hotel in New York in the early 1920s. The French country soup known as *potage parmentier* must have been the inspiration for this soup which reminded chef Diat of his boyhood days in Vichy. Vichyssoise is eaten cold.

4 potatoes, peeled and sliced
2 oz (50 g) butter
4 leeks, sliced
1 medium onion, chopped
Sea salt and white pepper
2 1/3 pints (1.25 litres) chicken stock
1/2 pint (275 ml) cream
Chopped chives

Melt the butter and add the leeks (from which you have removed the coarse green parts) and the onion. Allow to soften over a very low heat for about 10 minutes and then season and add the potatoes. Cook gently for a further 5 minutes and then pour on the chicken stock. Leave to simmer for about 45 minutes.

Purée the mixture in a food processor, put through a sieve into a clean bowl and allow to rest in the fridge overnight or for some hours. Before serving, stir in the cream and sprinkle with chives.

*"Potato soup. What wonderful stuff, and how likely you've never had it - not vichyssoise, which isn't potato soup at all, just a buttery-bland mouthful of weightless-seeming luxury for rich folk to start their gorging on..."*

*From* ***Simple Cooking*** *by John Thorne, 1987.*

## 15 JUNE

# POTATO SALAD WITH RADISHES AND CHIVES

If you grow radishes you will probably find yourself with far too many of them at some point. Here they are a main ingredient of the salad rather than a garnish and the more varieties you can include the more interesting the result.

1 lb (450 g) potatoes
1 small onion, finely chopped
1 tablespoon vinegar
4 tablespoons oil

1 lemon
Sea salt and freshly ground black pepper
2 large bunches radishes
Parsley and chives, chopped

Steam the potatoes and while still warm, peel and slice them. Heat the onion in a small pan with the vinegar. Leave it to reduce for a few minutes.

Take off the heat, add 3 tablespoons oil and seasonings. Mix with the potatoes.

Wash the radishes well, slice them thinly and mix with the remaining tablespoon of oil and the juice of a lemon. On a large plate, pile the potatoes in a pyramid in the centre and surround them with the radishes. Strew the salad with chives and parsley.

*In World War I, a 'potato-masher' was a slang term for a German hand-grenade that was thus shaped.*

## 16 JUNE

# NEW POTATOES WITH CREAM AND CROUTONS

This is just another excuse to eat cream.

1½ lb (700 g) new potatoes
¾ pint (400 ml) cream
4 oz (110 g) butter
A little nutmeg
Sea salt and freshly ground black pepper
Juice of ½ a lemon
Croutons

Steam the cleaned but unpeeled potatoes until just tender. Put them into a pan with the other ingredients except for the croutons. Heat gently and thoroughly.

Have the croutons ready prepared and serve with the potatoes.

*"Women are usually employed for picking up the Potatoes, one collecting the 'ware', or largest sound tubers, another the 'seed', or middle sized ones, and a third the 'chats' and 'tail', in which is included all the smallest, as well as diseased and broken ones, which are usually reserved for pig feeding or disposed of locally."*

*From **The Profitable Culture of Vegetables** by Thos. Smith, published 1911.*

## 17 JUNE

# SALAD OF POTATOES AND CUCUMBER

This simple combination of vegetables, put together while the potatoes are still warm, makes an exquisite dish.

1½ lb (700 g) potatoes
1 small cucumber
1 tablespoon cider vinegar
3 tablespoons olive oil
Sea salt and freshly ground black pepper
3 fl oz (75 ml) fromage blanc

Steam the cleaned potatoes and cut in rounds. Slice the cucumber. Mix the cider vinegar and olive oil with the seasoning and stir into the fromage blanc. Gently stir the vegetables into the dressing.

*"Oh! the Praties they are small over here - over here*
*Oh! the Praties they are small over here*
*Oh! the Praties they are small, and we dug them in the fall,*
*And we ate them skins and all, full of fear - full of fear."*

*Traditional Song.*

18 JUNE

# SESAME POTATO TWIST LOAF

This recipe comes from Gwen Robyns' excellent *Potato Cookbook.*

15 oz (425 g) potatoes, peeled
4 oz (110 g) butter
2 tablespoons sugar
2 teaspoons salt
8 fl oz (225 ml) scalded milk
2 packets active dry yeast
3 fl oz (75ml) warm water
1lb 6 oz (625 g) sifted all-purpose flour
1 egg white
Sesame seeds

Cook the potatoes and put through a sieve. In a large bowl, add the butter to the potatoes and stir until melted. Add the sugar, salt and milk and stir until the mixture is smooth and cooled to lukewarm.

Soften the yeast in water, then stir to dissolve; stir into potato mixture. Stir in 9 oz (250 g) of the flour, beating until smooth. Gradually stir in enough of the remaining flour to make a moderately firm dough which does not stick to the sides of the bowl. Turn out onto a floured surface and knead until smooth and elastic, about 10 minutes, working in additional flour as necessary to prevent dough from sticking.

Place the dough in a buttered bowl, turning to butter all sides. Cover and let it rise in a warm place until almost doubled, about 1 hour. Gently brush the tops of loaves with the egg white slightly beaten with a tablespoon of water. Sprinkle generously with the sesame seeds.

Bake at gas mark 6/400°F/200°C for 10 minutes. Reduce the heat to gas mark 4/350°F/180°C and bake for 35 minutes until golden brown. Turn out onto a wire rack to cool. It makes 2 loaves.

*'Mr Potato Head' was the first toy advertised on television.*

## 19 JUNE

# SALT BLOOM POTATOES WITH GARLIC AND MASCARPONE SAUCE

Mascarpone is an Italian cream cheese and one that is becoming, thank goodness, much more widely available. Cooked correctly, these potatoes take on a whitish bloom.

$1^1/_2$ lb (700 g) new potatoes
2 fat cloves garlic, very thinly sliced
$1^1/_2$ oz (40 g) butter
6 oz (175 g) mascarpone cheese
Freshly ground black pepper
Sea salt
Chives, chopped

Put the garlic into cold water and bring to the boil. Drain at once, then refresh in cold water.

Drain again then cook the garlic gently in the butter, taking care it doesn't burn. Add the mascarpone with 2-3 tablespoons water, stirring all the time to make a smooth sauce. Add pepper but no salt.

Clean the potatoes and put them in a wide pan with a covering of water and a generous helping of sea salt. Cook until they are barely tender and add extra salt and boil rapidly until the water evaporates.

Split the potatoes open and spoon over the sauce and a few chives.

*" A cheap and delicious mess is furnished in summer to those healthy and happy children educated in what are called the Maiden Hospitals of Edinburgh. Good potatoes, boiled, peeled and roughly broken, are boiled up with sweet milk, and a small proportion of butter".*

*From **The Cook and Housewife's Manual** by Mrs. Margaret Dods, 1826.*

20 JUNE

# POTATOES AND ARTICHOKES

These vegetables together are another divine inspiration. Globe artichokes are easy to grow and beautiful to look at.

$1^1/_2$ lb (700 g) potatoes
At least 1 artichoke per person, preferably 2-3
1 dessertspoonful ground coriander seed
Olive oil
Juice of 1 lime
Sea salt
Fresh coriander leaves

Steam the cleaned potatoes and at the same time cook the artichoke globes. This can be done by steaming or boiling in salted water. Then, using a sharp knife, remove the leaves, scrape off the hairy part of the centre until you are left with just the hearts.

Slice the warm potatoes and gently turn both vegetables in the coriander seed, the oil, lime juice and the salt. Sprinkle with a few coriander leaves.

*"The three worst things of all; small, soft potatoes, from that to an uncomfortable bed and to sleep with a bad woman."*

*Old Irish proverb.*

21 JUNE
ST JOHN'S DAY

# 246 LAYERED POTATOES

This recipe comes from the kitchens of the popular 1980's Restaurant 246 in London's Notting Hill Gate. Etorki is a sheep's milk cheese from Gascogne.

4 new potatoes, cleaned and sliced about $^1/_2$ inch thick
1 large tomato, sliced
4 oz (110 g) fine French beans
3 spring onions, coarsely chopped
4 oz (110 g) Etorki cheese, grated
2 oz (50 g) pine nuts
6 oz (175 g) cream
1 clove garlic, chopped

Layer the potatoes in a greased gratin dish with the tomato, the beans, the spring onion and the cheese. Sprinkle with the pine nuts.

Heat the cream to just below boiling point with the garlic and pour over the dish. Bake at gas mark 4/350°F/180°C for 45 minutes or until nicely browned on top.

*21 June, St John's Day, was the traditional day for digging the new potatoes.*

22 JUNE

# POTATO AND AVOCADO PURÉE

Serve this with a few extra slices of avocado and the whole trickled with a little lemon juice.

1 lb (450 g) potatoes, cooked and puréed
1 ripe avocado
Grated rind of half a lemon
Sea salt and freshly ground black pepper

Mash the avocado flesh with a fork and then mix it well with the potato purée. Add the lemon rind and the seasoning and reheat before serving.

*"Potatoes...take rank for universal use, profit and easy acquirement..."*
*From **American Cookery** by Amelia Simmons, 1796.*

## 23 JUNE

# POTATO FRITTERS

Much of the attraction of these fritters is their versatility. They are good eaten with meat dishes, or vegetables, or they can be eaten as pancakes with a sweet sauce. I like to eat them with *dulce de leche*, a delicious milk and sugar product seen everywhere in Argentina, but creatable in one's own kitchen by boiling a tin of condensed milk for a couple of hours.

2 medium potatoes
1/4 pint (150 ml) water
2 oz (50 g) butter
A little salt
4 oz (110 g) plain flour
2 eggs

Peel and boil the potatoes until tender and while they are cooking, heat the water, butter and salt until boiling. Immediately add the flour and stir vigorously until a ball is formed that leaves the side of the pan clean.

Remove from the heat and beat in the eggs. Allow to cool a little and then add the potatoes that have been well dried and put through a sieve.

Heat a little oil in a frying pan and cook tablespoons of the mixture until golden on both sides. Drain and eat at once.

*"Sublime potatoes! that, from Antrim's shore*
*To famous Kerry, form the poor man's store;*
*Agreeing with every place and state -*
*The peasant's noggin, or the rich man's plate.*
*Much prized when smoking from the teeming pot,*
*Or in turf-embers roasted crisp and hot.*
*Welcome, although you be our only dish;*
*Welcome, companion to flesh, fowl or fish;*
*But to the real gourmands, the learned few,*
*Most welcome, steaming in an Irish stew".*

*Thomas Crofton Crocker (1798-1854).*

## 24 JUNE
## MIDSUMMER'S DAY
# HAY BOX POTATOES

Now for the season of picnics and the great life outdoors. If you are camping and don't want to keep a bonfire burning all day, why not make a hay box? I've never tried it but I'm told it sometimes works.

To do this dig a hole twice the size of your cooking pot. Pack it very tightly with dried leaves of bracken, then push down your cooking pot to form a nest. Get a large paper bag, stuff it with more dried grasses to make a cushion and take out the pot - your hole is ready for use. (Better to mark it with two upright sticks lest the unwary fall into it.)

Put your cleaned potatoes into the pot and bring to the boil in salted water on the camp fire. Boil for 3 minutes then immediately transfer to the hole, tucking it well down. Put your cushion on top of the lid of the pot and leave it for at least 2 hours. Eat the cooked potatoes with foods gathered from the wild - perhaps nettles or samphire (sometimes known as sea asparagus) or whatever you have in your area - and perhaps some freshly caught fish.

*"And over that potato field*
*A lazy veil of sun*
*The Kerr's Pinks in a frivelled blue,*
*The Arran Banners wearing white."*

*From* ***Spraying the Potatoes*** *by Patrick Kavanagh.*

## 25 JUNE
# GRATIN OF NEW POTATOES AND COURGETTES

With a warm start to the summer, new-season courgettes should be coming into the kitchen. The smaller the better.

1 lb (450 g) new potatoes, cleaned and finely sliced
3 tablespoons olive oil
1 large clove garlic
4-6 small courgettes, sliced
4 eggs
3 fl oz (75 ml ) milk
Sea salt and freshly ground black pepper
2 oz (50 g) Cheddar cheese, grated

Heat the oil in a frying pan and add the potatoes. Fry gently for about 10 minutes, stirring occasionally. Add the courgettes and cook for a further 5 minutes.

Put the vegetables into a buttered ovenproof dish. Beat the eggs and stir in the milk and the seasoning. Pour over the vegetables, sprinkle with the cheese and cook at gas mark 5/375°F/190°C for 30 minutes.

*Cocaine is said to play a part in the planting of potatoes. In the Andes, coca leaves are placed in the ground with seed potatoes and sprinkled with corn beer.*

### 26 JUNE
### FEAST OF ST. PETER AND ST. PAUL
# POTATOES AND OYSTER MUSHROOMS

All through the year now different types of mushrooms are becoming available in the shops. We live in a mushroom producing area in Ireland so have the freshest possible crops available. Not as good, perhaps, as the fresh field mushrooms, but a good substitute. If you can't get oyster mushrooms, use the ordinary variety.

$1^1/_2$ lb (700 g) new potatoes, cleaned
2 oz (50 g) butter
$^1/_2$ lb (225 g) oyster mushrooms, sliced
1 clove garlic, chopped
Sea salt and freshly ground black pepper

Steam the potatoes until just tender. In a wide frying pan melt the butter and cook the mushrooms with the garlic for a few minutes. Add the potatoes and cook for another 5 minutes. Season and serve. You may wish to add a few tablespoons of cream but this is unnecessary.

*"The feast of St. Peter and Paul used to have culinary significance for us when I was growing up. It was the day when, as a special treat, we dug the first stalk or two of the new potatoes."*
*From* ***Full and Plenty*** *by Maura Laverty.*

## 27 JUNE

# SPICED POTATO PANCAKES

Grated raw potato, pressed into a pancake shape and fried in hot oil, must be one of the quickest, most adaptable and elegant ways of giving a sophisticated lift to food. Here the pancakes are served with smoked salmon and sour cream. Saffron is expensive (unless you have just been in the Middle East) so instead you can use paprika or turmeric.

2 lb (900 g) floury potatoes, peeled and grated
2 teaspoons saffron
1 teaspoon cumin
Sea salt and freshly ground black pepper
Oil for frying
8 slices smoked salmon
Sour cream

Squeeze out the excess liquid from the grated potatoes with your hand and then mix in the spices and the seasoning. In a non-stick frying pan heat a little olive oil and when it is very hot divide the potatoes into four and put into the hot oil pressing them down to make little pancakes.

Turn down the heat, cover with a lid and cook for about 5 minutes. Turn the pancakes over, raise the heat and cook until golden.

Drain well and put a couple of slices of smoked salmon on each, fold over and serve with a spoonful of sour cream.

*"There is no species of human food that can be consumed in a greater variety of modes than the potato."*

*Sir John Sinclair, 1828.*

## 28 JUNE
# SALADE NIÇOISE

It is very doubtful that a true Salade Niçoise contains potatoes, although, curiously, they are included in the recipe for the salad in *Larousse Gastronomique*.

1 lb (450 g) new potatoes, cleaned and steamed
3/4 lb (350 g) French beans
4 tomatoes, peeled and quartered
8 oz (225 g) can of tuna, flaked
4 spring onions, sliced
2 anchovy fillets, cut into pieces
4 oz (110 g) black olives
4 eggs, hard boiled and quartered

For the dressing:
1 clove garlic
4 fl oz (110 ml) extra virgin olive oil
3 tablespoons red wine vinegar
Sea salt and freshly ground black pepper

Snap the ends of the French beans and cook them until just tender in a little boiling salted water.

Rub the garlic around the sides of a large bowl and put in all the salad ingredients. Make the salad dressing and mix very gently into the salad.

*On the 28th June, 1715, the Court of Nancy issued a decree exacting a tithe, which was payable after 50 years of potato cultivation.*

29 JUNE

# POTATOES WITH WALNUTS AND GARLIC

Nut oils may seem expensive but they impart such a delicate flavour to anything they accompany, that it is well worth spending a little extra on a high quality product.

2 lb (900 g) new potatoes, washed and thickly sliced
Walnut oil
Sea salt and freshly ground black pepper
A little nutmeg
4 cloves of garlic, chopped
A few walnuts

Heat enough walnut oil to cover the base of a heavy skillet to about $^1/_8$ inch. Slide in the potatoes and gently cook, seasoning as you go. Cook for about 40 minutes or until the potatoes are tender (and turn them occasionally).

Stir in the garlic 5 minutes before the potatoes are cooked. Add walnuts to taste.

*"You may talk about your suppers grand*
*Of dishes covered with spices*
*Your turkeys, oysters and fine meats*
*And puddings, tarts and ices.*
*But better than them all combined*
*The Irishman's great trate is -*
*Taste it once, you'll surely find,*
*'Tis buttermilk and praties."*

*19th Century Ballad.*

30 JUNE

# POTATO SALAD IN THE PINK

This will be a better salad if made with home-made mayonnaise, but you may not have the time or the inclination.

2 lb (900 g) new potatoes, steamed and cut in little dice
2 tender celery stalks, sliced
1 pickled dill cucumber, sliced
1 small onion, chopped
4 oz (110 g) peas
3 tablespoons chopped parsley
10 fl oz (275 ml) mayonnaise
$^1/_2$ red pepper, de-seeded and chopped
1 teaspoon capers

Mix the celery and the cucumber with the potatoes. Add the onion, cooked peas and parsley.

With a blender mix together the mayonnaise, red pepper and the capers. Blend until smooth and pink. Turn the potatoes around in this dressing.

*In the* ***Encyclopaedia of Practical Cookery****, 1890, Theodore Garnett gives instructions for over 8 potato dishes, including potato sandwiches and potato crulles, decorative potato spirals.*

## 1 JULY

CANADA DAY

# NOVA SCOTIA (OLD ARCADIA) GRATED POTATO PIE

This recipe comes from the *Journal American,* published sometime in the 1950s. It would feed an enormous amount of people and would be fine for any celebration. Other names for this dish are Rappie Pie or Pâté à la Rapture. I reproduce it as it was passed on to me. It is obviously not a recipe to be tackled on one's own.

5 lb (2.3 kg) chicken
3 lb (1.4 kg) pork
2 large onions, quartered
1 lb (450 g) salt pork
Salt and pepper to taste
2 pecks (half a bushel) of potatoes

Cut up the chicken and the pork as for fricassée. Half of the salt pork should be in very small pieces. Salt and pepper to taste. Cook chicken, pork and onion in the biggest pan or pans you can find. Separate the meat from the bones and cut meat into small pieces.

While meat is cooking, peel and grate potatoes. Fill a cheesecloth bag with as much potato as it will hold and squeeze out the water. Continue until all the potato is dry. Discard the starchy water.

Put the potatoes in a large pan or bowl. Pour over them $^3/_4$ of the meat stock, a little at a time. Make sure the stock is boiling hot. Stir the mixture vigorously, so that the hot stock in effect cooks the potato. Add salt and pepper to taste.

Place a thick layer of the potatoes in the bottom of a large roasting tin. Over this place the meat and about 2 cups of stock, then spread another layer on top, leaving a hole in the centre. Leave some pieces of salt pork on top.

Bake at gas mark 5/375°F/190°C for $2^1/_2$-3 hours. Baste occasionally with a few spoonfuls of stock.

*"...Unskinned potatoes - this is not on: the point of restaurants is that someone does spud-bashing."*

*Jonathan Meades writing in the **Times Saturday Review**, 1991.*

2 JULY

# LEMON POTATOES

A perfect dish for a summer evening, eaten at dusk with a chicken roasted in butter and a plate of lightly dressed just-out-of-the-garden salad leaves.

$1^1/_2$ lb (700 g) small new potatoes
2 oz (50 g) butter
1 heaped tablespoon grated lemon
Juice of $^1/_2$ a lemon
Sea salt and freshly ground black pepper
Parsley and chives, chopped

Steam the potatoes and push off the skins when cool enough to handle. Melt the butter, stir in the lemon peel and juice, then the seasonings. Slide in the potatoes and roll them in the sauce so that they are evenly coated and heat through.

Sprinkle with chives and/or parsley.

*"Being boiled, baked or roasted and eaten with good butter, salt, juice or oranges and lemons and double refined sugar...they increase seed and provoke lust causing fruitfulness in both sexes."*

*From* ***The English Herbal*** *by William Salmon, 1710.*

3 JULY

# POTATOES WITH BRETON SAUCE

Here follows one of the most useful sauces a cook can know; it can be served with many different foods and has the great advantage that you can vary it enormously according to what herbs you have.

2 lb (900 g) new potatoes
2 egg yolks
Salt and pepper
1 teaspoon Dijon mustard
1 tablespoon white wine vinegar
Chopped herbs
2 oz (50 g) melted butter

Steam the potatoes and when they are tender, offer them with the following sauce:-

Beat the egg yolks, season and stir in the mustard and the vinegar followed by a tablespoon or so of finely chopped fresh herbs. Just before serving, melt the butter and pour over the other ingredients. The sauce will thicken if stirred gently in a bowl over a pan of barely simmering water.

*"I continue to mention the Potato Museum with enthusiasm and respect to all the relevant people I meet...I tell them to take the museum very seriously."*

*Kenneth Hudson, museum critic, writing 1980s.*

4 JULY

AMERICAN INDEPENDENCE DAY

# QUILTED GIRAFFE MASHED-POTATO SUSHI

Here is a recipe from the famous chef Barry Wine, of the Quilted Giraffe Restaurant in New York. America has absorbed so many different cultures over the years that her cuisine naturally reflects the international nature of her society. Nori is now available in Ireland.

2 large potatoes, peeled
2 tablespoons half-and-half (i.e. a tablespoon each of milk and cream)
2 tablespoons butter
1/2 tablespoon salt
1/4 teaspoon pepper
3 sheets nori (Japanese seaweed), 6x7 inches
1 small carrot, julienned
1 small red bell pepper, julienned
1/2 avocado, sliced 1/4 inch thick
4 shiso leaves (Japanese beefsteak plant) or 1 teaspoon ground beefsteak leaves (optional)
2 teaspoons spicy oriental mustard
2 cooked, peeled plums (fresh or canned) cut in 8 sections

Boil the potatoes until tender. Cut in cubes. Mash with the half-and-half (or milk and cream), butter, salt and pepper. Place a sheet of nori on a bamboo mat or cloth napkin and spread 1/4 of the mashed potato over 4/5 of the nori, leaving top 1/5 of the sheet clean.

Arrange half the carrot, red and yellow pepper and avocado across the middle of the potato. Top with half the shiso leaves. Lay half a nori sheet on top of the vegetables. Put 1/4 of the mashed potato on top of this sheet and spread with 1 teaspoon oriental mustard. Top with 1/2 the plum sections.

Use mat or cloth to help roll up the nori tightly, then roll back and forth one or two times and gently squeeze to make firmer. Unroll the mat or cloth. Slice the nori roll into 1/4 inch slices.

*"If something on the menu isn't selling, I put mashed potato with it. Then they can't get enough of it."*

*Michael Romano, chef of New York's Union Square Café.*

5 JULY

# SORREL AND POTATO SOUFFLÉS

Serve these little soufflés as a first course. A well-flavoured tomato sauce goes well with them but is not essential.

8 oz (225 g) potatoes
1 large handful sorrel leaves
1 oz (25 g) butter
2 oz (50 g) cottage cheese
2 oz (50 g) sour cream or fromage blanc
1 tablespoon chopped chives
2 eggs, separated
4 teaspoons grated Parmesan

Boil the cleaned potato and when cool enough to handle, push off the skins. Put the potato flesh through a sieve and weigh out the required amount.

Strip the coarse stems from the sorrel leaves, wash well and cook quickly in 1/2 oz (15 g) of the melted butter, turning around in the pan until the sorrel is just wilted.

Put the remaining butter around 4 ramekins and put a spoonful of the cooled sorrel in the bottom of each. Add the cottage cheese, the sour cream and chives to the potato. Beat in the egg yolks until the mixture is very smooth, then whip the egg whites stiffly and fold in.

Divide the mixture between the ramekins, sprinkle with the Parmesan and cook for 10 minutes in a hot oven (gas mark 7/425°F/220°C).

*In **Simmond's Vegetable Kingdom**, published c.1879, it is reported that a Professor Bollman of the Russian Agricultural Institute accidentally discovered that drying potato tubers at a sufficiently high temperature protected the plants against potato disease.*

## 6 JULY

# FOCACCIA WITH RED ONIONS

This very popular olive oil bread is easy to make. The presence of potato in bread helps to retain its moisture and makes it light.

4 oz (110 g) potatoes, cooked and puréed
12 oz (350 g) plain flour
2 heaped tablespoonfuls Quick-Action yeast
1 teaspoon sea salt
7 fl oz warm water
8 tablespoons good quality olive oil
12 oz (350 g) red onions, thinly sliced
Rosemary (optional)

Mix the flour with the yeast, salt, potatoes and water with 4 tablespoons of the olive oil. Make a dough, adding more flour if necessary and knead until smooth. (This can be done in a food processor).

Place in a covered bowl and leave to rise in a warm place until doubled in size - about 1½-2 hours. Meanwhile heat the remaining 4 tablespoons of oil and over a very low heat leave the onions to soften in this for about an hour.

Knock the dough back and press into an oiled 12 x 8 inch tin. Leave to rise again for about 20 minutes and then with a spoon make a few depressions on the surface of the dough.

Spread over the onion mixture and scatter the rosemary over the surface. Bake at gas mark 6/400°F/200°C for about 25-30 minutes until golden brown. The base should sound hollow when tapped.

*A World War II recipe suggested adding powdered egg, powdered milk and Bovril to mashed potatoes and, having thinned the mixture with water, frying in little pancakes on a griddle. These were known as Potato Panettes.*

## 7 JULY

# CAESAR SOUP

I recently came across the dreadful suggestion that left-over salads should be liquidized with potatoes to make soup. The piquant broth below, however, while sharing the same ingredients as the famed Caesar salad, uses fresh ingredients and is excellent in its own right.

12 oz (350 g) potatoes, peeled and thinly sliced
1 clove garlic, finely chopped
1 tablespoon olive oil
1 medium-sized lettuce, shredded
3 anchovy fillets, rinsed
2 pints (1.1 litre) chicken stock
Juice of $^{1}/_{2}$ lemon
Sea salt and freshly ground black pepper
Grated Parmesan cheese
Croutons

Heat the olive oil and cook the potatoes and garlic in this over a low heat. As soon as the potatoes take on a transparent appearance, add the lettuce and chicken stock. Bring to the boil and simmer for 20 minutes.

Add the anchovy fillets and the lemon juice and cook for another few minutes. Liquidize and then season. Serve with a dusting of Parmesan and a few croutons on each plate.

*"The rent of a cabin and potatoe (sic) plot in the county of Wicklow and neighbourhood is from one to two guineas; the family live on potatoes and buttermilk six days in the week and instead of 'an added pudding', the Sabbath is generally celebrated by bacon and greens. In those parts I found the price of potatoes to be eight shillings and four pence the barrel (twenty stone to the barrel) and three quarts of buttermilk for a penny. The price of labour was sixpence halfpenny per day."*

*John Carr, of the Honourable Society of the Middle Temple, writing in 1806.*

## 8 JULY

# SALAD OF POTATOES, TOMATOES AND WATERCRESS

Based on a recipe from Dorothy Hartley's *Food in England* this charming salad makes a good first course or a simple meal by itself. If you have no watercress, use ordinary cress.

2 lb (900 g) very small new potatoes
$^{1}/_{4}$ pint (150 ml) cream
Sea salt and black pepper
$1^{1}/_{2}$ lb (700 g) tomatoes, skinned and de-seeded
Bunch of watercress
3 tablespoons olive oil
1 tablespoon cider vinegar

Steam the potatoes and while still warm, slice thickly and add to the cream, seasoning as you go. Put this on to a flat plate and cover with the tomatoes. Season again.

Cover with tender watercress leaves and sprinkle over, just before serving, the oil and vinegar.

*"He turned my way. 'God further the work,'*
*He echoed an ancient farming prayer,*
*I thanked him. He eyed the potato drills.*
*He said: 'You are bound to have good ones there."*

*From **Spraying the Potatoes** by Patrick Kavanagh.*

## 9 JULY

# SALAD OF POTATO AND CHEESE

It would be hard to imagine a more simple salad than the following one, yet no elaborate amalgam of vegetables sitting in its blanket of mayonnaise could compare.

2 lb (900 g) very small new potatoes
2 red peppers, peeled, de-seeded and sliced peppers
8 oz (225 g) smoked cheese, cut in slivers
Sea salt
Extra-virgin olive oil

Steam the potatoes, rub off the skins and combine with the peppers and the cheese. Scatter a little salt over the salad and pour over olive oil.

*"And poet lost to potato fields,*
*Remembering the lime and copper smell*
*Of the spraying barrels he is not lost*
*Or till blossomed stalks cannot weave a spell."*
*From* ***Spraying the Potatoes*** *by Patrick Kavanagh.*

## 10 JULY

# POTATO PURÉE WITH WHIPPED CREAM

This purée can be put into a pre-baked pie crust (I once made it to advantage with a nut pastry) and put into the oven to brown, but it is not necessary. Extra effort, however, rarely goes unnoticed by the diners.

4 large potatoes, cleaned
4 oz (110 g) butter
2 egg yolks
Sea salt and freshly ground black pepper
A little nutmeg
$^1/_4$ pint (150 ml) whipped cream

Bake the cleaned potatoes and when cool, scrape out the centres. Put through a sieve and put the potato into a pan with butter, egg yolks, seasoning and nutmeg.

When smooth and white, add the whipped cream. The purée can now be served or put into a pastry case.

*"If angels ever ate mashed potatoes they would call on Pellew's chef to prepare them."*
*From* ***Hornblower and the Hotspur*** *by C.S. Forester, 1962.*

## 11 JULY
# OCOPA

Don't be put off by the combination of ingredients here. This is a Peruvian dish, substantial and with a beguiling flavour. It should include *huacatay*, a native herb belonging to the marigold family but, since there is no known substitute, it must be left out.

$1^1/_2$ lb (700 g) potatoes, boiled, peeled and cut in half
4 oz (110 g) raw peanuts
6 cream crackers
4 fl oz (110 ml) sunflower oil
1 small onion, chopped
1 medium tomato, chopped
1 clove garlic, chopped
1 green chilli, de-seeded and chopped
4 fl oz (110 ml) evaporated milk
4 fl oz (110 ml) water
1 teaspoon salt

Lettuce leaves
4 hard-boiled eggs
12 ripe olives

Put the peanuts into a hot oven, gas mark 7/425°F/220°C for about 4-5 minutes until the skins can be rubbed off in a clean cloth. Grind the nuts in a blender and reserve, then do the same with the crackers.

Heat 1 tablespoon of the oil and fry the onion, tomato, garlic and chilli for a few minutes and then put into a liquidizer with the remaining oil. Add the peanuts and crackers and blend well. Mix the milk and the water and pour into the sauce - you may need to add a little more water if the mixture is too thick. Pour over the previously cooked potatoes arranged on the lettuce leaves. Decorate with the eggs and the olives.

*In **Rariorum plantarum historia**, published 1601, the French botanist Carolus Clusius describes the potato as 'reddish or verging on purple, with as many as fifty tubers on a root'.*

## 12 JULY

# COFFEE POTATO DOUGHNUTS

The school holidays are long. Too long, some would say. A cooking session helps to make them happier and, with a little parental help, children can enjoy the making, as well as the eating, of these.

3 oz (75 g) cooked potato, mashed
10 oz (275 g) plain flour
1 teaspoon sugar
1/2 teaspoon salt
1/2 sachet Quick-Action dry yeast
1/2 oz (15 g) butter, melted
1 egg, beaten
Approx. 3 fl oz (75 ml) tepid milk
Oil for deep frying

For the icing:
5 oz (150 g) icing sugar
1 teaspoon coffee granules
1 tablespoon boiling water

Sift the flour, sugar and salt into a warmed bowl. Stir in the yeast, mashed potato, melted butter, the beaten egg and, lastly, enough milk to make a pliable dough. Knead well until silky smooth. (This can be done in a food processor.) Set aside in a warm place for an hour or so until the dough has doubled in size.

Knead again and then cut into about 12 pieces. I cut these with a wine glass and then cut a hole with a round *petits fours* cutter (a bottle top will do) in the middle of each one. Set aside again for 20 minutes until the doughnuts are again well risen.

Deep fry for 4 minutes or until they are golden brown, turning them over once during cooking. Drain on kitchen paper and cover with icing made by mixing the icing sugar with the coffee granules and boiling water.

*"Their food principally potatoes and oatmeal, very little meat...many of them live very poorly, sometimes having for three months only potato, salt and water."*

*From* ***A Tour in Ireland*** *by Arthur Young, 1780.*

## 13 JULY

# POTATO AND FRENCH BEAN SALAD

Don't attempt to make this potato salad unless you have a dense, waxy-fleshed potato such as Wilja, Cultra, Pink Fir Apple or Jersey Royals. A floury potato that collapses when sliced is a waste of time for salads. It is important to mix the dressing with the potatoes while they are still warm. A basic vinaigrette can hardly be bettered, made with oil and vinegar to a proportion of 3 to 1. Potatoes will absorb dressing so be generous with it. Fresh herbs can be added as they are available.

1 lb (450 g) potatoes
1 lb (450 g) French beans
Sea salt and freshly ground black pepper
2 tablespoons Dijon mustard
3 tablespoons wine vinegar
10 tablespoons olive oil
4 oz (110 g) black olives
Fresh herbs

Clean and steam the potatoes. Peel while still hot and have steaming the prepared French beans.

Slice the potatoes and add with the beans to the dressing. Prepare this by crushing the garlic with the salt and pepper, then add the mustard, vinegar and lastly the oil.

Add the olives and freshly cut herbs.

*"Potatoes are good when the white flower is on them*
*They are better when the white foam is on them*
*They are still better when the stomach is full of them."*
*Old Irish saying.*

## 14 JULY
## BASTILLE DAY
# POMMES DE TERRE LYONNAISE

This is one of those seemingly simple dishes that needs careful watching. The onions should not brown before they are added to the potatoes.

2 lb (900 g) waxy potatoes, peeled, boiled and cut in uniform rounds
8 oz (225 g) onions, very thinly sliced
Good lump of butter
Parsley

Take 2 frying pans and start by sautéeing the potatoes in butter. In the second pan, heat another lump of butter and cook the onions over a low heat.

When the potatoes are nearly cooked, add the onions and brown them and the potatoes together.

*"She rejected all potatoes*
*For a thousand nights and days*
*Till a Frenchman wooed and won her*
*With pommes de terre Lyonnaise."*
*From* ***Giving Potatoes*** *by Adrian Mitchell.*

15 JULY

# POTATOES WITH WHITE WINE AND HERBS

White wine and herbs - an irresistible combination.

1½ lb (700 g) potatoes, cleaned
1½ fl oz (40 ml) olive oil
1 medium onion, chopped
1 clove garlic, chopped
1 teaspoon flour
Sea salt and freshly ground black pepper
5 fl oz (150 ml) white wine
5 fl oz (150 ml) chicken stock
Small handful of chopped herbs

Use little potatoes, all of one size. If they are larger, cut in quarters. Heat the oil, add the onion and garlic and cook until they begin to change colour. Stir in the flour, add the seasoning and white wine and stock. Put in the herbs, bring to the boil and cook until the potatoes are tender and the liquid has reduced.

*When a dental expert visited the island of Tristan da Cunha he examined 150 of the islanders and found that 131 of them had perfect teeth. The eldest inhabitant, E. Samuel Swain, aged 75 was found to be a dental marvel. Potatoes are the mainstay of the islanders' diet.*

16 JULY

# TERRINE OF POTATOES WITH CARAWAY SEED

This will serve 6 people. Eat while still warm, with a salad or perhaps a chicken dish.

1½ lb (700 g) potatoes, peeled and thinly sliced
1 large onion, sliced
1 clove garlic, chopped
1 red pepper, sliced
1 green pepper, sliced
10 slices streaky bacon
3 eggs
½ pint (275 ml) milk
¼ pint (150 ml) cream
1 tablespoon English mustard
Sea salt and freshly ground black pepper
1 tablespoon caraway seeds
3 oz (75 g) grated cheese

Melt the butter and gently fry the onion, peppers and garlic until translucent. Stir in the potatoes and turn around in the pan for about 5 minutes.

Oil well a 2 lb (900 g) loaf tin and cover the base and long sides with the bacon, allowing it to overhang the edges. In a bowl combine the eggs, milk, cream, mustard, seasoning, caraway seeds and half the cheese.

Combine with the potato mixture and put into the loaf tin. Sprinkle with the rest of the cheese and then bring the overhanging bacon slices into the top of the terrine. Cook at gas mark 5/375°F/190°C for about 50 minutes or until the potatoes are cooked and the crust is golden.

*It has been estimated that those in pre-famine Ireland who relied totally on potatoes were consuming a stone a day - about 50 to 80 potatoes. Over a 50-year span, this meant eating a million potatoes.*

## 17 JULY

# POTATO BISCUITS

The preparation of these might amuse children for an hour or so. Cover them with melted chocolate and swirl the surface with a fork.

4 oz (110 g) cold mashed potato
4 oz (110 g) plain flour
4 oz (110 g) rolled oats
2 oz (50 g) sugar
1 teaspoon salt
3 oz (75 g) butter or margarine

Mix the flour, oats, sugar and salt and rub in the butter or margarine. Knead in the mashed potatoes and roll out thinly on a floured board.

Place on oiled baking trays and cook in a slow oven (gas mark 3/325°F/170°C) for about 20 minutes until crisp but not brown.

*In 1750, King Frederick William 1 of Prussia publicly ate potatoes on his balcony to encourage his subjects to eat the vegetable.*

## 18 JULY

# POTATO SAUCE

Potato Sauce - the words do not encourage immediate epicurean feelings but this, based on a sauce served at the Cipriani in Venice, has the advantage of good visual appeal - a rich cream flecked with saffron - as well as an agreeable affinity with a variety of foods. The dominant flavour is garlic; it is good with seafood, chicken, lamb and makes an interesting alternative to 'mash' with 'bangers'.

3 oz (75 g) potato, peeled, cooked and puréed
2 cloves garlic, peeled
4 fl oz (110 ml) olive oil
Large pinch of saffron
2 fl oz (50 ml) hot water
1 egg yolk
Sea salt and freshly ground black pepper

Crush the garlic roughly and leave to marinate in the olive oil for about 30 minutes. Pour the hot water onto the saffron.

While the potato purée is still warm stir in the egg yolk and the saffron liquid. Using a hand whisk, slowly add the strained olive oil until the sauce is smooth. You may need to add a little more water. Season well.

*"If you want to get that foreign taste, which many people fancy in mashed potatoes, try the following method:- when your potatoes are nicely boiled, and drained, turn them back into their saucepan, which, after the draining, you must rub lightly with garlic: go on as previously described, be liberal with your butter, and instead of the milk, add a little stock from the soup kettle. A dust of pepper, and a little nutmeg, will complete the purée, for remember that mashed potatoes abroad goes by the name of purée de pommes de terre, and is sent to table not nearly as stiffly moulded as ours."*

*From **Culinary Jottings for Madras** by "Wyvern", 1878.*

## 19 JULY

# POTATOES WITH LENTILS

Lentils are usually associated with the winter, yet can make a delightful summer lunch combined here with potatoes and a handful of fresh cut herbs.

1 lb (450 g) potatoes, scrubbed and diced
8 oz (225 g) green lentils

2 tablespoons olive oil
2 shallots, chopped
1 large clove garlic, crushed
$1^1/_2$ pints (900 ml) chicken stock
1 glass white wine
Sea salt and freshly ground black pepper
Sprig of thyme
Chopped herbs - parsley, basil, etc.

Wash the lentils and drain. Heat the olive oil and sauté the shallots and garlic for a few minutes. Stir in the lentils and cook for another few minutes, stirring all the time. Add the chicken stock, wine, seasoning and thyme and simmer for 30 minutes.

Add the potatoes and cook until they are tender. Sprinkle the herbs over the dish and serve.

*"What I say is that if a man really likes potatoes, he must be a pretty decent sort of fellow."*
*From* ***Not That It Matters*** *by A.A. Milne.*

## 20 JULY

# POTATO CANAPÉS

The imagination can be unfettered when it comes to ways of serving baby new potatoes as canapés - sort of upmarket crisps - with your cocktails.

Clean and steam the potatoes until tender and then cut in half lengthways. Slice a little piece off the bottom of the potato so that it stands squarely. With a teaspoon scoop a little out of the centre of each potato.

Serve with a variety of the following: sour cream topped with red and black caviar, taramasalata, pesto, quail's eggs, scrambled eggs dusted with paprika, anchovy butter, a salsa of mushrooms, cream cheeses, grilled peppers or whatever you will.

*"There is, I imagine, as much art in boiling a potato as writing tribal lays..."*
*From* ***The Epicure's Companion*** *by Edward and Lorna Bunyard, 1937.*

21 JULY

# POTATOES WITH SQUID AND FRESH HERBS

A Dublin friend who gave me this recipe is lucky enough to live next to an old-fashioned fishmonger who has regular supplies of squid, yet always manages to look surprised when anyone buys it. Buy it whenever and wherever you can, freeze what can't be eaten fresh because, unlike most fish, squid responds quite well to freezing.

2 lb (900 g) potatoes, cut into chunks
1½ lb (700 g) squid
2 tablespoons olive oil
2 cloves garlic, chopped
¼ pint (150 ml) white wine
1 dessertspoon tomato purée
½ pint (275 ml) water, perhaps a little more
Sea salt and freshly ground black pepper
Fresh parsley or chervil or basil

Clean the squid and slice into strips. Heat the oil, add the garlic and squid and cook briskly for a few moments.

Pour in the white wine, then stir in the tomato purée and the water. Allow this to cook for about 10 minutes before adding the potatoes and the seasoning. Cook gently until the potatoes are soft - this should take about 20 minutes or so. The squid should retain a slight rubbery quality.

Sprinkle with fresh herbs before eating.

*When Mrs Austen, around 1770, advised a tenant's wife in Hampshire to plant potatoes in her garden, she was told, "No, no, they are all very well for you gentry, but they must be terribly costly to rear."*

22 JULY

# SMOKED HADDOCK TERRINE

Terrines make lovely summer food served with salads. Offer this with a fresh tomato sauce made with garlic and basil just picked. If you don't have fresh spinach in the garden, you can use frozen spinach.

12 oz (350 g) potato, cleaned, cooked and puréed
12 oz (350 g) smoked haddock fillets
1/4 pint (150 ml) cream
3 fl oz (75 ml) milk
Sea salt and freshly ground black pepper
1 lb (450 g) spinach
4 eggs

Steam the fish until just cooked. Flake and remove any bones. In a large bowl put the fish and puréed potatoes and mix with the cream, milk and seasoning.

Wilt the spinach (barely cook it) and drain out any moisture. Chop finely. Separate the eggs and beat the yolks. Stir in the spinach.

Whisk the egg whites until dry and fold half into the fish mixture and half into the spinach. Put half the fish mixture into an oiled 2 lb (900 g) loaf tin followed by half the spinach. Repeat with the remaining mixtures and level the surface. Cover with a piece of greaseproof paper and put into a roasting tin half filled with hot water. Bake at gas mark 5/375°F/190°C for 45 minutes. Turn out and serve with the tomato sauce.

*In 1996, food writer John McKenna reported that the latest potato offering in restaurants was 'smash' - cooked potatoes crushed with a fork and infused with herb-flavoured oil.*

## 23 JULY

# POTATO AND SPINACH CAKES

Spinach should be plentiful now.

1 lb (450 g) potatoes, cooked and puréed
8 oz (225 g) cooked spinach, chopped
1 onion, chopped
1 clove garlic, chopped
4 oz (110 g) grated cheese
Wholewheat flour
A little sunflower oil

Mix the potato purée with the chopped spinach. Soften the onion and garlic in a little oil and mix with the potato. Add the grated cheese. Shape into little cakes, dust with wholewheat flour and fry in a little oil.

*"If you wish your potatoes to have a dry and mealy appearance, pour off every drop of water after cooking and shake the saucepan for a second or two in front of an open window. The potatoes will fluff up immediately and no further steaming will be necessary."*

*From **Things Worth Remembering, Good Housekeeping,** July 1923.*

## 24 JULY

# OMELETTE À LA SAVOYARDE

Potatoes and eggs are perfect partners. This recipe originated in the cheese-producing region of Savoy in France, where potatoes have a place of honour. This omelette is cooked more like a pancake.

4 medium potatoes, cleaned, cooked and sliced
4 oz (110 g) butter
8 eggs
Sea salt and freshly ground black pepper
2 oz (50g) Gruyère cheese, cut into little shavings or small dice

Melt the butter and brown the potato slices. Beat the eggs together and season. Mix the cheese with the eggs. Pour into the pan over the potatoes and cook like a pancake, turning it over as soon as it is browned on one side.

*La Cuisine Républicaine, published 1793, was the first French cookery book written by a woman, Mme. Meridiot. It was devoted entirely to the potato.*

25 JULY

# FINNAN HADDOCK WITH BACON AND POTATOES

True Finnan haddock is a mellow yellow. It has been smoked on the bone or as fillets and is a superior (kettle of) fish to the bright yellow haddock that is probably artificially dyed. It is well worth seeking out.

$1^1/_2$ lb (700 g) potatoes, cleaned, cooked and diced
1 lb (450 g) smoked haddock fillets
$^3/_4$ pint (400 ml) milk
2 tablespoons butter
4 rashers streaky bacon, chopped
2 tablespoons flour
Sea salt (if needed) and freshly ground black pepper
3 eggs, beaten
Chopped parsley

Poach the haddock in the milk for about 5 minutes until the flakes separate easily. Drain, reserving the milk and flake the fish removing any skin and bones.

In a saucepan, melt the butter and fry the bacon. Stir in the flour and then add the milk to make a smooth sauce. Add a little water if too thick. Put in the potatoes, fish and seasoning and heat through. Stir in the eggs over a gentle heat without boiling, then serve, sprinkled with the chopped parsley.

*Potatoes are said to have arrived in Japan via Jakarta. At first, they were known as the Jakarta Yam.*

### 26 JULY

# CORNISH BOUILLABAISSE

Based on another recipe by Madam Prunier, the flavour of this dish will depend very much on the variety of fish that is put into it. Red mullet, mackerel, cod, whiting, rock salmon, turbot - the choice of course depends on availability. It is a soup better made in large quantities and the amounts here will feed 10 to 12 people.

2 lb (900 g) potatoes, scrubbed and roughly sliced
5 leeks, thinly sliced
12 oz (350 g) tomatoes, skinned and de-seeded
3 small celery hearts, quartered
3 1/2 pints (2 litres) water
Sea salt and freshly ground black pepper
Bouquet garni
3 lb (1.4 kg) fish, cleaned and sliced, no bones
3 egg yolks
4 tablespoons cream
Croutons

Put the potatoes, leeks, tomatoes and celery into a large pan with the water, seasoning and bouquet garni. Bring to the boil and cook for 25 minutes.

Add the fish and cook gently for another 15 minutes. Remove from the heat. Mix the egg yolks with the cream and stir gently into the soup. On no account allow to boil again. Scatter the croutons over the soup before serving.

*"The potatoes never failed us...for each meal, they looked different and tasted different."*
*From **One Foot in America** by Yuri Suhl.*

27 JULY

# STIR FRY POTATOES

I think if there had to be a sudden evacuation of our kitchen and I could only take one object, it would be the wok. Or possibly the Chinese steamer?

8 oz (225 g) potatoes
2 tablespoons sesame or sunflower oil
4 baby sweetcorn
4 oz (110 g) mangetout peas
1 red pepper
4 baby courgettes
1 clove garlic
4 spring onions
A little soy sauce

First prepare your vegetables. Clean the potatoes and cut into very little dice. Keep separately from the other vegetables. Take any coarse parts off the peas and slice the pepper and courgettes. Chop the garlic finely. Prepare the spring onions.

Heat the oil in a wok (a large frying pan will substitute) and put in the potatoes. Allow to cook for a few minutes, stirring all the while, until they begin to soften. Add the remaining vegetables and stir fry until the vegetables are cooked but crisp.

Add a little soy sauce and eat at once.

*"Hors d'oeuvres of sardines, eggs and potato slices were followed by soup (probably Heinz). Then came camouflaged tinned salmon with a doubtful flavour...mutton (or goat) cutlets appeared next with potatoes and vegetables...next a joint of beef with more vegetables and the*

*same dish of potatoes - slightly cooler and fewer. Minced chicken cutlets, supported by the now fast congealing remnants of the potatoes, were, we fervently hoped, the last of the meat dishes, as a strawberry pudding followed them, but this was rapidly followed by snipe, roast with potato chips..."*

*From **A Dinner in India** by Marguerite Bunyard, 1937.*

## 28 JULY

# POTATO MUFFINS

Light as anything, these are wonderful with jam or just butter. This amount makes 8 muffins.

2 medium potatoes, cleaned, cooked and sieved
1/4 pint (150 ml) milk
1/2 oz (15 g) butter
1/2 sachet Quick-Action dried yeast
11 oz (310 g) flour
1/2 teaspoon salt
1 heaped teaspoon sugar
1 egg, beaten

Put the milk into a small pan with the butter and warm through. Mix the yeast, flour, salt and sugar and pour in the milk/butter. Add the egg and the potatoes and knead until you have a smooth dough. (This can easily be done in a food processor).

Put the dough into a clean bowl, cover with a cloth and leave to double in size for a couple of hours in a warm place.

Punch the dough down and with a biscuit cutter cut out into muffin shapes. Leave to rise for another 20-30 minutes and then cook in a hot oven, gas mark 7/425°F/220°C for 15 minutes, turning once during the cooking time.

*"The barrels of blue potato spray*
*Stood on a headland of July*
*Beside an orchard wall where roses*
*Were young girls hanging from the sky."*

*From **Spraying the Potatoes** by Patrick Kavanagh.*

29 JULY

# GARLIC POTATO PURÉE

This is glorious food.

2 lb (900 g) potatoes
6 fat cloves garlic
2 oz (50 g) butter
1 tablespoon flour
A little grated nutmeg
1/2 teaspoon French mustard
1/2 pint (275 ml) boiling milk
2 oz (50 g) butter
3 tablespoons cream

Blanch the garlic heads for 1 minute in boiling water. Drain and peel. Boil or steam the potatoes and while they are cooking melt 2 oz (50 g) of butter and add the garlic cloves. Crush them with a wooden spoon in the butter. Let them soften over a gentle heat for about 7 minutes and then stir in the flour, nutmeg and mustard. Pour over the hot milk blending to make a smooth sauce.

Purée the cooked potatoes, stir in another 2 oz (50 g) of the butter and spoon by spoon, mix in the garlic sauce.

*"...I usher*
*Such an unexpected dainty bit for breakfast*
*As never yet I cook'd; 'tis not Botargo,*
*Fried frogs, potatoes marrow'd, cavear..."*
*From* ***Curiosities of Literature*** *by Isaac D'Israeli, 1791.*

30 JULY

# POTATOES À LA GREQUE

*An Bord Glas*, Ireland's Horticultural Department, provided this recipe to which I have added fresh coriander leaves. Coriander does not respond very well, for me at any rate, to the Irish climate, but it does make an attempt at growing and the leaves are even more precious because of their scarcity.

2 lb (900 g) potatoes
1/2 pint (275 ml) dry white wine
1/2 pint (275 ml) water
4 tablespoons olive oil
Juice of a lemon
2 garlic cloves
2 tablespoons coriander seeds
Sprig of thyme
1 teaspoon black peppercorns
Chopped coriander leaves

Clean the potatoes and boil or steam until just tender. While they are cooking, put all the other ingredients except the coriander leaves into a pan and simmer for 15 minutes.

Cut the potatoes into pieces if they are not very small and put them into a bowl. Pour over the dressing while both are still hot. Leave to cool and serve, sprinkling with the coriander leaves.

*"Take away your baked potato*
*In your fusty musty van*
*Take away your baked potato*
*You potato-skinned old man."*

*From* ***Giving Potatoes*** *by Adrian Mitchell.*

31 JULY

# NEW POTATOES WITH PRAWNS

Divided between 8 ramekin dishes, this will make an excellent first course for that number of people. Otherwise, the amount will serve 4 as a main course eaten with a salad.

1½ lb (700 g) very small new potatoes, cleaned
2 oz (50 g) butter
8 oz (225 g) peeled and cooked prawns
2 oz (50 g) carrot, grated
5 fl oz (150ml) yoghourt
1 tablespoon mayonnaise
5 fl oz (150 ml) meat stock
4 large tomatoes, sliced
4 oz (110 g) grated cheese

Steam the potatoes and keep warm. Melt the butter, add the prawns, allow to warm through and then put in the potatoes and carrots. Stir in the yoghourt, mayonnaise and meat stock and heat without boiling.

Put into a wide gratin dish, cover with sliced tomatoes, sprinkle with the cheese and brown under a grill.

***How to Cook and Dress Potatoes in One Hundred Different Ways*** *by Georgiana Hill, published in 1866, was the first all-potato American cookbook. Georgiana Hill also turned her attention to eggs and apples.*

# GREEN GODDESS SOUP

This soup, served chilled, is based on a recipe given to me by the chef at Jury's Hotel, Dublin.

1 lb (450 g) potatoes, peeled and sliced
1 medium onion, sliced
1 tablespoon butter
1 fat bunch watercress, chopped
3 tablespoons chopped parsley
2 large artichoke hearts
2 teaspoons fresh tarragon, chopped
1 pint (570 ml) chicken stock
1/2 pint (275 ml) milk
1/4 pint (150 ml) cream
Sea salt and freshly ground black pepper
Cooked shrimps for garnish

Cook the potatoes and onion in the butter until translucent. Add the watercress (reserving a little for the garnish) and parsley, the artichoke hearts and the tarragon. Cover with stock and cook until the vegetables are soft. Add the milk and cream and cook another minute.

Liquidize the ingredients and season. Chill and serve garnished with the shrimps and watercress.

*One of the largest collections of potato recipes is the Russian cookbook **500 Blyud iz Kartoffelya**, or **500 Potato Dishes**.*

2 AUGUST

# SUMMER FLOWER SALAD

Although the idea of eating flowers is an old one, it doesn't have much appeal to me. When Bernard Shaw was asked why he didn't have cut flowers in his house, he replied that he liked children but didn't want to cut their heads off. However, nasturtiums are so prolific and easily grown (besides being full of taste) that it seems a shame not to include them in cooking. Add a few borage flowers with their vivid blue and pink hues.

2 lb (900 g) new potatoes, cleaned
1 avocado, peeled and sliced
Sea salt and freshly ground black pepper
1 teaspoon sugar
1 teaspoon Dijon mustard
2 tablespoons wine vinegar
6 tablespoons extra virgin olive oil
Nasturtium flowers (different colours if possible)
Marigold petals

Steam the potatoes; while still warm, peel and put in a bowl with the avocado. Make a dressing with the seasonings, vinegar and olive oil and pour over the potatoes and avocado. Strew flowers over the salad and serve.

*The Irish practice of commemorating successful potato growers resulted in the slang terms 'Murphys' and 'Crokers' which are said to have been used as early as 1640.*

## 3 AUGUST

# STUFFED POTATO SHELLS

This recipe from the actress Nanette Newman is a perfect summer lunch for 6 people. The potatoes are twice baked, thus making crisp shells. The filling should be added at the last moment, otherwise the shells will become soggy.

6 large potatoes
2 oz (50 g) melted butter for brushing

For the fillings:
3 sticks celery, chopped
A few spring onions, sliced
2 large dessert apples, peeled and chopped
4 oz (110 g) walnuts or salted peanuts
Ground nutmeg
Sea salt and freshly ground black pepper
12 oz (350 g) cottage cheese
8 oz (225 g) button mushrooms, sliced
2 smallish courgettes, sliced
1 red onion, finely chopped
$^{1}/_{4}$ pint (150 ml) soured cream
2 tablespoons chives

Bake the potatoes in their jackets in a moderately hot oven ( gas mark 6/400°F/200°C) for about an hour or until they are cooked through. Leave them to cool slightly, then cut each one in half and scoop out the middle using a small spoon.

Leave a fairly thick skin, then brush the shells with melted butter, both insides and out, and place them in a baking tray. Put them back in the oven for a further 20 minutes, or until the shells are really crisp. For the cottage cheese filling mix together the chopped celery, spring onions and apples with the nuts, a good sprinkling of nutmeg, seasoning to taste and the cottage cheese.

For the vegetable filling mix together the mushrooms and courgettes, the onion and the soured cream. Shortly before eating, fill 6 of the shells with the cottage cheese filling and 6 with the mushroom and courgette and sprinkle with the chopped chives.

*Potatoes are an important food source in at least 128 of the world's 173 nations.*

4 AUGUST

# AJIACO DE OLLOCUS

Ollocus are potatoes grown in Latin America that are tuber shaped, small and yellow and are sometimes flecked with red. Their inclusion in this aromatic brew may be largely aesthetic but also necessary because they don't break up when cooked. A small, waxy potato such as the knobbly Pink Fir Apple will substitute. At any rate, use two distinct varieties of potatoes here, as near a yellow and a white as is possible.

1 lb (450 g) waxy potatoes, cleaned and thinly sliced
1½ lb (700 g) old potatoes, cleaned, cooked and diced
2 fl oz (50 ml) oil
2 medium onions, chopped
2 cloves garlic, chopped
Chilli pepper to taste
Sea salt and freshly ground black pepper
½ pint (275 ml) good stock
4 oz (110 g) cheese, crumbled
Chopped parsley

Heat the oil and fry the onions, garlic and chilli pepper until the onions are transparent.

Add the waxy potatoes and move around the pan until they are just taking colour. Add the cooked and diced potato and the stock and cook over a fairly brisk heat for 5 minutes. Add the cheese, the parsley and correct the seasoning. For authenticity, eat with boiled rice.

*"Peruvians like their food picante...I like to speculate about the use of yellow in the food...There are potato dishes that are a symphony of yellow and white, perhaps honouring the sun god and the moon goddess."*

*From **The Book of Latin American Cooking** by Elizabeth Lambert Ortiz, 1984.*

5 AUGUST

# POTATOES WITH LETTUCE AND NASTURTIUM BUTTER

This makes a charming and unusual summer salad. Use as many different coloured nasturtium flowers as you can find. I sometimes add a sprinkling of roasted pine nuts over this salad but this could be considered over-the-top.

1 1/2 lb (700 g) baby potatoes, cleaned
2 Little Gem lettuces
4 oz (110 g) butter
4 tablespoons nasturtium flowers, chopped
1 tablespoon lemon juice

Steam the potatoes and while this is in progress, cut the lettuces in quarters and soak in salted water, without cutting further. Drain well and put 2 quarters on each plate.

Melt the butter, add the nasturtium flowers and the lemon juice. Arrange the cooked potatoes around and about the lettuce quarters and pour over the warmed butter.

*Potato diggers appeared on Irish stamps commemorating An Gorta Mor (The Big Hunger ) from 1945-1950.*

6 AUGUST

# BARBECUED POTATOES WITH MINT

Any herb you like can substitute for the mint. These potatoes can be cooked in charcoal on a barbecue or put into the smouldering embers of a wood fire and left to cook slowly while you do something else. Instead of the usual large baking potatoes, try cooking bundles of new potatoes which will take less time to cook.

Prepare a double layer of foil and brush the surface with oil. Place the cleaned potatoes and chopped herbs on this and fold into a packet. Cook for approximately 40 minutes but this will depend on where you are cooking them. If you use an oven, bake for 40 minutes at gas mark 6/400°F/200°C.

*"I have borne this baked potato*
*O'er the Generation Gap*
*Pray accept this baked potato*
*Let me lay it in your heated lap."*
*From **Giving Potatoes** by Adrian Mitchell.*

7 AUGUST

# SALAD OF POTATOES, TOMATOES AND BASIL

Because of the visual appeal, it is important that you should use the tiniest potatoes and tomatoes you can find. The result makes an attractively coloured first course for a summer dinner.

1 lb (450 g) potatoes
1 lb (450 g) cherry tomatoes
6 tablespoons hazelnut or olive oil
2 tablespoons lemon juice
A little chopped shallot or spring onion
Fresh basil

Steam the potatoes, peel and toss with the other ingredients including the chopped basil. Eat while the potatoes are still warm.

*'Quite the clean potato' was a 19th century expression meaning the best or most apposite thing.*

8 AUGUST

# SAUTÉ POTATOES WITH HAZELNUT SAUCE

This is extravagant, because hazelnut oil is expensive, and a little tricky because it needs careful watching and once prepared, the dish must be eaten immediately. But it is worth the money spent and every minute taken in its preparation. One of the best potato recipes that ever came into this house.

1-1 $^{1}/_{2}$ lb (450-700 g) medium-size potatoes
1 oz (25 g) hazelnuts

Hazelnut oil
$^{1}/_{4}$ pint (150 ml) cream
Squeeze of lemon juice
Sea salt and freshly ground black pepper

Steam the potatoes in their skins until barely tender. Drain and cool. Simmer the hazelnuts in a little water for 3-4 minutes, then drain, skin and dry. Gently fry them in a little hazelnut oil until brown and set aside to cool. Crush roughly. Peel the potatoes and slice thinly. Sauté in hazelnut oil, just using enough to brown the potatoes without becoming oily. Remove to a heated serving plate.

The preparation of the sauce must be done as quickly as possible or the potatoes will become soggy. Add 1-2 tablespoons of fresh hazelnut oil to the pan and when quite hot, add the cream. Boil, stirring all the time, until the mixture combines and thickens. Once it is reduced to a coating sauce, add a squeeze of lemon juice and the seasonings. Pour over the potatoes, scatter with the crushed hazelnuts and serve.

*"If the Englishmen were Romans, one of their household gods would no doubt have the shape of a potato."*

*Marcel Boulestin.*

## 9 AUGUST

# CAUSA WITH TUNA AND AVOCADO

The International Potato Centre in Peru provided me with several recipes using *causa*, potatoes mashed with oil, chilli peppers and lemon juice. This is one of them - it makes good picnic food.

2 lb (900 g) floury potatoes, peeled, cooked and puréed
6 tablespoons olive oil
1 green chilli, seeded and finely chopped
Juice of 2 lemons

Sea salt
1 large can tuna
5 fl oz (150 ml) mayonnaise
1 hard boiled egg, chopped
1 large ripe avocado, sliced
1 red pepper, thinly sliced
6 olives, sliced
Salad leaves to garnish (optional)

In 2 tablespoons of the olive oil, liquidize the chilli and stir with the remaining olive oil into the potato with the lemon juice and salt to taste.

Mix together the tuna and the mayonnaise. Divide the *causa* mixture into 3 portions. Spread one of the portions in a shallow dish. Cover with half the tuna mixture. Make a second layer of the *causa* and cover with the remaining tuna. Arrange the egg, avocado slices, pepper and olives on the tuna layer. Cover with the remaining *causa*. Leave for at least an hour in a cold place. Turn out, surround by salad leaves if liked, and serve.

*In Peru, the potato was grown in the same high valleys where the coca leaf grows. The potato offered nutrition; the coca leaf a numbness from the pain of daily living.*

## 10 AUGUST

# NEW POTATOES IN MUSTARD

Don't attempt to make this unless you have Dijon mustard.

1½ lb (700 g) new potatoes, cleaned
2-3 oz (50-75 g) butter
2 tablespoons Dijon mustard
Sea salt and freshly ground black pepper
Fresh herbs

Steam the potatoes until barely tender, drain and when cooled rub off the skins. Melt the butter in a wide pan and stir in the mustard and seasonings. Add the potatoes, turning so that all the surfaces are covered with the mustard. Sprinkle with the herbs and serve.

*"Those who do not get milk to their potatoes, eat mustard with them, raising the seed for the purpose. The population of the country increases exceedingly..."*

*From **A Tour in Ireland** by Arthur Young, 1780.*

## 11 AUGUST

# DILL POTATOES WITH GARLIC MOUSSELINE

A mousseline is a name given to preparations that contain whipped cream.

1 1/2 lb (700 g) small new potatoes, cleaned
Dill
2 egg yolks
1/2 teaspoon French mustard
Juice of 1/2 a lemon
2 cloves garlic
1/4 pint (150 ml) olive oil
Sea salt and freshly ground black pepper
1/4 pint (150 ml) cream

Steam the potatoes with a sprig of dill and when tender, put them in a warmed dish with a little chopped dill. Serve with the following sauce.

Ensure the ingredients are at room temperature. Beat the egg yolks and then beat in the mustard, lemon juice and squeezed garlic (use a garlic press). Then add the oil, drop by drop, until the sauce thickens. Towards the end the oil can be added faster. Season and add a tablespoon of boiling water. Whip the cream and fold into the mayonnaise.

*"I could eat water-gruel with thee a month, for this jest my dear rogue. O by Hercules, 'tis your only dish; above all your potato or oyster pies in the world."*

*From **Cynthia's Revels** by Ben Johnson, 1601.*

## 12 AUGUST
## GROUSE SHOOTING STARTS
# GAME CHIPS

The practice that still lingers of serving commercial crisps with game is, I think, a repulsive one. Home-made potato crisps are simple to make and far superior. They can be made in a variety of shapes; straws by coarsely grating the potato, or in corkscrew shapes by peeling the potato with a peeler.

1 lb (450 g) potatoes, peeled and very thinly sliced
Oil for deep frying
A little sea salt

Allow the potato slices to soak in cold water for 10 minutes and then dry very thoroughly. Heat oil to 350°F/180°C and deep fry. .Drain and salt lightly.

*"I have to declare my interest in the matter of deep-fried potatoes. They are most unsuitable for making in the ordinary family kitchen."*

*From **Jane Grigson's Vegetable Book**, 1978.*

## 13 AUGUST
# RESIN POTATOES

When you read the following instructions you will see why the preparation of resin potatoes is beyond the capabilities of most of us. Nevertheless, I reproduce it for its interest as it was given to me by an American friend who regularly cooks it up on his farm in Virginia.

"Place chunk resin (solid) in a suitable container. We use a cast-iron pot about 22 inches in diameter. Put fire to bottom of the pot - charcoal is the best fuel we have found - peat or coal would surely be just as good.

When resin has come completely to a boil (surface will boil first) place potatoes into boiling resin. They will sink below the surface. In approximately 20 minutes they will come to the surface. Allow the potatoes to cook for 20 more minutes as they float on the surface.

Using tongs, very carefully take a potato from the surface and place it in the middle at one end of a single sheet of newspaper. Roll the potato into the paper and twist the ends. To eat: do not unroll the paper. With a fork, spear 3 times across the middle of the potato and break into two parts. Either eat the potato with a spoon from each half or scoop the potato from the shell.

Butter is the only condiment we ordinarily use, although sour cream, chives etc may be..."

*"A small lifetime has passed but I can still recall the cries of ravenous diners in bathing suits (returning from a fourth or fifth dip in the surf) demanding that the potatoes be served before the moon rose."*

*From* ***Greene on Greens*** *by Bert Greene, 1984.*

## 14 AUGUST

# A PICNIC OMELETTE

This is ideal to be eaten while sitting on warm grass under, one hopes, a cloudless sky.

2 medium potatoes, cleaned
1 small onion, thinly sliced
2 tablespoons olive oil
Small handful spinach
3 eggs
Sea salt and freshly ground black pepper
1 tablespoon water

Steam the potatoes until tender. Drain and skin. Cook the onion gently in the olive oil. Have the spinach ready cooked, dried and chopped and add this to the pan with the potatoes.

Beat the eggs, add the seasonings with a tablespoon of water and, raising the heat, add to the pan. When the omelette is almost set, invert a plate over the pan and remove the omelette, tipping the frying pan over. Put the pan back on the heat, adding more oil if necessary, then slide the omelette back with the cooked side uppermost. Turn out onto a plate, allow to cool and take with you on your picnic, served cut in slices.

*'The Brandenberg Potato Paper' was an edict issued by Frederick the Great of Prussia, ordering farmers to plant potatoes or risk losing their ears and noses. Not surprisingly, soon afterwards potatoes became a staple part of the Prussian diet.*

15 AUGUST

# SMOKED DUCK BREAST, ROCKET AND POTATO SALAD

Rocket deserves to be better known outside restaurants. I would never have a vegetable garden without it. Smoked duck breast is a fairly new product and one that also, deserves wider recognition. It is not dissimilar to Parma ham but very much cheaper.

1 lb (450 g) very tiny new potatoes
4 oz (110 g) smoked duck breast
A large handful of rocket leaves
3 tablespoons fruity olive or hazelnut oil
2 tablespoons lemon juice
Sea salt and freshly ground black pepper

Steam the potatoes. Do not remove the skins but while still warm roll them in the oil, lemon juice and seasonings. Gently add the rocket leaves and place on the salad little pieces of the duck breast.

*In **The Diary of Edward Wynne** the Welsh squire and agriculturalist reports that he brought potato seed from Ireland and in 1730 had three 'potato gardens'.*

16 AUGUST

# SPINACH AND POTATO ROULADE

My daughter brought this recipe back from France but, during the journey, managed to forget what little of the French language she had learned. We found it difficult to imagine that the instructions given by her hostess and that she had written down were the correct ones. For example, the roulade had to be boiled! We attempted this, but it resulted in disintegration. Baking yielded better results. This amount will serve 6-8 people as an accompaniment to meat.

1 lb 2 oz (500 g) potatoes
1 lb (450 g) spinach
$1^1/_2$ oz (40 g) butter
2 eggs
3 oz (75 g) Parmesan cheese
Sea salt and freshly ground black pepper
4 oz (110 g) flour

Wash the spinach and cook in salted water for 3 minutes or until wilted. Refresh in cold water and drain. In a pan melt the butter, add the spinach and cook for 5 minutes. Season. Add 1 egg and the Parmesan and mix together.

Cook the potatoes in salted water, drain and put through a sieve. Mix with the flour and the other egg. Work this into a dough and, on a clean tea towel that has been lightly sprinkled with flour, roll it into a rectangle to a thickness of about 1 cm. Cover with the spinach and roll up as you would for a Swiss roll. Transfer it gently onto a greased baking tray. Pour a little melted butter over the roulade and bake at gas mark 6/400°F/200°C for 20-25 minutes until just browned. Cut in slices to serve.

*On August 16th, 1845, a Dr. Salter wrote in the Gardeners' Chronicle that a disease was affecting potatoes grown in the south of England. Within weeks of the first recording of its existence, few healthy potatoes could be found on sale at Covent Garden Market.*

17 AUGUST

# PURÉE OF POTATO WITH BASIL

In a warm summer basil should be plentiful, but sadly for those who live in towns, it rarely seems to reach the shops.

2 lb (900 g) potatoes, peeled, cooked and puréed
3 oz (75 g) basil leaves
1/4 pint (150 ml) good quality olive oil
Sea salt and freshly ground black pepper

Put the potato purée into a warmed dish. Liquidize the basil leaves with the olive oil. Stir into the potato purée. Season.

*'Hot potato' was rhyming slang for a waiter. The words probably originated in the music halls in the 1880s.*

18 AUGUST

# SPICED NEW POTATOES

Use the smallest potatoes you can find, and they must have no knobs, or the spices will not cover them properly.

2 lb (900 g) small new potatoes, cleaned
2 oz (50 g) butter
1 medium onion, chopped
1 teaspoon chilli powder
1 teaspoon turmeric
1 teaspoon salt
2 teaspoons garam masala

Heat the butter, add the onion and all the spices except the garam masala, stir together for a few moments.

Add the cleaned but unpeeled potatoes and, over a gentle heat, allow to cook until the potatoes are tender, shaking every few minutes so that the potatoes cook evenly. When nearly done, stir in the garam masala.

*An old remedy for softening and removing blemishes from hands involves making a paste from cooked, mashed potato mixed with glycerine, a tablespoon of safflower oil and a few drops of rosewater. Apply to the hands, then leave for half an hour before washing off.*

19 AUGUST

# POMMES FIFINE

Who is Fifine? Alas, I have not been able to find out. The charm of this recipe lies in its visual appeal with golden cubes of potato served around half an egg shell containing the raw yolk. The diners stir this into the hot potatoes.

1 1/2 lb (700 g) potatoes, cleaned
4-5 tablespoons olive oil
1 oz (25 g) butter
Sea salt and freshly ground black pepper
4 egg yolks
Chives

Steam the potatoes for 10 minutes, rub off the skins and cut into cubes. Fry in the hot oil and butter until golden. Serve, sprinkled with chives, around the half shell of an egg, filled with the yolk, for each person.

*Sir Francis Drake was thought by many to have been responsible for the introduction of the potato into Europe. Enough Germans thought so to have a statue of him erected holding a potato flower. This was pulled down by the Nazis in the 1940s.*

## 20 AUGUST

# PAUPIETTES OF SEA TROUT

Paupiettes are thin slices of meat or fish, rolled into the shape of corks, secured with little skewers and braised in liquid.

4 medium potatoes, cleaned, steamed and cut into thin slices
4 fillets of sea trout
5 fl oz (150 ml) white wine
5 fl oz (150 ml) cream
Sea salt and freshly ground black pepper

Roll up the trout fillets and secure with a wooden cocktail stick. Put the white wine, cream and seasonings into a bowl and mix well. Lay the sliced potatoes at the bottom of an ovenproof dish and put the trout fillets on top. Cover with the cream and wine and bake at gas mark 6/400°F/200°C for 15 minutes.

*In* ***The Arran Islands****, J. Millington Synge records the myth that the death of a child (in other words, its removal by the fairies) was marked by the turning red of the flesh of a seed potato.*

## 21 AUGUST

# DESSERT OF POTATO WITH PEACHES

Any fruit in season could be used in this dessert - even citrus fruits are good.

4 medium potatoes, cleaned and very thinly sliced
2 oz (50 g) granulated sugar

$^1/_2$ pint (275 ml) water
4 large peaches, skinned and sliced
1 tablespoon runny honey
4 oz (110 g) clarified butter

Make a syrup by dissolving the sugar in the water, bringing to the boil and simmering for about 3 minutes. (Flavourings - spices, vanilla essence, ginger etc. - may be added). Add the peach slices and allow them to cool in the syrup.

Wash the potato slices in cold water and then dry well. Stir the honey into the butter and dip the potato slices into this. Arrange them on a greased baking tray in little rounds of overlapping circles. Bake at gas mark 7/425°F/220°C for about 10 minutes until the slices are tender and golden. Carefully remove (they will tend to separate) and put on 4 serving plates with the peaches and syrup spooned over them.

*"Then a sentimental passion of a vegetable fashion must excite your languid spleen.*
*An attachment á la Plato for a bashful young potato..."*
*W.S. Gilbert.*

22 AUGUST

# SEAFOOD SALAD WITH POTATOES AND AÏOLI

Serve this on a large plate with the aioli like a full moon in the middle and the fish and vegetables strewn almost carelessly around.

2 lb (900 g) potatoes, scrubbed
$1^1/_2$ lb (700 g) fresh white fish
$^1/_4$ pint (150 ml) white wine
$^1/_4$ pint (150 ml) water

Bay leaf
2 pints (1.1 litres) cooked mussels
A few prawns, peeled
A few lettuce leaves
4 oz (110 g) black olives
1 medium onion, thinly sliced

For the aïoli:
3 cloves garlic, finely chopped
1 egg yolk
Sea salt and freshly ground black pepper
$^{1}/_{4}$ pint (150 ml) olive oil
1 tablespoon lemon juice (approximately)

Boil or steam the potatoes. Poach the white fish gently in the wine, water, and bay leaf. Do not overcook. Make the aïoli by crushing the garlic, adding the egg yolk and seasoning and then, adding the oil, drop by drop, until the sauce amalgamates and thickens. Add the lemon juice to taste.

Put the salad leaves on the bottom of the serving dish, then the fish, the potatoes and finally the onion and olives. Spoon the aïoli into the centre and serve.

*The English are said to have introduced the potato into Flanders during the wars against Louis XIV.*

## 23 AUGUST
# ITALIAN POTATO CAKES

My sister who lives in Tuscany makes these to use up leftover chicken. She serves them on a rocket salad.

6 oz (175 g) potatoes, cooked and sieved
4 oz (110 g) cooked chicken, finely chopped
4 oz (110g) mortadella sausage, finely chopped

2 oz (50 g) Pecorino cheese, grated
1 clove garlic, finely chopped
1 tablespoon parsley, chopped
1 large egg, beaten
Breadcrumbs
Oil for frying

Mix together the first 6 ingredients. Bind them together with the egg. Form into little cakes and roll in the breadcrumbs. Fry in the hot oil.

*In 1770 a cargo of potatoes was sent to Naples to relieve famine. The citizens refused to eat them.*

## 24 AUGUST

# POTATO SUBRICS

Subrics are like the little croquettes normally served in France as an *hors d'oeuvre* or small *entrée*. To clarify butter, heat it over a gentle heat until the oil separates from the whitish part and then put through a muslin sieve.

1 lb (450 g) potatoes, peeled and cut into little dice
1 oz (25 g) butter
3/4 pint (400 ml) béchamel sauce
1 egg, beaten
3 egg yolks
Sea salt and freshly ground black pepper
A little nutmeg
Clarified butter for frying

Parboil the potato dice for 2 minutes. Drain and cook lightly in the butter for a few minutes. Stir into the béchamel sauce and then add the beaten egg and egg yolks and seasonings.

Heat the clarified butter and drop little spoonfuls of the potato mixture into the pan. Fry until golden on both sides.

*"Stir-about and potatoes are what the people live on. All they buy from the shopkeepers is tea and drapery."*

*From* ***In Castle and Cabin*** *by George Pellew, 1888.*

25 AUGUST

# POTATOES AND MUSHROOMS

If you cannot buy crème fraîche, make a version by slightly whipping 8 fl oz (250 ml) double cream, adding 8 fl oz (250 ml) sour cream and leaving in a warm place overnight. Chill in the fridge. This should keep 2-3 weeks.

1 1/2 lb (700 g) potatoes
1 tablespoon oil
1 medium onion, sliced
1 lb (450 g) mushrooms, sliced
1/2 pint (275 ml) crème fraîche
2 tablespoons dill
Sea salt and freshly ground black pepper

Steam the potatoes and when cool and, only if necessary, peel. If large, cut into quarters. Heat the oil and gently cook the onion and mushrooms. Stir in the crème fraîche, the chopped dill and the salt and pepper. Add the potatoes, allow to heat through and serve.

*Wild South American potatoes set flower and seed and this seed was originally brought back to England as well as tubers. Both were used in potato production. In his* ***Seeds of Change*** *(1985) Henry Hobhouse writes that by 1650 the white potato was "a garden crop or cattle food in every other European country....in Ireland...it had become a staple."*

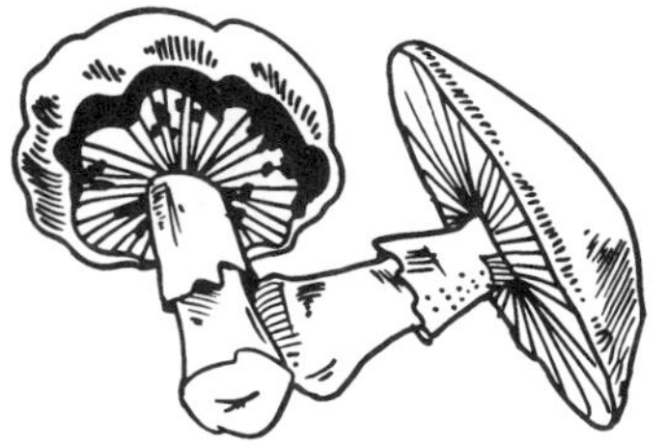

## 26 AUGUST

# SMOKED FISH SOUP WITH LOVAGE AND MARIGOLD PETALS

The petals of marigolds are a poor man's saffron. I keep a jar of them dried for use throughout the winter. They give colour, have no intrusive taste, and should be in abundance at this time of year. This lovely soup is always welcome - I know someone who eats it for breakfast.

1 lb (450 g) potatoes, peeled and thinly sliced
2 oz (50 g) butter
2 medium onions, chopped
1 fat head of Florence fennel, chopped
1 lb (450 g) smoked fish (haddock or cod)
Sea salt and freshly ground black pepper
Nutmeg
Handful fresh lovage leaves, chopped
$1^1/_4$ pint (700 ml) of milk
$^1/_2$ pint (275 ml) cream

Melt the butter in a heavy-based pan, and gently cook the onion, fennel, the potatoes and the fish (removed from the bone and roughly cut up).

When translucent, season and add the lovage leaves, reserving a few as a garnish. Cover with the milk, bring to the boil and simmer very gently (making sure the mixture doesn't stick to the bottom of the pan) until the potatoes are tender. Stir in the marigold petals and the cream. Reheat and serve. A handful of prawns added at the last moment and you have something quite exquisite.

*"The potato is one of nature's best designed products; it is born in a sturdy package, with wonderful shelf life. Yet we haul it from field to factory, peel and slice it by machine, cook it in hot grease, dose it with additives, wrap it in a petroleum or natural gas derivative, freeze it, store it in a frozen warehouse, haul it across the country in a diesel refrigerated truck, store it in another freezer warehouse, deliver it to a supermarket freezer, move it to a kitchen freezer, and, eventually, we reheat it. Then we eat it."*

*American writers, John and Karen Hess.*

27 AUGUST

# POTATOES COOKED WITH TOMATO AND CUCUMBER CONCASSÉ

The soothing flavour of this beautiful saffron-coloured dish contrasts well with the sharper taste of the barely cooked filling. The little baked cases make a good first course.

1 lb (450 g) potatoes, cleaned
1 oz (25 g) butter
Nutmeg
Salt and pepper
2 egg yolks
2 tablespoons tomato purée

For the concassé:
4 large tomatoes, skinned, de-pipped and cut in little dice
1/4 cucumber, chopped
A nut of butter
1 teaspoon grated lemon rind
Finely chopped parsley

Boil or steam the potatoes, drain and dry well. Put through a sieve and then put into a saucepan with the butter and the seasonings. Beat well with a wooden spoon until the mixture leaves the sides of the pan. Stir in the egg yolks and the tomato purée and cook for a further few minutes over the heat.

Using a piping bag, pipe the mixture into 8 little rounds, leaving a centre hole in each, onto a greased and floured baking tray. Put in a hot oven, gas mark 7/425°F/230°C, for 5-10 minutes, until just browned.

While the cases are in the oven, melt the butter and quickly heat through the tomatoes and the cucumber. Stir in the lemon rind and chopped parsley and put a spoonful in the centre of each potato case.

*"The potatoes are the love of my heart*
*They don't require a kiln or mill*
*Only to be dug in the field*
*And left on the fire."*
*Proverb from Co. Monaghan*

## 28 AUGUST

# AROMATIC POTATOES AND TURNIPS

Good with grilled meat and a green salad. I don't think turnips should ever be allowed to get bigger than golf-ball size.

1 lb (450 g) tiny new potatoes
1 medium onion, chopped
4 small turnips, halved
1/2 pint (275 ml) vegetable stock
1/2 pint (275 ml) water
4 tablespoons olive oil
Fresh herbs, coriander leaves if possible
Sea salt

Put the potatoes, onion and turnips into the stock and the water. Bring to a boil and cook, uncovered, until all the liquid has gone. Add the oil, brown for a few minutes, then add the salt and herbs and serve.

*Mrs C. De Witt Owen of Dixon, Illinois lays claim, perhaps, to the most winsome title for a potato cookbook. She called her volume* ***Murphy's Pets****. Other books written by this lady include* ***Miss Salad and Her Trousseau, Delicious Desserts for Dainty Diners*** *and* ***Sixteen Studies in White and Gold****.*

## 29 AUGUST
# POTATO BOATS

These little biscuits, like *petits fours,* are good served with fruit fools and all kinds of cream puddings. The amount given below makes about 36 biscuits.

4 large potatoes, cleaned
4 oz (110 g) butter, melted
4 oz (110 g) caster sugar
2 oz (50 g) plain flour
2 yolks of eggs
A little salt
1 whole egg, beaten

Bake the potatoes and when cooked remove enough of the centres to provide 12 oz (350 g) of potato. Put through a sieve and allow to get cold. Add the butter and when smooth, add the sugar, flour and the egg yolks and salt. Mix into a smooth dough.

Turn out onto a floured surface and cut into 4 equal parts. Roll each part out and make into little balls the size of a walnut. Shape into little boats, coat with the beaten egg and bake at gas mark 4/350°F/180°C for 20 minutes.

*When Addison Q. Thatcher was elected Mayor of Toledo in 1931 on his platform of relief for the poor, his friends said congratulations on the potato trucks that were destined for the soup kitchen that Thatcher had maintained for the poor of the town.*

## 30 AUGUST
# PROVENÇAL POTATOES

Fresh herbs should be abundant now, so add what you have to this casserole. Basil, or marjoram, oregano, parsley, chervil, hyssop, fennel, dill and many more all add interest to potato dishes.

$1^1/_2$ lb (700 g) potatoes, cleaned
$1^1/_2$ lb (700 g) tomatoes
2 tablespoons olive oil
2 tablespoons tomato purée
$^1/_2$ pint (275 ml) water
Sea salt and freshly ground black pepper
2 cloves garlic, chopped
8 black olives

Steam the potatoes in their skins for 10 minutes and then slice them thickly. Remove the skin from the tomatoes by plunging in boiling water and then slice thickly. Heat the oil and cook the tomatoes with the purée, water, seasoning and garlic until the sauce is a little reduced.

Put into a casserole with the potatoes and the olives and bake at gas mark 5/375°F/190°C for an hour or until the potatoes are tender.

*In Parmentier's home town of Montpelier, a memorial statue to the potato pioneer shows people taking potatoes from the royal experimental gardens while the guards are away.*

31 AUGUST

# POTATO AND LEEK PURÉE

With some experimention with sowing dates, I believe leeks should be available throughout the year, as they are in France.

1 lb (450 g) potatoes, peeled and cut into inch-size pieces
6 medium leeks
1 oz (25 g) butter
$^1/_4$ pint (150 ml) single cream
Sea salt and freshly ground black pepper
A little ground nutmeg

Clean the leeks very well, remove any coarse green parts and cut into inch lengths. Cook the potatoes and the leeks together in boiling salted water. Drain and dry and then purée together. Add the other ingredients and eat at once.

*"We have so many museums for war; why not one for a plant that sustains life?"*
***Washington Magazine*** *on the Potato Museum.*

# POTATO AND BEAN SOUP WITH TURNIP TOPS

This soup originates in Galicia in north-west Spain. Different meats are added and often served separately after the soup.

1 lb (450 g) potatoes, peeled and quartered
8 oz (225 g) dried haricot beans
4 pints (2.3 litres) water
1 large onion, chopped
8 oz (225 g) streaky pork rashers, cut into pieces
1 lb (450 g) shoulder of bacon, cut into pieces
$1^{1}/_{2}$ lb (700 g) turnip tops or kale, chopped
2 chorizo sausages
Sea salt and freshly ground black pepper

Soak the beans overnight. Drain and rinse and bring them to a boil in a large pan with the water, onion, pork and bacon. Simmer for about $1^{1}/_{2}$ hours, then add the potatoes and the turnip tops and cook for another half hour.

Add the sausages 10 minutes before the end. Season and serve.

*"The poor will not eat potatoes if they can get anything else."*
*Thomas Ruggles, writing in 1794.*

## 2 SEPTEMBER

# POTATO AND TOMATO PURÉE

The best tomato I have ever eaten was grown by my mother who brought a tomato back from Italy and allowed the seeds to dry out all winter on a saucer. The following summer she grew the sweetest, most succulent fruits.

1½ lb (700 g) potatoes
1½ lb (700 g) very ripe tomatoes
1 fat clove garlic, chopped
A little butter
A few fresh herbs ( basil, chervil, parsley etc.) chopped

Boil or steam the potatoes and prepare a purée. Meanwhile, plunge the tomatoes in boiling water to remove the skins. Cut open and remove the seeds. Cook gently with the garlic in the butter for a few minutes.

Put through a sieve and stir into the potatoes with the herbs.

*Potatoes were the only vegetable served at **Food and Wine** magazine's wine tasting for chefs and restaurateurs in Aspen, Colorado. Yukon Golds were mashed or fried and served to the 1,200 wine tasters.*

## 3 SEPTEMBER

# RABBIT WITH ROSEMARY AND POTATOES

This recipe was a winner in the *Independent on Sunday*'s Game Cookery competition. You could substitute the rabbit with chicken but there is no substitute for the rosemary.

1 lb (450 g) potatoes, peeled and thinly sliced
1 rabbit, jointed
A few sprigs of rosemary
3 cloves of garlic
Sea salt and freshly ground black pepper
Olive oil
Dry white wine or chicken stock
Juice of $^1/_2$ lemon

Cover the base of the pan with olive oil, heat, and add the rabbit and the garlic. Fry until browned. Add the lemon juice and about a wine glass of wine or chicken stock. Season, add the rosemary and leave to simmer for a couple of minutes before transferring to a roasting tin.

Cover the meat with a layer of potatoes. Pour over more stock so the base of the tin is covered but not the whole rabbit pieces. Sprinkle with salt and cook in a moderate oven for about 45 minutes or until the potatoes are cooked through. You may need to add more liquid during the cooking.

*"Gave them for Supper a couple of Rabbitts smothered in onions, some Hash Mutton and some rosted Potatoes. We were exceedingly merry all the night."*

*From* ***The Diary of a Country Parson (1778)*** *by James Woodforde.*

4 SEPTEMBER

# POTATO GALETTE WITH THYME

Based on a recipe created by Portuguese chef Jose Lampreia of La Maison Blanche in Paris, these little galettes delight the eye and the mouth. This quantity is enough to fill 4 crumpet ring moulds and makes a charming first course.

1 lb (450 g) potatoes, peeled, cooked and puréed
4 tablespoons olive oil
Sea salt and freshly ground black pepper
1 tablespoon fresh thyme leaves

4 large ripe tomatoes
Sea salt and freshly ground black pepper
Chervil or parsley, chopped
4 eggs

Stir the olive oil, seasoning and thyme into the puree. Divide the mixture between 4 oiled ring moulds and set on a baking tray. Bake for 15 minutes at gas mark 7/425° F/220° C.

While these are cooking slice the tomatoes and arrange around the edges of 4 serving plates. Strew with the herbs. Remove the galettes from the oven and put the baking tray over a high heat for 2 minutes or so to form a crust on the bottom. Meanwhile poach the eggs. Remove the potato from the moulds, putting a galette on each plate, topped with an egg.

*"Once cuisines nouvelle and minceur had gained a hold on the imagination of the restaurant-going public (and on the greed of restaurateurs) the potato was among the first ingredients of traditional cooking to be banished from the gourmet's table."*

*Top chef Jean-Louis Palladin.*

## 5 SEPTEMBER

# WILLIAM POTATOES

I'm not sure about one food dressed up to look like another, but for those who are, William potatoes may amuse. The taste is excellent anyway. Good for a party, too.

2¼ lb (1 kg) potatoes, peeled and cut into even-size pieces
Sea salt and white pepper
Grated nutmeg
2 egg yolks
1 oz (25 g) butter
Seasoned flour
2 eggs, beaten
Breadcrumbs
Oil for deep frying
1 extra potato

Boil the potatoes in a little water until soft. Drain and dry over a low heat. Purée and season the potatoes. Add the egg yolks and butter and mix well. Shape into little pear shapes and then dust first with the seasoned flour, then dip in the beaten eggs and finally the breadcrumbs. Deep fry until brown and crisp. Have ready the extra potato sliced and cut into matchsticks. Briefly deep fry and place one in each potato to resemble the stem of the pear.

*"Take away your fried potatoes*
*Use them to clean your ears*
*You can eat your fried potatoes*
*With birds-eye frozen tears".*

*From **Giving Potatoes** by Adrian Mitchell.*

## 6 SEPTEMBER

# SALADE CAUCHOISE WITH AVOCADO CREAM

This lovely autumnal salad is from *Jane Grigson's Fruit Book.*

12 oz (350 g) new potatoes, cleaned, cooked, peeled and diced
1 head of celery
3 good-flavoured dessert apples, peeled, cored and diced
Lemon juice
3 1/2 oz (95 g) walnuts
2 oz (50 g) smoked ham
2 small ripe avocados, peeled and stoned
Oil and wine vinegar
Sea salt and freshly ground black pepper
Crisp lettuce

Remove the coarse stalks of the celery and chop the centre. Sprinkle the apples with lemon juice before mixing with the celery and potatoes. Add the chopped walnuts and the ham, cut into matchstick strips.

To make the dressing, liquidize the avocados with two tablespoons of the vinegar and enough oil to make the consistency thick but pourable. Season with salt and pepper. Just before serving, line the serving bowl with lettuce leaves, mix the dressing with the salad and turn gently into the bowl.

*"For where will Ireland be, in the event of a universal potato rot?"*
*Dr Lindley, Editor, **Gardener's Chronicle**, 1845.*

## 7 SEPTEMBER

# POTATO LASAGNE

An Italian would no doubt consider this with horror but lasagne made with potato is - dare I say it - as good as authentic lasagne made with pasta dough. The quantities given below will feed 6.

1 lb (450 g) potatoes, cleaned
2 tablespoons olive oil
1 large onion, chopped
1 carrot, diced
1 stick celery, sliced
1 lb (450 g) good quality mince
1 clove garlic, chopped
2 tablespoons tomato purée
1 glass red wine
1/2 pint (275 ml) water
Bouquet garni
2 large flat field mushrooms, sliced
A little oil
1 1/2 pints (900 ml) béchamel sauce
Sea salt and freshly ground black pepper
2 oz (50 g) Parmesan cheese, grated

First heat the olive oil and let the onion, carrot and celery sauté gently until just transparent. Add the mince and stir over a brisk heat for a few minutes. Put in the garlic, tomato purée and then the wine, water and bouquet garni. Bring to the boil, then turn down the heat and allow to cook for 10 minutes. In a separate pan sauté the mushrooms in enough oil to prevent them sticking to the pan.

Peel the potatoes and slice in 1/8 inch thick slices. Steam until just tender. In a large ovenproof dish put a layer of the ragu, then a layer of the béchamel sauce and then the field mushrooms. Arrange the potato slices on this, seasoning as you go. Cover with the rest of the meat mixture and pour over the remaining béchamel sauce. Sprinkle with the Parmesan and cook at gas mark 6/400°F/200°C for 20-25 minutes until the cheese is bubbling.

*In the 18th century, a duel is said to have taken place between two Irish hairdressers, whose seconds loaded the pistols with boiled potatoes. Real bullets were thought to be the preserve of the aristocracy.*

## 8 SEPTEMBER

# POTATO SALAD WITH COCKLES AND MUSTARD

I rarely ever make salads with mayonnaise. Dressings of olive oil, flavoured vinegars or lemon juice seem to have an affinity with potatoes, in particular. In this instance, the mustardy emollient taste seems to create a good background for potatoes and cockles. Cleaning the shellfish is done in much the same way as with mussels. The shells are soaked in several changes of cold water and then steamed over a high heat.

1 lb (450 g) very small new potatoes, scrubbed
6 fl oz (175 ml) fromage frais
3 tablespoons mayonnaise
2 tablespoons Dijon mustard
Sea salt and freshly ground black pepper
1/4 pint (150 ml) cockles, cooked and removed from their shells
A few fennel leaves, chopped

Put the potatoes on to steam or boil. Meanwhile, make the dressing by mixing the fromage frais with mayonnaise, the mustard and the seasoning. Put the drained potatoes into a bowl with the cockles and toss them in the dressing. Decorate with the fennel leaves.

*" If there had been a slice of Double Gloucster in the larder of Tullyra, I should not have minded the absence of the salmon. But to be told I must dine off two eggs and a potato, so that his conscience should not be troubled during the night, worried me, and I am afraid I cast many an angry look across the table."*

*George Moore writing about a visit to Tullyra Castle.*

9 SEPTEMBER

# JOHN TOVEY'S POTATO AND MUSHROOM FLAN

Here is an adaptation of a recipe of John Tovey's. He is chef / patron of Miller Howe in Lake Windermere. He was inspired by what he described as a "baked upside-down potato gâteau with fresh grated truffles" that he ate in Provence.

1 1/2 lb (700 g) potatoes, cleaned
Olive oil
3 oz (75 g) butter
12 oz (350 g) mushrooms, sliced
8 oz (225 g) onions, sliced
1 large clove garlic
1 teaspoon ground cumin
1/2 pint (275 ml) cream
1 egg and 1 egg yolk

Peel and thinly slice 1 lb (450 g) of the potatoes and fry on one side in a little olive oil and 1 oz (25 g) of the butter until browned. Drain on kitchen paper and arrange around the bottom and sides of a 1x8-inch loose bottom flan tin (I line it with silver foil), reserving enough potatoes to cover the top. The cooked side goes outside.

Cook the onion and the garlic with the rest of the butter for a few minutes. Add the mushrooms. Drain and keep. Grate the remaining 1/2 lb of potatoes and layer in the flan tin with the mushroom mixture.

Beat the eggs with the cream and cumin powder, season and pour over the flan. Put the remaining potato slices on top and cook at gas mark 6/400°F/200°C for about 45 minutes. A lovely dish.

*"As a producer of problems for Food Controllers, the potato has no rival in the vegetable or animal world."*

*Sir William Beverage, 1928.*

## 10 SEPTEMBER

# POTATOES OF THE GRAPE GATHERERS OF BURGUNDY

It was the name of this dish that first captivated me. Its charm, however, is not only in its name. Visually, gastronomically and for simplicity of assembly, Potatoes of the Grape Gatherers of Burgundy is an unrivalled dish.

1½ lb (700 g) potatoes, peeled and very thinly sliced
12 oz (350 g) smoked streaky bacon
3 oz (75 g) grated cheese
12 oz (350 g) unsmoked low salt bacon
3 oz (75 g) butter

In an ovenproof dish lay half the smoked bacon. Put half the potato slices in a layer on the bacon. Sprinkle with a little cheese. Cover with the unsmoked bacon, then the rest of the potatoes and remaining grated cheese. Finish with a layer of smoked bacon. Dot with little pieces of the butter.

Cover with damp greaseproof paper and cook for 1 hour at gas mark 7/425°F/220°C. During the last 20 minutes cooking time take off the paper so the whole dish develops a magnificent golden crust. Turn out onto a large warmed dish and eat very hot.

*"I am told that the Burgundians are forbidden to make use of these tubers, because they are assured that the eating of them causes leprosy, and they call them the artichokes of the Indies."*
*From **Prodromos** by Gaspard Bauhin, 1620.*

## 11 SEPTEMBER

# SAVOURY SUMMER PUDDING

This rather quirky dish is perhaps best eaten as part of a larger buffet, since its appearance scores over its taste. Nevertheless, worth a try.

1 large potato, peeled
$1^1/_2$ lb (700 g) raw beetroot, peeled
1 small onion, chopped
A few tender lovage leaves, chopped
$^3/_4$ pint (400 ml) chicken or vegetable stock
Sea salt and freshly ground black pepper
1 small loaf stale brown bread, sliced and de-crusted

Grate the beetroot and potato and put in a saucepan. Add the onion and the lovage with the stock to the pan. Season. Bring to the boil and simmer for 15 minutes.

Line a buttered pudding basin with the bread slices. Spoon in the vegetable mixture, together with the juice and cover with further slices of bread. Cover with foil and put overnight under a heavy weight. Turn out and serve with perhaps a sauce of yoghourt mixed with a little chicken stock, some chopped chives and sprinkled with lovage leaves.

*Chefs at the Travellers' Club in Paris thought highly enough of their potatoes to serve them stuffed with truffles and shrimps and named after the distinctly un-potato-like dancer, La Belle Otero.*

## 12 SEPTEMBER

# FISHERMEN'S POTATOES

In the West of Ireland fishermen are said to dig a hole about 2-inches deep, put a potato into each hole and cover with sand. A fire is lit on top and the potatoes, it is said, will be cooked in half an hour. I've never had the patience to try it but it would give children something different to do on holiday.

*"We stop the Press, with very great regret, to announce that the Potato Murrain has unequivocally declared itself in Ireland. The crops about Dublin are suddenly perishing."*

*From **The Gardener's Chronicle**, 12th September, 1845.*

13 SEPTEMBER

# CARROT, CELERY, POTATO AND LOVAGE SOUP

Lovage is, in fact, a very good substitute for celery in soups but in this case you will use both.

6 oz (175 g) potatoes, peeled and cubed
1 medium onion, sliced
2 large sticks celery, sliced
10 oz (275 g) carrots, peeled and sliced
1 oz (25 g) butter
2½ pints (1.4 litres) good chicken stock
Sea salt and freshly ground black pepper
Fresh lovage leaves

Cook the onion, celery and carrots in the butter until softened. Add the potatoes and stock and simmer until cooked.

Remove from the heat, liquidize with the lovage leaves and serve, reheated, with a little sprinkling of chopped lovage leaves.

*It is said that if you bury little new potatoes in a sealed tin in sand in the garden, you will be able to dig them up on Christmas Day as fresh as the day you put them there.*

14 SEPTEMBER

# POTATOES BAKED WITH CHEESE AND OLIVE OIL

Fruity and pungent olive oil makes this dish. As far as the cheese is concerned, experiment with what you have at hand. I have used ricotta, Gruyère, but mostly just Cheddar. Accompanied by a salad and a piece of crusty bread to absorb the last traces of oil, anything else would be superfluous.

2 lb (900 g) potatoes, peeled and thinly sliced
1 lb (450 g) tomatoes
2 medium onions
4 oz (110 g) cheese, grated
Sea salt and freshly ground black pepper
Fresh thyme
3 fl oz (75 ml) olive oil

Layer the potato slices in an oiled gratin dish with the sliced tomatoes and onions. Sprinkle as you go with the cheese and seasonings.

Pour over the olive oil and bake, covered, in a moderate to hot oven for 45 minutes or until the potatoes are cooked.

*A 'couch potato' is American slang for a television addict.*

15 SEPTEMBER

# WILD MUSHROOM AND POTATO MOULD WITH A SAUCE OF DRIED MUSHROOMS

The fields, after a warm, wet summer, may now be full of mushrooms for the creation of a wide range of lovely vegetable dishes. This dish can be made with farmed mushrooms but will inevitably loose some of its flavour. Dried mushrooms, especially the Italian *porcini* - or dried *ceps* - are available in most good delicatessens.

1lb (450 g) potatoes, peeled
2 oz (50 g) butter
8 oz (225 g) field mushrooms
1 clove garlic

3 eggs, beaten
Sea salt and freshly ground black pepper
Handful of chopped parsley

For the sauce:
2 oz (50 g) dried mushrooms, covered with hot water and soaked $^1/_2$ hour
2 shallots, chopped
1 oz (25 g) butter
$^1/_4$ pint (150 ml) cream
2 tablespoons lemon juice

Boil or steam the peeled potatoes. While they are cooking, melt half the butter in a pan and cook the sliced mushrooms with the chopped garlic clove. Raise the heat at the end to evaporate some of the liquid.

Purée the cooked potatoes and stir in the beaten eggs and the seasoning with the remaining butter. Butter a $2^1/_2$ pint (1.4 litre) pudding bowl or soufflé dish, put in the mushroom mixture and then the potatoes. Smooth the surface and cover with buttered paper. Place in a bain-marie and bake in the oven at gas mark 6/400°F/200°C for 30 minutes. Leave to rest for 5 minutes or so, and then turn out.

While the mould is cooking make the sauce. Drain the mushrooms. Reserve the liquid and make up to 1 pint (570 ml). Fry the chopped shallots gently in the butter, add the mushrooms and, after a few minutes, the mushroom liquid. Cook until this has almost evaporated. Add the cream and lemon juice and serve with the mushroom and potato mould.

*"Mashed potato is the gentile's chicken noodle soup. It's nature's tranquillizer. I take it instead of Valium."*

*From **Love after Lunch** by Andrew Payne.*

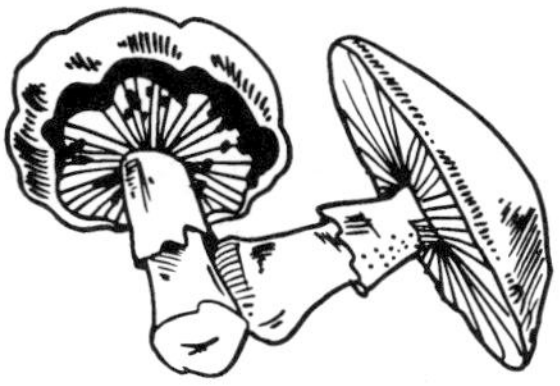

## 16 SEPTEMBER

# HEDGEHOG POTATOES

The idea for this dish is based on a creation by Joachim Splichal, chef-proprietor of Patina restaurant in Hollywood.

1 1/2 lb (700 g) potatoes, peeled
1 large potato, unpeeled
6 oz (175 g) butter, clarified
1/4 pint (150 ml) hot milk or cream
Sea salt and freshly ground black pepper
2 medium leeks, thinly sliced
A little oil, sesame or olive

Put the peeled potatoes on to boil. Slice the large potato as thinly as possible and put the slices in a hot oven (gas mark 7/425°F/220°C) with the clarified butter for about 10-15 minutes until golden. Púree the boiled potatoes with the milk or cream and keep warm. Fry the leeks quickly in the hot oil.

Spread the purée on a warm serving plate and stick the chips all over the surface. Surround with the leeks.

*Elvis Presley is said to have eaten mashed potato every night for the last year of his life.*

## 17 SEPTEMBER

# WHITE FISH SOUP WITH LEMON GRASS AND POTATO ROUILLE

Everything about this soup delights; its deep amber colour flecked with the muted greens of the herbs; the aroma takes you straight to the Mediterranean. The bread is warmed in the oven, spread with the almost fluid potato/olive oil mixture with which the pieces of fish and vegetables are scooped up out of the aromatic lemon broth. The name 'rouille', incidentally , comes from the French word meaning 'rust' that refers to the colour imparted by the paprika.

For the soup:
1 lb (450 g) white fish
Bayleaf
1 tablespoon oil
1 large onion, sliced
1 large carrot, sliced
2 sticks celery, sliced
4 tomatoes, skinned and loosely chopped
2 cloves garlic, chopped
Sea salt and freshly ground black pepper
1 glass white wine
1 piece lemon grass
Chopped parsley and chervil

For the rouille:
4 oz (110 g) cooked potato
1 egg yolk
6 tablespoons olive oil
Pinch of paprika

Simmer the fish in water with the bayleaf until just barely cooked. Drain and reserve both fish and liquid. There should be about 1½ pints (900 ml) of the cooking liquid. Discard any fish bones and skin.

Heat the oil and gently cook the onion, carrot and celery for 5 minutes. Add the tomatoes and the garlic. Allow to cook for a few more minutes and then cover with the white wine and the fish water. (You may need to add a little more water). Add the lemon grass, bring to the boil and allow to simmer very gently until the vegetables are tender. Add a generous sprinkling of chopped herbs and the fish.

For the rouille: mix together ( a food processor is ideal for this) all the ingredients until very smooth. Add a little fish stock if too thick. Serve spread on warmed French bread or toast.

*"The potato can, and generally does, play a twofold part; that of a nutritious food, and that of a weapon ready forged for the exploitation of a weaker group in a mixed society."*
*From **The History and Social Influence of the Potato** by Redcliffe Salaman, 1949.*

## 18 SEPTEMBER

# POTATOES WITH CHEESE, TOMATO AND ONION SAUCE

This is a recipe from Elizabeth Lambert Ortiz's *Book of Latin American Cooking*. It is a rich, dense dish, food for the hungry.

6 large potatoes, cleaned
1 oz (25 g) butter
1 medium onion
2 large tomatoes, peeled and chopped
Salt and freshly ground black pepper
$^{1}/_{4}$ pint (150 ml) double cream
4 oz (110 g) Cheddar cheese

Boil the potatoes until tender. Drain, peel and keep them warm. Heat the butter and sauté the onion until it is softened. Add the tomatoes, salt and pepper to taste. Cook for about 5 minutes.

Add the cream and the cheese, stirring until the cheese is partially melted. Pour over the potatoes.

*Chuno and Tunta, made from freeze-dried potatoes, have fed the Indians of South America for centuries. Produced in the coldest mountain regions, these foodstuffs were carried down to the lower valleys on the backs of llamas.*

## 19 SEPTEMBER

# AUTUMN GRATIN

Summer vegetables struggle to survive against early frosts, wind and lack of sun. Those that survive often lack the potency of summer growth, yet respond well to inclusion in dishes such as the one below.

$1^1/_2$ lb (700 g) potatoes, peeled and thinly sliced
8 oz (225 g) spinach
1 onion, sliced
2 tomatoes, sliced
2 courgettes, sliced
Sea salt and freshly ground black pepper
8 fl oz (220 ml) cream
Fresh parsley or chervil, chopped

Leave the potatoes to soak in cold water for 10 minutes to reduce the starch. Wash the spinach and wilt briefly in a little hot butter. Allow to cool and roughly chop.

Season the onion, tomato and courgette slices. Layer in a gratin dish with the well-dried potatoes and other vegetables, seasoning as you go. Put some fresh parsley into the cream and pour over the vegetables. Cook in any way that is convenient to you, either for 40 minutes or so in a hot oven or better still, longer cooking in a slow oven. A very adaptable dish.

*The potato is alleged to have reached Italy from Spain carried by bare-footed friars.*

20 SEPTEMBER

# LOMO SALTADO

Here is another wonderful recipe from Peru. The potatoes are peeled and sliced into small finger sizes - smaller than for normal chips but larger than julienne.

$1^1/_2$ lb (700 g) potatoes
$1^1/_2$ lb (700 g) fillet steak, cut into bite-size pieces
1 oz (25 g) butter
$1^1/_2$ lb (700 g) onions, thinly sliced
2 tablespoons oil
$1^1/_2$ lb (700 g) tomatoes, skinned and roughly chopped
8 oz (225 g) peas
1 clove garlic, chopped
1 teaspoon fresh oregano, chopped
Sea salt and freshly ground black pepper
Chopped parsley to garnish

Fry the meat pieces in the butter until tender. Remove and keep warm. Add a little oil to the pan and fry the onions until transparent, add the tomatoes, peas and garlic. After a couple of minutes put in the meat, oregano and seasoning and move quickly over a high heat but on no account allow to go mushy.

Remove from the pan and keep warm. Put more oil into the pan so it is about 3 inches deep and add the potato fingers. Fry until crisp then add to the meat and vegetables and dust with chopped parsley. Eat with rice.

*"The potato is not yet an article of so much importance in France..."*
*From* ***Symonds' Vegetable Kingdom****, written in 1853.*

21 SEPTEMBER

# POTATO CASSEROLE WITH PORK

An ideal supper dish, this is simple to prepare and will not spoil by keeping.

1 1/2 lb (700 g) potatoes, peeled and sliced
1 lb (450 g) belly of pork
2 large onions, sliced
Sea salt and freshly ground black pepper
A little chopped sage
3/4 pint (400 ml) good meat stock

Cut the pork into strips about the size of a finger. Layer the potatoes and onions with the pork in a casserole dish, finishing with the potatoes and seasoning as you go with sage and salt and pepper.

Cover with the stock. Put uncovered in a hot oven (gas mark 7/425°F/220°C) for 30 minutes then lower the heat to gas mark 3/325°F/170°C for a further 40 minutes or so until the crust is well browned. This cooking time is only a rough estimate and this casserole will fit in happily with different oven temperatures and times according to what else is cooking.

*"Quayle gets Baked, Mashed and Fried" screamed a tabloid headline the day after Vice-President Dan Quayle corrected a 12-year-old child for his "mis-spelling" of the word "potato". The perplexed child, at Mr. Quayle's urging, added an "e". It was a small mistake for which the Vice-President paid dearly.*

## 22 SEPTEMBER

# DOLMADES

Leave the bacon out of this and you have a very good vegetarian dish.

1 lb (450 g) potatoes, cooked and puréed
1 small cabbage
4 rashers streaky bacon, cut into little strips
1 oz (25 g) butter
1 large onion, chopped
1 stick celery, finely sliced
6 oz (175 g) mushrooms, sliced
Sea salt and freshly ground black pepper
2 dessertspoons tomato purée
1 heaped tablespoon flour
1 pint (570 ml) beef or vegetable stock

Separate the cabbage leaves and blanch them for about 4 minutes in boiling salted water. Drain. Fry the rashers until crisp, then remove from the pan and reserve. Melt the butter in the same pan and sauté the onion, celery and mushrooms for about 5 minutes. Season and stir in the tomato purée. Put in the bacon and then combine with the potato purée.

Put spoonfuls of this mixture onto the cabbage leaves. Roll up and make into little parcels. Dust them with flour and put into a shallow casserole dish. Pour over the stock and bake the dolmades at gas mark 4/350°F/180°C for about 40 minutes.

*The Incas produced a variety of pots made in potato shapes. The National Museum in Lima has probably the largest collection of these. Very often the pots were human caricatures, sometimes with sexual connotations.*

23 SEPTEMBER

# PARCELS OF POTATO AND IRISH FARMHOUSE CHEESE

Filo pastry is now widely available and is not difficult to deal with as long as you remember to keep the spare sheets of it covered with a damp cloth until you use them. Filo pastry also has the great advantage that it can be refrozen if you have any to spare. The amount below makes 4 parcels. They can be prepared well in advance and cooked at the last minute.

4 medium potatoes, boiled and diced
A little oil
1 onion, chopped
Sea salt and freshly ground black pepper
4 sheets filo pastry
Melted butter
3-4 oz (75-110 g) Cashel Blue cheese

Heat the oil and quickly fry the onion and potato until lightly browned. Season and set aside. Lay out 1 sheet of filo pastry and paint with the melted butter. Repeat with the remaining 3 sheets and then, using scissors, cut into 4 rectangles.

Lay a quarter of the potato mixture in the middle of each rectangle and cover with little slivers of cheese. Pull up the sides of the rectangle to make little parcels and give the pastry a twist at the top. Paint with more melted butter and cook on a baking tray for 15 minutes at gas mark 4/350°F/180°C until golden coloured.

*"These things have neither smell nor taste, not even the dogs will eat them, so what use are they to us?" The answer received by Frederick the Great, who, in 1774 sent a wagonload of potatoes to the starving people of Kolberg.*

24 SEPTEMBER

# MUSHROOM TOPPING FOR MASHED POTATOES

To 'mash' or to 'purée'? As will be obvious to readers of this book, I belong to the latter category. 'Mash' is one of the ugly words of cookery.

To make a good purée, a floury potato is essential. Put unpeeled, even-sized potatoes, cut in quarters, in cold salted water, bring to a boil and simmer gently until the potatoes are cooked. The Roux brothers recommend putting a quarter of lemon in the cooking water to prevent break-up. As soon as the potatoes can be handled push off the skins and steam dry under a cloth for 5-10 minutes on a warm stove.

Paul Bocuse recommends pushing the potatoes through a fine sieve with a pestle - but working top to bottom and never with a circular or horizontal movement. Good purées can also be made with a mouli but never with a food processor. A potato masher tends to crush the life out of potatoes - I prefer a whisk. Put the resulting purée in a clean pan and add the seasonings. Mix, using a spatula to achieve a silken finish. Warm milk, cream, egg yolk, chopped onion, olive oil, lemon juice, grated orange, yoghourt - even Guinness - are just a few of the additions that give interest and variety to purées.

Chef Joel Robuchon, whose restaurant has 3 Michelin stars, has raised potato purée to divine heights. His potatoes are puréed by hand with warm milk in a mouli, then 9 oz (250 g) of the best chilled butter is added per kilo of potatoes. The purée is then pushed through a sieve with a wooden fork.

A good purée needs no accompaniment. However, the following addition is very good. Use different varieties of mushroom if possible.

1 large onion, sliced
1 lb (450 g) mushrooms, sliced
3 tablespoons olive oil
2-3 cloves garlic, chopped
Sea salt and freshly ground black pepper
Fresh chopped parsley

Sauté the onion in the olive oil until just transparent then add the mushrooms, raise the heat and stir fry for a few minutes. Add the garlic and seasonings and cook over a gentle heat for a few more minutes. Sprinkle with parsley and serve on top of the purée.

*Grated or peeled potatoes can be used to clean normal or oily skins.*

## 25 SEPTEMBER

# CARAPULCHRA

A rare tasting amalgam of meat and vegetables, this Peruvian stew is usually made with dried potatoes and has the great virtue of providing an entire meal in one dish although, it must be said, the Peruvians eat it with rice and yucca.

2 lb (900 g) potatoes, peeled and halved if large
1 lb (450 g) chicken meat, cut into cubes
1 lb (450 g) lean pork, cubed
1/2 pint (275 ml) oil
3 medium onions, chopped
1/2 red chilli pepper, sliced thinly
2 cloves garlic, chopped
Sea salt and freshly ground black pepper
1 teaspoon cumin seed
3 cloves
4 oz (110 g) finely chopped peanuts
5 fl oz (150 ml) sweet wine or port

Fry the chicken and pork in the hot oil until well browned. Remove and keep on one side. In the same oil, fry the onions, chilli pepper and garlic until the onion is transparent.

Add the meat and the chicken stock and bring to the boil. Now add the potatoes. Simmer for 1 hour, stirring every now and then to prevent sticking. Add the cloves, peanuts and port after 30 minutes. Once the stew is thick and creamy, adjust the seasoning and serve.

*Potato hunter Carlos Ochos was collecting potatoes in north Peru in the 1970s when he heard a cry "Catch him alive!". His attackers rolled rocks down at him but he escaped unhurt by hiding in a trench. "They must have thought I was a treasure hunter," he said afterwards. "And they were right. Potatoes are much more precious than a jewel."*

## 26 SEPTEMBER

# KARTOFFELKRAPFEN

German cuisine includes some of the most innovative and varied ways of cooking potatoes. This recipe originated in Bavaria.

14 oz (400 g) potatoes, peeled
Salt
3 fl oz (75 ml) milk
1 oz (25 g ) butter
A little ground nutmeg
2 oz (50 g) flour, sifted
2 eggs
Oil for deep frying

Cook the potatoes in salted water until soft. Drain, dry and put through a sieve. Bring the milk, butter and nutmeg to the boil and mix in the flour.

Over the heat, stir the mixture until it leaves the sides of the pan clean. Add the eggs one by one and finally the potato. Mix until smooth. Take soupspoonfuls of this mixture and fry until golden.

*The writer Mark Twain, a great potato lover (he is said to have brought his American cook to London out of reluctance at being parted from her creamed potatoes), was guest of honour at a banquet hosted by Kaiser Wilhelm II of Germany. The one thing he remembered about the evening was the potatoes which reminded him of his boyhood in Missouri. An apprentice on a newspaper, he used to steal potatoes from the editor's cellar and cook them on the print shop's stove.*

27 SEPTEMBER

# SPICED POTATO CAKE

This makes a moist rich cake which improves with keeping.

4 oz (110 g) potatoes, cooked and puréed
4 oz (110 g) butter
8 oz (225 g) caster sugar
2 oz (50 g) melted chocolate
2 eggs, well beaten
4 oz (110 g) plain flour
1 level teaspoon baking powder
$^1/_2$ level teaspoon cinnamon
2 pinches ground nutmeg
Pinch of salt
4 oz (110 g) almonds, blanched and chopped
4 tablespoons milk

Prepare an 8-inch square cake tin (or approximate size). Cream the butter and sugar and stir in the potatoes. Add the melted chocolate and beat in with the eggs.

Sift the dry ingredients and stir in with the almonds and milk. Bake at gas mark 5/375°F/190°C for 12 minutes and then turn down the heat to gas mark 4/350°F/180°C for a further 45-50 minutes. Allow to cool in the tin for 5 minutes before turning out.

*One of the first published recipes for potatoes appeared in Germany in 1581, in* ***Ein Neues Kochbuch*** *by Markus Rumpolt. It read: "Boil diced potatoes, roast them in bacon fat and simmer the result in milk."*

28 SEPTEMBER

# ITALIAN STUFFED POTATOES

If Italians have eschewed potatoes in favour of pasta, when they do serve the potato they treat it with perhaps greater respect than nations who have embraced it with more fervour. This way of cooking potatoes, served with a basil-spiked tomato sauce, makes a complete meal.

4 large potatoes
8 oz (225 g) good quality minced beef
2 tablespoons fresh breadcrumbs
4 tablespoons Parmesan cheese (freshly grated if possible)
Sea salt and freshly ground black pepper
1 clove garlic, chopped
1 tablespoon parsley
1 egg
A little olive oil
1 medium onion, sliced
A little piece of celery, sliced
2 lb (900 g) tomatoes, skinned and de-seeded
1/2 teaspoon sugar

Wash and peel the potatoes and, with a potato peeler, scoop out the centres of the potatoes, leaving a shell about a quarter inch thick. Put the potato shells in cold salted water and put the centres into a little water to cook until they are tender. Drain and mash.

Meanwhile, in a non-stick frying pan, sauté the mince until browned and then mix with the potato purée, breadcrumbs, cheese, seasoning, garlic and parsley and beaten egg. Stuff this mixture into the potato shells. Heat the oil and sauté the onion and celery. Add the potatoes and cook them carefully until the shells are golden.

Remove the potatoes, then add the tomatoes and sugar. Stir to amalgamate and then put back the potatoes, cover and cook gently for half and hour or so, until the potatoes are tender when tested with a skewer.

*Writing in 1601, Clusius reports that for the sake of his health, the Papal Legate cooked potatoes like carrots or parsnips.*

29 SEPTEMBER

# HOT POTATO AND CHICORY SALAD

Unlike many warm salads, the dressing is added and then the whole dish is reheated.

2 lb (900 g) potatoes, peeled
8 oz (225 g) smoked bacon
2 small or 1 large head chicory
1/4 pint (150 ml) warmed milk
3 tablespoons red wine vinegar

Boil or steam the potatoes until just tender. Meanwhile, cut the bacon in little strips and fry quickly. Drain, reserving separately the fat and the bacon. Wash the chicory and cut into 1-inch lengths. Put in a warmed dish. Purée the potato and stir in the milk. Put on top of the chicory and then add the bacon pieces.

Using the pan in which you fried the bacon, heat the remaining fat and pour over the vinegar, allowing to cook for a few moments. Put back the potato mixture and allow to cook gently until the chicory is just tender. Serve at once.

*"Depending on how caterers wish to promote their image they should choose whether to list chips or French fries on the menu. 30% of customers regard fries as modern, compared to only 5% for the old chip. So, if your restaurant is modern, serve fries."*
*Advice from the Dutch Potato Bureau.*

30 SEPTEMBER

# CHOCOLATE AND HAZELNUT POTATO CAKE

The presence of potato in this recipe may seem lacking in significance, because of the small amount, nonetheless the result is a moist, dense cake that will serve at least 10 people.

3 oz (75 g) purée of potato
8 oz (225 g) butter
14 oz (400 g) sugar
4 eggs
3 oz (75 g) good quality plain chocolate
1 teaspoon cinnamon
1 teaspoon grated orange peel
1/2 teaspoon nutmeg
10 oz (275 g) plain flour, sifted
1 teaspoon baking powder
1/4 pint (150 ml) milk
1 tablespoon lemon juice
4 oz (110 g) hazelnuts, chopped
Whipped cream

Cream the butter and the sugar, add the eggs one at a time and beat well. Beat in the melted chocolate, potatoes, cinnamon, orange peel and nutmeg. Put the soda with the flour and the lemon juice with the milk and then add to the cake mixture in alternative spoonfuls. Stir in the nuts.

Put into a greased 9 inch cake tin and cook for about 1 1/4 hours at gas mark 4/350°F/180°C but watch that the top doesn't burn and, if necessary, turn down the heat. Split and fill with whipped cream when cool or put the cream on top with a dusting of grated chocolate.

*"The potato...the Englishman's Sunday would be a day of mourning if bereft of its presence."*
*From **The Epicure's Companion** by Edward and Lorna Bunyard, 1937.*

# MRS MURPHY'S SOUP

The eponymous Mrs Murphy is an American of Irish extraction who has a seemingly endless supply of recipes including 'taties' or 'spuds' with which to feed her enormous (and growing) family in her adopted Virginia. This soup is both nourishing and delicious.

12 oz (350 g) potatoes, peeled and cut into small dice
4 tablespoons butter
2 medium onions, chopped
6 oz (175 g) mushrooms, sliced
Large handful of spinach, washed and finely chopped
3-4 oz (75-110 g) oatmeal
2 pints or 1 litre good stock
Sea salt and freshly ground black pepper
$^{1}/_{4}$ teaspoon ground cloves

Melt the butter, add the potatoes, onions and mushrooms and cook gently until softened. Add the spinach to the soup and cook for a few moments.

Put in the oatmeal, stir around, then cover with the stock and seasonings and cook for about 20 minutes. Serve with a spoonful of cream.

*By cross-breeding domestic varieties with a wild Bolivian potato species which is inedible, the Centro International de la Papa in Lima, Peru has developed a 'hairy potato' that is resistant to all major potato pests and costs less to produce."The hair isn't on the potatoes,"reassured one of its entomologists, "It's on the foliage."*

## 2 OCTOBER

# GRATIN OF POTATOES AND CELERIAC WITH FROMAGE BLANC

Celeriac, a kind of edible celery root, is not hard to grow but not easy to find in shops. It makes a good purée, cooked with equal quantities of potato with the last-minute addition of cream and butter. The gratin below will serve 6 people as a side dish or 4 if it is eaten as a main course.

$1\frac{1}{2}$ lb (700 g) potatoes, peeled and thinly sliced
1 large celeriac, peeled and thinly sliced
3 oz (75 g) butter
Sea salt and freshly ground black pepper
$\frac{1}{2}$ pint (275 ml) fromage blanc
$\frac{1}{2}$ pint (275 ml) cream

Blanch the celeriac in boiling salted water for 3 minutes. Butter a gratin dish and fill with alternative layers of potatoes and celeriac, seasoning as you go. Mix together the fromage blanc and the cream and pour over the vegetables. Dot with the remaining butter and cook uncovered at gas mark 6/400°F/200°C for 1 hour.

*"To make this condiment your poet begs*
*The pounded yellow of two hard-boiled eggs*
*Two boiled potatoes, passed through kitchen sieve*
*Smoothness and softness to the salad give."*
***A Poet's Salad** by Sidney Smith, 1843.*

## 3 OCTOBER
## DAY OF GERMAN UNITY
# KARTOFFELKUCHEN

We found this recipe at the back of an old drawer here in my husband's home where the family have lived for 8 generations. No one remembers having tried this recipe before. Bitter almonds are very difficult to find. They are occasionally to be found in Oriental shops. You can substitute sweet almonds and add a few drops of bitter almond essence (plain almond essence will not do), but again this is hard to obtain. You will probably have to settle for using ordinary sweet almonds and the result will be very good, if not totally authentic.

1 lb (450 g) cooked potatoes, rubbed through a sieve
9 eggs, separated
12 oz (350 g) sugar
1 heaped teaspoon lemon peel
2 oz (50 g) blanched sweet almonds, finely chopped
1 oz (25 g) blanched bitter almonds, finely chopped

Beat the yolks of the eggs with the sugar. Originally, German cooks had to beat the mixture for a half-hour but with an electric hand mixer it can be done in 5 minutes or until the whisk leaves heavy tracks in the mixture.

Fold in the lemon peel, the potatoes and the almonds. Beat the egg whites until they are a stiff snow and fold into the cake mixture. Put into a cake tin and bake at gas mark 4/350°F/180°C for 1 hour 15 minutes. You may have to cover the cake with greaseproof paper if it becomes too brown.

*The Germans called the potato 'kartoffel' in the 18th century but at first even starving people put up a great resistance to a food considered fit only for pigs. Its inclusion in workhouse soups in Munich had to be kept secret.*

## 4 OCTOBER

# POTATOES WITH BEANSPROUTS

Some say that beansprouts can be easily grown on the windowsill. Not on mine.

$1^1/_2$ lb (700 g) potatoes, peeled and sliced in half-inch sizes
4 hard-boiled eggs, peeled and sliced
1 pint (570 ml) béchamel sauce, well-flavoured with nutmeg
8 oz (225 g) fresh beansprouts
Breadcrumbs

Cook the potato slices in a little salted water until just tender. Layer the egg slices with the potatoes in a shallow casserole dish. Bring the sauce to near boiling point, add the beansprouts for 1 minute and pour at once over the eggs and potatoes. Sprinkle the top with breadcrumbs and brown under a grill.

*"The pasty taste, the natural insipidity, the unhealthy quality of this food, which is flatulent and indigestible, has caused it to be rejected from refined households and returned to the people, whose coarse palates and stronger stomachs are satisfied with anything capable of appeasing hunger."*

*From* ***Histoire de la Vie Privée des Français*** *by Legrand d'Aussy, 1783.*

## 5 OCTOBER

# POTATO, ROCKET AND BREAD SOUP

Here is an Italian soup that deserves to be better known. All-year-round supplies of rocket can be achieved by regular sowings of rocket between February and October.

1 lb (450 g) floury potatoes, peeled and thickly sliced
1 large handful rocket, washed and any tough stalks removed
Sea salt and freshly ground black pepper
4 slices of stale French or Italian bread
6 tablespoons olive oil
1 large clove garlic, crushed

Cover the potatoes with cold, salted water and bring to the boil. Cook for about 10 minutes and then add the rocket. Cook until the potatoes are very soft. Add the bread and stir well.

In a frying pan, heat the oil and fry the garlic for just a few moments. This is to flavour the oil — the garlic is then removed and the oil stirred into the soup.

*In the 18th century, the self-styled Count Rumford (who was born Benjamin Thompson in Massachusetts) attached himself to the Bavarian Elector as a soldier, tackling at the same time the problems of Bavaria's vast beggar population. Rumford Soup came into existence and this potato and bread soup was alleged to have fed 6,000 people.*

## 6 OCTOBER

# SPICED POTATO, CAULIFLOWER AND PUMPKIN

Pumpkin is an agreeable vegetable. With its bland taste it adapts well to different dishes.

1 lb (450 g) potatoes, cleaned and diced (only peeled if necessary)
1 small cauliflower, broken into florets with the thick stalk discarded
1 lb (450 g) pumpkin flesh, diced
3 tablespoons sunflower oil
1 onion, chopped
1 clove garlic, chopped
3 cardamom pods
1 teaspoon ground cumin
1 teaspoon crushed coriander seeds
1 teaspoon salt

Heat the oil and add the onion and garlic. Remove the black seeds from the cardamom pods and put into the pan with the other spices. Allow to cook for a few minutes and then put in the potatoes. Cover the pan and leave to cook over a low heat for about 10 minutes, stirring from time to time.

Add the cauliflower and about half a pint of water. Cook for another 5 minutes and then add the pumpkin. The vegetables should be ready to serve in another 10 minutes or so. Do not overcook - the vegetables should be *al dente.*

*An article written by a doctor that appeared in* ***The Countryman*** *magazine in the 1950s, making claims for the nutritional value of the potato, quoted an experiment in which a man lived for eleven months solely on potatoes and vegetable margarine flavoured with onion. He argued, too, that consumption of the vegetable was bringing down the Danish death rate.*

## 7 OCTOBER

# VEGETABLE TERRINE

You can eat this either hot or cold and as a vegetable or with a salad as a light lunch dish. To retain the fresh taste of the vegetables I resist the temptation to add herbs to this terrine.

14 oz (400 g) potatoes, peeled and chopped
4 oz (110 g) carrots, peeled and chopped
4 oz (110 g) turnip, peeled and chopped
4 oz (110 g) spinach
1 oz (25 g) butter
A small pinch salt
1 teaspoon ground nutmeg
1 beaten egg

Cook the potatoes, carrots and turnip separately in a little water. Do the same with the spinach but trim well and shred the leaves before cooking. Drain and purée all the vegetables, again separately (a little bit time consuming but worth it) then flavour each with a little butter and salt.

Add the beaten egg to the potato and divide between the three other vegetables. Oil a 1 lb (450 g) loaf tin and spread, first the carrot mixture, then the turnip and finally the spinach.

Put in a roasting tin half filled with boiling water. Bake at gas mark 5/375°F/190°C for 1-1$^1/_2$ hours until set. Leave to stand for 10 minutes before turning out.

*"The Rev. Patric Bronte had grown to gigantic proportions on potatoes; he knew no reason why his children should fare differently."*

*From **The Life of Charlotte Bronte** by E. Gaskell, 1857.*

## 8 OCTOBER

# POTATO SCONES

Eat these warm from the oven, split in half and covered in butter.

6 oz (175 g) potatoes
8 oz (225 g) self-raising flour
1 teaspoon salt
3 oz (75 g) butter or margarine
2-3 fl oz (50-75 ml) milk

Boil or steam the potatoes and put through a sieve. Sift the flour and salt and rub in the butter or margarine. Mix in the warm potato and lastly enough milk to make a soft dough. On a floured surface, shape into a round about half an inch thick and cut into scones (using a 2$^1/_2$ inch cutter the yield will be about 12 scones).

Put on a greased baking tray and cook at gas mark 6/400°F/200°C for 20 minutes or until golden brown.

*"...We will just wonder why, while in France many dishes containing potatoes are called à la Parmentier, there are, all ungratefully, none in England named after Walter Raleigh."*

*Marcel Boulestin, c.1932.*

## 9 OCTOBER

# POTATOES HUANCAINA

A friend from Uruguay gave me this recipe that reads unpromisingly yet produces a most delightful lunch dish. I prefer to substitute yoghourt for the cottage cheese and tomatoes, just drizzled with olive oil, instead of the salad leaves.

1 lb (450 g) potatoes, peeled
1 large Philadelphia cream cheese
1 small cottage cheese or 4 oz (110 g) plain yoghourt
A small clove garlic
A little milk
A few drops of Tabasco (optional)
2 tablespoons olive oil
A little lemon juice
Salt and pepper
A few lettuce leaves or a few sliced tomatoes .
4 hard boiled eggs
A dozen olives

Boil the potatoes and while they are cooking prepare a sauce by putting the cheeses (and yoghourt, if using) in a blender with the olive oil, lemon juice, garlic, salt and pepper. Add the milk very slowly at the end so that the mixture is not too thick nor too liquid. Add the Tabasco sauce if you like.

Purée the potatoes, adding a little more olive oil. Season and shape into a round. Place the lettuce leaves or tomatoes on a large platter. Put the potato on this, cover with the cream mixture and finish with the slices of hard-boiled eggs and olives around the plate.

*Since the days of the Incas, potato planting in South America has been a community activity, often accompanied by elaborate rituals and the singing of a chant in which the word "triumph" is repeated.*

## 10 OCTOBER
# HILTON POTATOES

There are, obviously, people all over the world like ourselves who cook potatoes in this way but I have a problem with the naming of this dish. It is a sort of ratatouille, but without the long cooking time; it is also an excellent way of conjuring a vegetarian dish out of almost nothing and can be adapted to what is available in the kitchen. The only basic requirements are potatoes and tinned tomatoes and who would ever be without those?

1½ lb (700 g) potatoes, cleaned and diced
2 tablespoons oil
2 green peppers
1 small aubergine, sliced (optional)
2 cloves garlic, chopped
2 tins tomatoes
Sea salt and freshly ground black pepper
1 teaspoon sugar
Fresh chopped herbs

Heat the oil and put in the peppers, aubergine and garlic and sauté over a low heat for a few minutes. Put in the tinned tomatoes and seasoning and bring to the boil. Add the diced potatoes and simmer until the potatoes are tender. The vegetables should retain their shapes.

*"And is the potato to become extinct like the moly?"*
*From **Aurora Leigh** by Elizabeth Barrett Browning, 1857.*

## 11 OCTOBER

# BUCKWHEAT CRÊPES WITH POTATO FILLING

The famous crêpes of Brittany are made with this flour. It can be bought at most healthfood shops. The amount below makes 4 large pancakes, good vegetarian fare, and excellent served with a cheese sauce. This can be made using leftover pieces of cheese melted in a little heated cream.

For the filling:
1 lb (450 g) potatoes
2 medium onions
1 large red pepper, de-seeded and chopped
3 tablespoons olive oil
2 tablespoons lemon juice
Sea salt and freshly ground black pepper

For the pancakes:
2 eggs, beaten
2 oz (50 g) plain flour
2 oz (50 g) buckwheat flour
A pinch of salt
Approximately 2 fl oz (50 ml) milk
A little water
1 oz (25 g) butter with a little oil for frying

Peel the potatoes and put on to boil in salted water. While they are cooking, prepare the pancake batter by incorporating the beaten eggs into the flours and salt and adding enough milk until you have the consistency of thick cream. Allow to rest for 20 minutes or so. Before cooking add enough water to bring the consistency to one of thin cream.

Fry the onions and red pepper for a few minutes in 2 tablespoons of the olive oil. Drain the cooked potatoes, dry and cut into dice. Put in with the onions and peppers and add the remaining oil, lemon juice and seasoning. Remove from the heat.

Cook the pancakes on one side only. Lay them out with the cooked side upwards and spread a quarter of the potato mixture onto each. Roll up and, seam side down first, fry in the butter and hot oil until browned on all sides.

*Despite the general misconception, potatoes are not fattening. A small boiled potato has no more calories than an apple or an orange.*

## 12 OCTOBER

# GRATIN WITH BEER

This is much nicer than it sounds as the beer gives the potatoes a robust and almost meaty flavour.

1½ lb (700 g) potatoes, scrubbed and thinly sliced
2 oz (50 g) butter
3 medium onions, thinly sliced
Sea salt and freshly ground black pepper
¾ pint (400 ml) beer
¼ pint (150 ml) milk

Using 1 oz (25 g) of the butter grease a gratin dish and into this put the potatoes and onions in layers, seasoning as you go. Dab with the rest of the butter in little pats.

Pour over the beer and cook at gas mark 7/425°F/220°C for 10 minutes, then lower the heat to gas mark 4/350°F/180°C for another 40 minutes or until the potatoes are tender. Pour over the milk and cook for another 10 minutes or until the top is brown and crusty.

*"To Clean an Old Silk Dress - 'Unpick the dress, and brush it with a velvet brush. Then grate two large potatoes into a quart of water; let it stand to settle; strain it off quite clear, and sponge the dress with it. Iron it on the wrong side, as the ironed side will be shiny.'"*
*From **Useful Receipts for Housekeepers and Servants** in **Warne's Model Cookery and Housekeeping Book**, (1868).*

13 OCTOBER

# HERRING AND POTATO SALAD WITH CRÈME FRAÎCHE

Regrettably, since they are easily available, rollmop herrings will not do in this salad. *Matjes* herrings, much harder to find, are sweeter and gentler since they are cured in sugared brine.

12 oz (350 g) very small new potatoes, cleaned
8 oz (225 g) *matjes* herring fillets
1 cucumber, diced
1 beef tomato, diced
1 tablespoon parsley, chopped
3 tablespoons olive oil
2 tablespoons crème fraîche
Sea salt and freshly ground black pepper
1 small red onion, chopped

Steam the potatoes and, meanwhile, cut the herring fillets into bite-size pieces. Marinade the cucumber, tomato and parsley in the olive oil and crème fraîche. Season.

As soon as the potatoes are tender, stir them into the salad. Add the herring fillets, sprinkle with the red onion and serve.

*"After a word of grace we dipped our hand into the pot and took out a potato, hot and mealy, and with another we took a nip out of the silvery flank and the herring nearest us. It was a mouthful for a king, Sir!"*

*From* ***Nether Lochaber*** *by Rev. Alexander Stewart, 1883.*

## 14 OCTOBER
# BUBBLE AND SQUEAK

The name, presumably, comes from the noises that emanated from the frying pan while cooking. Traditionally this was made with leftovers. This version is up-to-date and all the ingredients are freshly cooked. It is a meal in itself.

1$^1/_2$ lb (700 g) potatoes, scrubbed and boiled until just tender
Beef dripping (or sunflower oil if you prefer)
8 oz (225 g) chorizo sausages, sliced
Sea salt and freshly ground black pepper
12 oz (350 g) cabbage, very thinly sliced
1 fl oz (25 ml) balsamic vinegar
2 fl oz (50 ml) meat jelly or good stock

As soon as the potatoes are cool enough to handle, slice them roughly. Heat the dripping or oil and add the potatoes. Cook them until they are well browned and at the last moment add the sausage and heat through. Season well.

Remove from the pan and keep warm. Add a little more dripping or oil and over a brisk heat cook the cabbage for a few minutes. It needs to retain its crispness. Remove from the heat and spoon onto the potatoes. Return the pan to the heat, add the vinegar to deglaze and then the stock. Allow to cook fiercely for half a minute and then pour over the potatoes and the cabbage. Eat at once.

*'Kotero' was a Maori way of dealing with potatoes that involved putting them in a bag and immersing them in a running stream for up to 6 months. The potatoes were then skinned, formed into cakes and baked in ashes.*

15 OCTOBER

# THREE ONION AND POTATO SALAD

Good food is, I think, about contrast in flavours, colours and textures. Sometimes this contrast can become conflict and taste is sacrificed in the cause of novelty. This salad is full of contrast - warm and cold, sharp and bland, red and white - which I think works well.

1 1/2 lb (700 g) very small new potatoes
2 oz (50 g) butter
2 medium red onions, thinly sliced
2 medium white onions, thinly sliced
2 spring onions
1 small clove garlic
Sea salt and freshly ground black pepper
2 teaspoons Dijon mustard
2 teaspoons red wine vinegar
6 tablespoons olive oil

Melt the butter in an ovenproof dish and put in the cleaned potatoes. Bake in a hot oven, gas mark 7/425°F/220°C for 20-30 minutes until they are well browned.

Meanwhile, put the onions into a wide bowl. Make a dressing by crushing the garlic in the salt and pepper, stirring in the mustard and then the vinegar and oil. Pour over the onions and leave to marinade. When the potatoes are cooked, add them immediately to the onions and serve at once.

*"Come, acushla, turn the clay.*
*And show the lumpers the light, gossoon;*
*For we must toil this autumn day,*
*With heaven's help till the rise of the moon.*
*Our corn is stocked, our hay secure,*
*Thank God! and nothing, my boy, remains,*
*But to pile the potatoes safe on the floor*
*Before the coming November rains..."*

*From* ***The Potato Digger's Song*** *by Thomas Caulfield Irwin.*

## 16 OCTOBER

# GRATIN DAUPHINOISE

Opinions differ about the definitive version of this classic French dish. Escoffier and Paul Bocuse cook it with cheese and eggs, as does Larousse. Elizabeth David leaves them out. Perhaps the character of this dish has changed with time because most chefs today cook this lovely gratin with cream, or cream and milk, and garlic.

1 1/2 lb (700 g) floury potatoes, cut wafer thin
3 oz (75 g) butter
3 cloves garlic, chopped
Sea salt and freshly ground black pepper
1 teaspoon flour
15 fl oz (400 ml) double cream

Wash the potato slices in cold water and dry well. Butter a wide gratin dish and layer the potatoes in it with the garlic and seasoning.

Sift the flour into the cream — this will prevent the cream separating — and pour over the potatoes. Cook for 1 hour at gas mark 6/400°F/200°C.

*"The potatoe...is a very useful root, being either boil'd or roasted in hot embers, and after it is boiled and beaten in a Mortar, it is used to thicken Sauces for making of rich Puddings."*

*From **The Country Housewife and Lady's Director** by Richard Bradley., 1736.*

## 17 OCTOBER

# GREEN RAVIOLI WITH TWO POTATO FILLINGS

Without a pasta machine (the hand-cranked variety is excellent) I would not recommend making ravioli. Rolling pasta by hand is time-consuming and difficult. With a machine, the whole process becomes very pleasurable. This amount will serve 4 as a main course.

For the ravioli:
7 oz (200 g) plain white flour
A pinch of salt
2 oz (50 g) spinach, cooked and very finely chopped
2 eggs

For the fillings:
8 oz (225 g) potato, steamed and cut into very small dice
2 oz (50 g) chorizo sausage, cut into very small dice
1 egg, beaten
Sea salt and freshly ground black pepper
4 oz (110 g) leeks, very thinly sliced
1 tablespoon olive oil
3 tablespoons cream

Make the ravioli by combining all the ingredients in a bowl and mixing to a smooth dough — this is very easily done in a food processor. You may need to add a little more flour to make a dry paste. Wrap in cling film and leave for 15 minutes.

Make the fillings by dividing the diced potato into 2 bowls. In the first bowl add the sausage and combine with the egg and seasoning. Cook the leeks very quickly in the olive oil and stir in the cream and seasonings and combine with the second batch of diced potato. Leave to cool.

Make the ravioli by rolling out the pasta to wafer thin sheets. If you don't have special ravioli cutters, a biscuit cutter will do well to cut out circles. Divide the 2 fillings between these, putting enough of the filling into each circle so that you can make moon-shaped pasties. Damp the edges with milk and press well together. Leave to dry for a half hour.

Cook the ravioli by plunging them into boiling salted water for about 2 minutes. Serve them sprinkled with grated Parmesan and melted butter.

*The potato was grown for many years in Italian gardens as an ornamental plant.*

## 18 OCTOBER

# OVEN FRIED CHIPS

A great success with children. Once I discovered how to make these potatoes I was freed for ever from the tyranny of the chip pan.

Potatoes, cleaned and peeled if necessary
Sunflower oil
Paprika
Salt

Prepare the potatoes into chip sizes. Dry well and put into a large bowl containing enough oil so each chip is just coated, but not soaked. Put into a roasting tin and cook at gas mark 7/425°F/220°C for about 20 minutes.

Remove from the oven, turn them in the tin, sprinkle with the paprika and salt (the paprika browns the chips) and cook for another 15 minutes or so until the chips are nicely browned.

*"Spam and Fried Chips*
*Say the BBC Pips!"*
*Wartime Version of Oranges and Lemons.*

## 19 OCTOBER

# SEGRESSE

The excellence of this dish lies in its simplicity. Any left overs could be liquidized with a little stock to make soup.

1 1/2 lb (700 g) potatoes, cleaned and sliced
1 1/2 lb (700 g) leeks, cleaned and sliced
2-3 oz (50-75 g) butter
Sea salt and freshly ground black pepper

Melt the butter in a heavy pan, layer the leeks and potatoes alternatively. Season, cover and simmer over a medium heat for about 45 minutes or until the vegetables are cooked.

*"The raising of that useful root, the potatoe, is coming into fashion; and several parts of the country grow considerable quantities."*

*From* ***The Beauties of England and Wales*** *by Rev. Evans, 1812.*

## 20 OCTOBER

# SALMON WRAPPED IN STRAW POTATOES WITH FENNEL SAUCE

This is a thoroughly elegant dish and one that could be accomplished by that unenviable figure, the cook/hostess, since most of the preparation is done in advance.

4 medium potatoes, peeled and cut into julienne strips
6 tablespoons lemon juice
Salt and freshly ground black pepper
4 salmon fillets or steaks
2 tablespoons olive oil
A bunch of fennel, chopped
4 oz (110 g) butter
1/4 pint (150 ml) fish stock

Place the potato strips in a bowl with the lemon juice and season. Press around the salmon fillets or steaks, wrap in a damp cloth and refrigerate for at least a half hour. Heat the oil and gently cook the fish 5 minutes or so on each side.

Meanwhile have ready the fennel blended with the butter (again, well chilled) and just before serving put little pieces of this butter into the frying pan in which you have cooked the salmon. Add the stock and blend together. Serve with the salmon.

*The Staffordshire Pottery works made a series of potato pots with open spouts. It is thought that these pots were either to be used as gin bottles or filled with hot water and used to warm the hands of those that carried them around hidden in muffs.*

21 OCTOBER

# BREAST OF CHICKEN WITH POTATO AND HERB STUFFING

The Crookedwood Restaurant in Mullingar, Co. Westmeath gave me this recipe. It is important to use fresh herbs - many are still available at this time of year.

1 lb (450 g) potatoes
2 oz (50 g) butter
1 small onion, chopped
2 oz (50 g) streaky bacon, diced
2 tablespoons mixed fresh herbs
Sea salt and freshly ground black pepper
4 breasts of chicken

Boil the peeled potatoes in salted water. Drain and purée. Melt the butter and soften the onions in this until translucent. Remove from the pan and quickly fry the bacon dice until crisp.

Combine with the potato purée, onions, herbs and seasoning. Make an incision halfway through each chicken breast and cut horizontally to make a pocket. Fill with the stuffing and pan fry the chicken breasts.

*In Ireland in the years between the mid 1700s and 1808 silver potato 'rings' became fashionable. Potatoes were served in the rings which were placed over white damask napkins to absorb any dampness. The best of these rings are to be found in the National Museum in Dublin.*

22 OCTOBER

# POTATO AND APPLE CAKE - CÁCÁ PRÁTAÍ AGUS ÚLL

This traditional Irish recipe is more of a pie than a cake. The crust is more biscuit-like than normal pastry and keeps a separate identity from the filling. This will serve 6.

1 lb (450 g) potato, peeled and boiled
2 oz (50 g) butter
4 oz (110 g) demerara sugar
6 oz (175 g) self-raising flour
1/2 teaspoon ground ginger
1 lb (450 g) cooking apples
2 oz (50 g) caster sugar
4 oz (110 g) raisins
A pinch of cinnamon
A few cloves

Make a purée with the potatoes, and while still warm stir in the butter. Add the demerara sugar, flour and ginger to make a dough. Divide the mixture into two portions and roll out one half to fit the bottom of a 9-inch flan dish.

Peel and slice the apples and put them on the pastry with the caster sugar (you may need a little more depending on the tartness of the apples), the raisins, cinnamon and cloves.

Roll out the remaining pastry and cover the top, leaving a slit open. Bake at gas mark 5/375°F/190°C for about 45 minutes, watching that the top doesn't brown too much. If this happens, cover with greaseproof paper.

*"Spent the night pleasantly and quietly eating apples, burning nuts, drinking tea and eating apple-cake. That is how I finished the Autumn season."*

*From the diary of Humphrey O'Sullivan, October 31st, 1831.*

23 OCTOBER

# BAKED POTATO WITH SESAME BUTTER

Nut butters are very good, not just on toast.

4 large potatoes
3 oz (75 g) sesame seeds
Sea salt and freshly ground black pepper
3 oz (75 g) butter

While the potatoes are baking, lightly toast the sesame seeds. Stir into the slightly softened butter with the seasoning, and mix well. Serve the potatoes with a spoonful of the butter in each.

*"I'll give you a song, 'tis a true Irish strain*
*Our cruiscins and glasses, my boy, let us drain.*
*Our voices in chorus now manfully lend*
*And sing the potato's the Irishman's friend.*
*With my Ballinamona oro, a laughing potato for me!"*

*From* ***The Irish Potato****, 19th Century Ballad.*

24 OCTOBER

# AUTUMN CASSEROLE

This is a most accommodating recipe; it goes well with almost anything, is very simple to prepare and can be easily adapted to suit varying numbers of people. It does need a long cooking time but it can be kept waiting and is ideal for a party. The quantities given below would feed 4 people as a vegetarian dish, or 6 people with a meat or fish dish.

1 lb (450 g) potatoes, washed and cut into small dice
1 small aubergine (8-12 oz/225-350 g), diced
1 green pepper, diced
1 red pepper, diced

8 oz (225 g) onions, finely chopped
1 lb (450 g) courgettes, sliced
A few okra (optional), sliced
2 cloves garlic, chopped
Chopped parsley
2 tablespoons tomato purée or 1 tin tomatoes
4 teaspoons paprika
5 tablespoons olive oil
Sea salt and freshly ground black pepper
1 lb (450 g) tomatoes

Put all the vegetables into a casserole dish with the garlic and parsley and then stir in the paprika, 3 tablespoons of the oil and the seasoning. Slice the tomatoes over the top and sprinkle with the rest of the oil.

Cook uncovered at gas mark 7/425°F/220°C for 20 minutes, then lower to gas mark 3/325°F/170°C for a further 1 to 1½ hours or until the vegetables are cooked through. Can be eaten hot or cold.

*"The King (George III)...complained that he had not what he liked to eat. 'Why not?' said Willis. 'If it is to be had in your Three Kingdoms your Majesty shall have it.' 'Shall I? Then let me have beef and potatoes'."*

*From* ***A Year with the Ladies of Llangollen*** *by Elizabeth Mavor, 1971.*

## 25 OCTOBER

# ALIGON À MA FAÇON

This is a little tricky to perfect. It is important that the purée is not over-heated, yet the cheese should melt. The only accompaniment needed is a green salad.

2 lb (900 g) potatoes, cleaned
Sea salt and freshly ground black pepper
A little nutmeg
2 oz (50 g) butter
8 oz (225 g) mild Cheddar, cubed
8 oz (225 g) ricotta, cubed
A small garlic clove, chopped

Boil the potatoes in their skins. Drain, peel and purée. Season and put the purée in a heavy saucepan with the butter and cook over a low heat until the butter is melted.

Take off the heat, add the cheeses and garlic, lifting the mixture with a fork as you go. The cheese will make long strands.

Put back on a gentle heat before you serve.

*"....there is no use talking for or against emigrating.... Educated youth who leave who have had the maps of the world before their eyes for years are not likely to sit down for life on a potato patch".*

*David Moriaty, Bishop of Kerry, writing to Lord Dufferin in 1868.*

## 26 OCTOBER

# STEAK PIE WITH POTATO CHEESE PASTRY

The potato is present in both the pastry and in the pie filling. This is a useful way of making a pound of steak serve four people.

8 oz (225 g) potatoes, peeled
1 lb (450 g) rump steak, cubed
1 oz (25 g) flour
Sea salt and freshly ground black pepper
*Bouquet garni*
1 medium onion, sliced
4 oz (110 g) mushrooms, halved
2 tablespoons vegetable oil

For the pastry:
3 oz (75 g) butter
2 oz (50 g) Cheddar cheese
6 oz (150 g) sieved, cooked potato
4 oz (110 g) plain flour, sifted
1/2 teaspoon mustard powder
1 small egg yolk, beaten

Boil the potatoes for the pie filling in salted water for 10 minutes. Cut in pieces. Season the meat cubes with flour and salt and pepper.

Heat the oil and brown the steak. Remove the meat and add the onion and mushrooms and cook for a few minutes. Return the meat, cover with water and add *Bouquet garni* and simmer for 40 minutes or until the meat is cooked. Layer in a 9-inch flan dish with the potatoes.

To make the pastry, melt the butter and add it with the coarsely grated cheese to the sieved potato. Add the flour, mustard powder and egg yolk. Form into a soft dough. Chill at least 20 minutes before covering the pie, leaving a hole in the centre of the pastry for the steam to escape. Cook at gas mark 5/375°F/190°C for 35-40 minutes until golden brown.

*"Potatoes, one of the best vegetables - and which would cost twice as much as truffles if they were only half as rare."*

*Marcel Boulestin.*

## 27 OCTOBER

# POTATO AND HAZELNUT SOUP

A thick, creamy soup ideal for the hungry on a cold evening. Soups made with nuts are to be found in South America. I like the taste of hazelnuts and so concocted this. It serves 4-6 people.

1 lb (450 g) potatoes, peeled and sliced
4 oz (110 g) hazelnuts
2 medium onions, sliced
1 oz (25 g) butter
Sea salt and freshly ground black pepper
1 pint (570 ml) chicken stock
$^{1}/_{4}$ pint (150 ml) cream
Chives, chopped

Put the hazelnuts to roast in a hot oven for a few minutes until well browned. Rub off the skins in a clean cloth and put the nuts in a liquidizer.

Cook the onions and the potatoes until transparent in the melted butter. Season, cover with the stock and then cook until the vegetables are soft. Strain, setting aside the liquid, and add the vegetables to the nuts and liquidize.

Slowly add the stock and then put back into a clean pan with the cream. If the consistency is a little thick add some more stock. Cook gently for about 10 minutes and then serve with a sprinkling of chives.

*At festival time in the Andes, workers searched for the largest possible potato in a field. This was then thrown as far as possible; it is thought this was to ensure future growth of large potatoes.*

## 28 OCTOBER

# FISH AND POTATO TIMBALE

Cook this in a 2-pint ring mould and decorate with a few fresh prawns. Serve with a red coloured salad using tomatoes, red peppers and red apples.

1 lb (450 g) potatoes, cooked and puréed
1 oz (25 g) butter
4 tablespoons grated cheese
Sea salt and freshly ground black pepper
A few brown breadcrumbs
12 oz (350 g) cooked white fish
6 tablespoons béchamel sauce
Chopped parsley
1 egg yolk
Grated rind of 1/2 lemon
A few fresh prawns to garnish

Melt the butter and add the potato, cheese and seasoning. Brown the breadcrumbs and sprinkle the inside of a well-greased ring mould. Line it with the potato mixture, reserving enough to cover the top. Flake the fish and mix with the sauce and the parsley, egg yolk and grated lemon.

Place in the lined mould, cover with the rest of the potato and bake in a moderate oven (gas mark 5/375°F/190°C) for 30-40 minutes. Allow to rest for 5 minutes and then turn out onto a warmed dish and serve.

*"A blight in the Bintje, blue-murder on the Mizen but, please, save our glorious Golden Wonder."*

*From a letter in* ***The Irish Times****, 1990.*

29 OCTOBER

# MASH OF NINE SORTS - STWMP NAW RHYW

This is based on a Welsh recipe that was traditionally cooked for Hallowe'en and served in a communal dish. Concealed in this mash was a wedding ring.

8 oz (225 g) potatoes, peeled and diced
4 oz (110 g) carrots, peeled and diced
8 oz (225 g) turnips, peeled and diced
8 oz (225 g) parsnips, peeled and diced
8 oz (225 g) peas
8 oz (225 g) leeks
5 fl oz (150 ml) milk
2 oz (50 g) butter
Sea salt and freshly ground black pepper

Cook the first 4 ingredients together in a little salted water until soft, drain and purée. Cook the peas and, using a potato masher, add to the purée.

Cook the leeks in the milk until they are soft (about 5 minutes) and then mash in the other vegetables. Add the butter and season.

*"Oh, it will not bear polish, the ancient potato*
*Needn't be nourished by Caesars, will blow anywhere*
*Hidden by nature, counted-on, stubborn and blind.*

*You may have noticed the blush it pushes to air,*
*Comical, delicate, sometimes second-rate flowers*
*Awkward and milky and beautiful only to hunger."*

*From* ***The Beautiful Changes and Other Poems*** *by Richard Wilbur, 1947.*

## 30 OCTOBER

# POTATO BARM BRACK

Barm Brack is an Irish cake traditionally eaten at Hallowe'en. Potato is not normally an ingredient but gives it a respectable chewiness.

8 oz (225 g) potatoes, cooked and puréed
1 lb (450 g) self-raising flour
8 oz (225 g) sugar
2 teaspoons mixed spice
6 oz (175 g) sultanas
2 oz (50 g) raisins
2 oz (50 g) glacé cherries, quartered
10 fl oz (275 ml) milk

In a large bowl mix the potatoes with all the dry ingredients and lastly stir in the milk.

Grease an 8-inch ring tin and spoon the mixture into this. Bake at gas mark 4/350°F/180°C for 1 hour or until firm to the touch. Cool in the tin for 10 minutes, then turn out and serve warm in slices with butter.

*"Tea is frequently an abundant and delightful meal owing to the varieties of bread which are put on the table. Barm brack is an Irish word meaning 'speckled cake' and besides barm bracks you will often have on the table, scones and farls of wheaten, soda and Indian meal bread, oat cakes, slim cakes, seed cakes, loaves, potato bread, or fadge, and various other sorts of bread. You may not have all these on the table at once, but you will have a good number of them if you are invited to share the hospitality of a prosperous farmhouse."*

*From* ***Home Life in Ireland*** *by Robert Lynd, 1909.*

## 31 OCTOBER
## HALLOWE'EN
# COLCANNON (CALLY)

Fresh kale with its vivid green shoots is a luxury at this time of year. This is a traditional Irish way of dealing with it and often eaten at Hallowe'en with the inclusion of a gold ring, a thimble, a button and a sixpence. The Oxford Dictionary has claimed that the word derives from 'cole' meaning cabbage and 'cannon' referring to the pounding of the mixture with a cannon ball. This would seem to arise out of the usual Anglo-Irish misunderstandings and it is more likely that the word comes from *cal ceann fhionn* - white headed cabbage. In his *History and Social Influence of the Potato,* Redcliffe Salaman writes that in the 17th century "Colcannon...was much favoured and found its way to the tables of the upper classes in England. It was composed of a mash of potatoes and brussel sprouts, highly flavoured with ginger and the like..." It sounds about as authentic as Swiss Roll.

1 lb (450 g) potatoes, peeled and boiled
1 lb (450 g) curly kale or Savoy cabbage
4 oz (110 g) butter
1/4 pint (150 ml) milk or cream
6 chopped scallions (spring onions)
Sea salt and freshly ground black pepper

Drain and purée the potatoes. Meanwhile have your kale cooking - either steamed or boiled.

Add the scallions to the milk or cream and bring to the boil, at which point add to the potatoes, beating well until a smooth mixture is attained. Finely chop the kale and add this, together with the butter. If necessary reheat. Serve with more butter.

*"Did you ever eat Colcannon*
*When 'twas made from thickened cream,*
*And the kale and praties blended*
*Like the picture in a dream?*
*Did you ever take a forkful*
*And dip it in the lake*
*Of the clover-flavoured butter*
*That your mother used to make?*

*Oh, you did; yes you did.*
*So did he and so did I,*
*And the more I think about it,*
*The more I want to cry,*
*Ah God be with the happy times,*
*When troubles we had not,*
*And our mothers made Colcannon*
*In the little three-legged pot."*

# RUMBLEDETHUMPS

This wonderful word comes from 'rumbled' meaning mixed or mashed and 'thumped' meaning to be beaten down. The dish itself is said to originate in the border region of Scotland; there are, of course, various versions.

1 lb (425 g) potatoes, peeled and boiled
1 large onion, sliced
1 lb (450 g) cabbage, cut into strips
2 oz (50 g) butter
Grated cheese

While the potatoes are boiling, in a separate saucepan boil the cabbage and onion together until just tender. Melt the butter and mash the potatoes, cabbage and onion together. Sprinkle with the cheese and brown under a grill.

*"May I ask, with all due solemnity, what are Rums?"*

*From* ***Noctes Amrosianae*** *by Christopher North, writing in Blackwood's Magazine, c. 1820.*

## 2 NOVEMBER

# CALDO VERDE

This is a simple version of the famous Portuguese cabbage and potato soup that is traditionally served with a corn bread called *broa*. Kale can be substituted for the cabbage.

1 lb (450 g) potatoes, peeled and sliced
1 lb (450 g) cabbage, very finely shredded
2 pints (1.1 litre) water
2 tablespoons olive oil
Sea salt
Grated cheese

Cook the potato slices in salted water until soft. Remove and purée them with the olive oil, then return to the cooking liquid. Bring to the boil, add the cabbage and cook for no more than 8 minutes. Serve with a sprinkling of cheese.

*In 1719, a group of Irish emigrants brought potato plants to Londonderry, New Hampshire, USA. The vegetables were greeted with suspicion until members of the local aristocracy began serving them regularly at their tables.*

## 3 NOVEMBER

# CHILCANO SOUP

This is a nourishing, inexpensive and very typical Peruvian soup. The soup is usually made with the head and bones of a large white fish, but finding these hard to come by, I use instead the freshest white fish I can buy.

1 large potato, peeled and diced
2 tablespoons oil
1 leek, thinly sliced
1 large tomato, peeled and de-seeded
Oregano (optional)
1 clove garlic, chopped
1 lb (450 g) fish (with bones)

Sea salt and freshly ground black pepper
1 carrot, sliced
2 oz (50 g) rice
Roughly chopped parsley

Heat the oil and gently fry the leek, tomato, oregano and garlic for 5 minutes. Add the fish and cover with water - about 2 pints. Bring to the boil and simmer for 20 minutes.

Strain into a clean pan, season and add the carrot, potatoes and rice. Cook for another 20 minutes or until the vegetables and rice are cooked. Serve strewn with parsley.

*"A packet of chips, a packet of chips,*
*Wrapped in the Daily Mail,*
*Golden juicy and fried for a week*
*In the blubber of the Great White Whale."*
*From **Giving Potatoes** by Adrian Mitchell.*

4 NOVEMBER

# POTATO AND BUTTER BEAN CURRY

A curious pulse, the butter bean, rather under regarded by food lovers and over regarded by school cooks.

6 medium potatoes, peeled and diced
2 tablespoons clarified butter
1 medium onion, chopped
A small piece of ginger
1 teaspoon turmeric
1/2 teaspoon cumin
1 teaspoon ground coriander
1/2 teaspoon chilli
1 teaspoon sea salt
1 teaspoon garam masala
1 tablespoon lemon juice
1 can butter beans or 8 oz (225 g) dried butter beans

If using dried butter beans soak them overnight and cook before adding to the potatoes.

Heat the butter and fry the onion gently. Add the spices and cook for a few minutes, then add the potatoes, together with 1 pint (570 ml) water and bring to the boil. Simmer for a half hour, then put in the butter beans and the lemon juice.

*"Hello Old Potato" was the greeting used by Alfred E. Smith to Franklin D. Roosevelt in 1932 after the two friends had been estranged for several years.*

5 NOVEMBER

# FOIL-BAKED CHILLI POTATOES

Romantics could cook these in the embers of a bonfire. A more reliable method is in the oven.

4 large potatoes, cleaned, unpeeled, sliced 1/4 inch thick
Sea salt and freshly ground black pepper
4 slices bacon, fried until crisp
1 medium onion, chopped
8 oz (225 g) Cheddar cheese, grated
2 green chillies, finely chopped
4 oz (110 g) butter

Lay out 4 large squares of aluminium foil and divide the slices of potato on these. Season. Crumble the bacon over the potatoes and then divide the onion, cheese and chillies between the four parcels. Dot with little pats of butter.

Bring up the edges of the foil and seal tightly. Bake at gas mark 4/350°F/180°C for an hour.

*"It is not correct to speak of a jacket of a suit. The correct name is coat. It is acceptable to speak of a jacket potato."*

*The British royal dressmaker, Sir Hardy Amies.*

## 6 NOVEMBER

# LOCRO

Locro is a potato and cheese soup from Ecuador. The cheese in this soup must not be allowed to cook, but added at the last minute and off the heat so that it just melts. The soup has a pinkish glow and is rich and sustaining. Brussels sprouts are one of my favourite vegetables; picked when small and steamed they are a lovely addition to this soup, although, of course, not at all in the Latin American tradition.

1lb (450 g) potatoes, thinly sliced
2 onions, thinly sliced
A little sunflower oil
1 tablespoon paprika
2 pints vegetable stock
$^{1}/_{4}$ pint (150 ml) milk
A little cream (optional)
4 oz (110 g) grated cheese (Cheddar type)

Cook the onions until transparent in the oil. Stir in the paprika and then the potatoes. Cover with the stock and cook until the potatoes begin to disintegrate.

Add the milk and the cream, bring to the boil and then take off the heat and stir in the cheese. Eat at once with any addition of steamed vegetables.

*" He who likes to work a lot and to eat potatoes, can spend many happy hours in Franconia."*

*German proverb.*

## 7 NOVEMBER

# POTATO AND CHEESE SOUFFLÉ

With its golden crust and its centre still liquid, this makes a perfect first course. The sour cream gives it a slightly tart flavour.

10 oz (275 g) potatoes, peeled and boiled
4 oz (110 g) very mature Cheddar cheese
1 small leek
4 oz (110 g) butter
1 clove of garlic
1 oz (25 g) flour
1/4 pint (150 ml) soured cream
4 tablespoons yoghourt
5 eggs
Sea salt and freshly ground black pepper
A little nutmeg

First, preheat the oven at gas mark 6/400°F/200°C. When the potatoes have cooled, grate them. Grate the cheese and chop very thinly about 2 inches of the green part of the leek. Melt the butter in a heavy-bottomed pan and add the leek and the chopped garlic.

Cook very gently for a couple of minutes and then stir in the flour and the sour cream and yoghourt. Stir over a low heat for 3 minutes and then remove from the heat. Stir in the egg yolks and add the grated potato. Season and add the grated cheese. (This preparation can be done a few hours before cooking.) Whip the egg whites until stiff and fold into the mixture. Put into a soufflé dish and cook for 25 minutes. Serve immediately.

*"While Gabriel and Miss Daly exchanged plates of goose and plates of ham and spiced beef, Lily went from guest to guest with a dish of hot floury potatoes wrapped in a white napkin."*
*From **Dubliners** by James Joyce, 1914.*

8 NOVEMBER

# BAKED POTATOES WITH SPICED CHICK PEA FILLING

One of the best uses of a freezer is the storage of cooked pulses. So often one needs them in small quantities, yet the cooking and preparation is time-consuming. I have never understood why people choose to spend their summer days preparing vegetables for the freezer in preference to spending time in the garden putting in vegetables for fresh use during the winter.

4 large potatoes
5 oz (150 g) cooked chick peas
2 tablespoons yoghourt
1 tablespoon lemon juice
1 fat clove garlic
1 dessertspoon fresh herbs (chervil or parsley)
Sea salt and freshly ground black pepper
2 tablespoons sesame seeds

Scrub and bake the potatoes. Purée the chick peas with a masher or a food processor, taking care not to over-process. Add the potato flesh, the yoghourt, lemon juice, garlic, herbs and seasoning.

Spoon the filling into the potato skins, sprinkle with the sesame seeds and bake for a further 20 minutes at gas mark 7/425°/220°C and then serve immediately.

*"An Englishman neither knows how to grow, how to boil, nor how to relish a potato."*
*Charlotte Elizabeth, traveller, writing in 1948.*

9 NOVEMBER

# POTATO WAFFLES

These are the best waffles I've ever eaten - sweetish, crisp, very light and amenable in cooking. This recipe makes 10 waffles.

12 oz (350 g) cooked potatoes, mashed
2½ oz (60 g) butter
2 fl oz (50 ml) water
2 tablespoons brown sugar
2 tablespoons golden syrup
2 eggs, separated
7 fl oz (200 ml) milk
6 oz (175 g) plain flour

Put the butter, water, brown sugar and golden syrup in a pan and stir over a low heat until the sugar is dissolved. Bring to the boil without stirring and take off the heat at once. Allow to cool. Beat the egg yolks and add the butter/sugar mixture, stir in the milk and the sifted flour and the potatoes. Beat the egg whites until soft peaks are formed and gently fold into the batter.

Heat and grease (I use butter) the waffle iron and drop in spoonfuls of the batter. Close the iron and cook for about 4 minutes, turning the iron once so both sides cook. These waffles can be made in advance and reheated in a hot oven for a few minutes.

*The word 'spud' originated in Scotland where it first referred to the three-pronged fork used to lift potatoes.*

10 NOVEMBER

# HORSERADISH POTATOES

These potatoes have the consistency of a thick soup and are delicious, of course, with a rare fillet of beef.

2 lb (900 g) potatoes
1/4 pint (150 ml) cream
2 cloves garlic
1 tablespoon fresh grated horseradish
Sea salt
Juice of 1 lemon
2 oz (50 g) butter

Peel and cook the potatoes in salted water. Drain and dry well and make into a purée. Heat the cream with the chopped garlic and horseradish and allow to cook for a few minutes.

Stir in the potatoes with the salt, lemon juice and the butter.

*"Why do you sing about the rose? It is the aristocrat of flowers. Why don't you sing the praise of the democratic potato, which is food for the people?"*
*Heinrich Heine.*

## 11 NOVEMBER

# CHILD'S DELIGHT

Here is a supper dish popular with children.

4 large baked potatoes
2 fl oz (50 ml) warmed milk
2 oz (50 g) grated cheese
8 frankfurter sausages
4 tomatoes

Cut the baked potatoes in half and scoop out the centres. Mix with the milk and cheese. Pour hot water over the frankfurters and leave to heat through for a few minutes.

Drain the sausages and put one in each half potato shell. Spread the potato mixture over the top. Cut the tomato in slices and divide between the potato shells. Cook in a hot oven (gas mark 7/425°F/220°C) for 10 minutes.

*'The Potato Plan,' published in **The Times** in January 1943, urged people to serve potatoes for breakfast on three days a week, make a main dish of potatoes one day a week, refuse second helpings of other foods except potatoes and to be more adventurous in the cooking of the vegetable.*

## 12 NOVEMBER

# POTATO CAKES WITH TOMATO

There are infinite varieties of potato cakes and, in a household like ours where potatoes have recently appeared in many different guises, this has been voted as one of the favourites.

1 lb (450 g) potatoes
1/2 oz (15 g) butter
2 teaspoons finely chopped parsley

Sea salt and freshly ground black pepper
1 shallot or small onion, chopped
2 tomatoes, skinned and finely chopped
1 oz (25 g) Parmesan cheese, grated
2 oz (50 g) flour
Oil for frying

Peel and boil or steam the potatoes and then press through a sieve. Mix with the melted butter, parsley, seasoning, onion, tomatoes, cheese and finally the flour.

Mix well together, roll out on a well-floured board to an inch thick and cut in circles with a cutter. Fry in hot oil until evenly browned. Dry on kitchen paper and serve at once.

*"Excellent potatoes, smoking hot, and accompanied by melted butter of the first quality, would alone stamp merit on any dinner: but they are as rare on state occasions, so served, as if they were of the cost of pearls."*

*From* ***The Original*** *by Thomas Walker, 1835.*

## 13 NOVEMBER

# CHOCOLATE AND MARMALADE POTATO CAKE

Marmalade is a subtle addition to chocolate cake, imparting its sharp orange taste to other flavours.

3 oz (75 g) cooked potato, puréed
4 oz (110 g) butter
4 oz (110 g) sugar
1 tablespoon cocoa
3 oz (75 g) self-raising flour
A pinch of salt
2 eggs, beaten
2 tablespoons marmalade
2 tablespoons milk

Cream the butter and the sugar and add to the puréed potato. Fold in the sifted flour, cocoa and salt alternatively with the beaten eggs. Stir in the marmalade and the milk.

Turn into a greased and lined sandwich tin and cook for 20 minutes in a moderate oven - gas mark 5/375°F/190°C.

*King Philip II of Spain is said to have paid homage to the Pope in Rome with a gift of potato tubers because they bore a resemblance to his name (Pappas).*

## 14 NOVEMBER
# GARLIC POTATOES

This recipe apparently originated in that popular 1960's London restaurant, Nick's Diner.

2 lb (900 g) potatoes
Oil for deep frying
3 cloves blanched garlic
3-4 oz (75-110 g) butter
Chopped herbs

Parboil the potatoes until barely tender, then deep-fry until golden crisp. Mash roughly with a fork with the blanched garlic, butter and herbs.

*French food was not to the liking of the men from Northern Ireland working on the building of Euro Disney outside Paris, so a special consignment of Irish potatoes was shipped from Belfast to Paris.*

## 15 NOVEMBER
# FARMERS' BREAKFAST

And why not anyone else's breakfast too?

Gently fry in a little oil some cut-up potatoes from a previous day's boiling. Beat up 2 eggs per person, a little milk and salt and pepper.

Add to the potatoes, moving around gently until just cooked. Eat immediately.

*"We have come to you with the Potato-man*
*Who no longer can contain himself in the field*
*Seeing how cold and wet it now is*
*He demands a feast of bacon and pancakes."*
*From* ***La Mythologie des Plantes*** *by A. de Gubernatio, 1882.*

## 16 NOVEMBER

# GALETTE OF POTATOES AND PARSNIPS

By slicing the vegetables so thin that they are almost transparent and then cooking them in a wide uncovered vessel you can achieve a crisp almost biscuit-like finish to this galette.

1 lb (450 g) potatoes, peeled and very thinly sliced
1 lb (450 g) parsnips, peeled and very thinly sliced
Sea salt and freshly ground black pepper
4 oz (110 g) butter, melted

Layer the vegetables in an 11-inch flan tin and season as you go. Pour over the melted butter and cook in a hot oven, gas mark 7/425°F/220°C for about 50 minutes until the galette is well browned. Turn out on a plate and serve.

*"A diet of whole milk and potatoes would supply almost all of the food elements necessary for the maintenance of the human body."*
*U.S. Department of Agriculture.*

## 17 NOVEMBER

# POTATOES STUFFED WITH CHICKEN LIVERS AND MUSHROOMS

A potato, baked and stuffed with a substantial filling, served with a salad, makes an ideal supper dish.

4 large potatoes, cleaned
6 oz (175 g) chicken livers, roughly chopped
4 oz (110 g) mushrooms, thinly sliced
Butter

Bake the potatoes and when cooked, remove from the oven. Keep them warm. Sauté the chicken livers in the butter with the mushrooms.

Scoop out the centre of the potato, put through a sieve and stir into the liver and mushrooms. Pile back into the potato shells and eat at once.

*Parmentier gave a banquet at which all the courses were made from potatoes. One of the guests, Marie Antoinette, was persuaded to wear potato flowers in her hair.*

## 18 NOVEMBER

# ROSEMARY POTATO GALETTE

The wonderful pungent aroma of rosemary, redolent of the Mediterranean, will fill the kitchen during the cooking of this dish.

1½ lb (700 g) potatoes
5 tablespoons unsalted butter
Rosemary leaves (about 2 tablespoons)
Sea salt and freshly ground black pepper

Scrub the potatoes and slice very thinly, dropping the slices into a bowl of cold water as you proceed. Melt 2 tablespoons of the butter in a wide frying pan and remove from the heat. Drain and pat dry the potato circles and arrange 1/3 of them in a spiral, starting in the centre and working to the outside of the pan.

Cut another tablespoon of the butter into little pats and dab over the potatoes. Sprinkle with half the rosemary leaves and season. Repeat twice using 1/3 each time of the remaining potatoes and 1 tablespoon of butter.

Cook over a gentle heat for about a half hour or until the bottom is crisp and golden brown. Invert the galette onto a flat plate and put it back into the pan. Continue cooking until the other side is golden. Cut into wedges and serve.

*Mr A.H. Roberts, Chief Instructor of the Army School of Catering at Aldershot, won gold medals in 1954 and 1959 at Hotel Olympia for his baskets made out of plaited strands of ribboned potatoes. The strips were softened in vinegar and water and woven into elaborate designs.*

## 19 NOVEMBER

# TREACLE PUDDING

A luscious, dark, moist pudding ideal for a cold November day.

8 oz (225 g) potatoes
4 oz (110 g) self-raising flour
2 oz (50 g) white breadcrumbs
3 oz (75 g) shredded suet
4 oz (110 g) sultanas
3 tablespoons black treacle
2 oz (50 g) caster sugar
1 tablespoon milk

Peel, boil and purée the potatoes. Mix with all the other ingredients - this is easily done with a food processor. Turn into a greased pudding basin, cover with greaseproof paper, secure a piece of aluminium foil or a pudding cloth over the whole and steam for 2 hours.

*John Hawkins, in his ship Jesus of Lubeck, visited Venezuela in 1565, where he received presents of hens, pineapples and potatoes, "the most delicate that may be eaten". Opinions differ as to whether these were sweet potatoes or the Solanum tuberosum.*

20 NOVEMBER

# PURÉE OF POTATOES AND CELERIAC

When cooking celeriac, it is important to work fast as raw peeled celeriac discolours quickly.

1½ lb (700 g) potatoes
1 lb (450 g) celeriac
2 oz (50 g) butter
3 fl oz (75 ml) cream
Sea salt and freshly ground black pepper

Boil the potatoes in the usual way and dry well. While they are cooking, peel and cut the celeriac into little cubes. Boil until soft and then purée.

Purée the potatoes and combine the two vegetables with the butter and the hot cream and the seasonings.

*"A Banquet! - Well, potatoes and eringoes*
*And, I take it, cantharides! Excellent!"*
*From* ***The Loyal Subject****, a play by John Fletcher, 1617.*

21 NOVEMBER

# IRISH STEW

How very rarely one eats a good Irish stew - so often there is too much liquid or it is spoiled by the inclusion of carrots or barley. Eliza Acton says that the potatoes should be cooked to a mash, but I prefer to do as suggested by Paul and Jeanne Rankin of Roscoffs, Belfast and use half of the potatoes to thicken the stew and the other half eaten whole. (I also follow their recommendation to add cream to the finished stew, but purists may disregard this.) Early recipes for Irish stew sometimes include mushroom ketchup, ham and celery, but I don't think these improve it.

2 lb (900 g) potatoes, peeled
2 lb (900 g) neck chops of lamb, trimmed of all fat, bone and gristle
1 lb (450 g) onions, sliced
1 tablespoon chopped parsley
1 bay leaf
A sprig of thyme
Sea salt and freshly ground black pepper
2 pints (1.1 litre) good meat stock (approx.)
10 fl oz (275 ml) cream (optional)

Layer half the potatoes, the lamb and the onions in a deep pan with the seasonings and cover with the stock. Bring to the boil, cover and simmer for about 1 hour and 15 minutes. Shake the pan vigorously to break up the potatoes and then add the remaining potatoes. You may need to add more stock at this stage.

The cooking time will depend on the quality of the meat. Remove the lid for the last half hour to allow the sauce to reduce. Add the cream, if using, to heat just before serving.

*"On the following day the parson expressed his kindness in a more liberal way, and desir'd us to dine with him: we had but one dish for entertainment, and that so crammed with such varieties of God's creatures that this dish seem'd to me to be the first chapter of Genesis: there was such beef, mutton, goat's and kid's flesh, bacon, roots, etc....and this was one point of their husbandry, to boyle all together to save charges."*

*Written in 1673, from* ***Scenes from Irish Clerical Life*** *by R. Wyse Jackson, published 1941.*

22 NOVEMBER

# SOUFFLÉ BAKED POTATO WITH SMOKED HADDOCK

This recipe is useful if you have a little left-over smoked fish. Ricotta cheese is becoming more widely available; if you can't get it substitute cottage cheese.

4 large potatoes
4 tablespoons cooked, smoked haddock
6 oz (175 g) ricotta cheese
1 tablespoon chopped parsley
2 eggs
Sea salt and freshly ground black pepper

Bake the potatoes and when cooked, scoop out the centre and put through a sieve. Add the fish, cheese, parsley, beaten egg yolks and the seasoning.

Whip the egg whites until stiff and fold into the potato mixture. Divide between the four shells and put back in a moderate oven ( gas mark 5/375°F/190°C) for 15 minutes.

*"And all you have for your labour is the potato?" "That's all, ma'am, that's all; and it's many of us that can't get a sup of milk with 'em, no, nor the salt; but we can't help it, we must be content with what the good God sends us."*

*From **The Bible in Ireland** by Asenath Nicholson, c.1840.*

23 NOVEMBER

# ORANGE CROQUETTE POTATOES

These little croquettes go well with casseroles of chicken or game. Since I try to avoid deep frying, I cook them in a frying pan with a little sunflower oil or clarified butter. Either cooking method will do.

1 lb (450 g) potatoes, peeled and boiled
Grated rind of an orange
1 tablespoon chopped parsley
2 egg yolks
Sea salt and freshly ground black pepper
A beaten egg
Breadcrumbs
Fresh oil for deep frying

Purée the potatoes. Add the orange rind, parsley, egg yolks and seasoning.

Allow to get cold. Shape into croquettes, dip in the beaten egg and then the breadcrumbs. Fry until an even, golden brown. Drain on kitchen paper and serve at once.

*Books about potatoes published in the 1980s include* ***The Potato Experience - Wonderful Ways with Potato Outers and Innards*** *by Lisa Tanner and* ***Toute la Pomme de Terre*** *by French poet Lucienne Desnoues. The Pusa Institute Ladies' Association of Bombay, India published* ***Potato Dishes*** *with the sub-heading* ***So slim a book, so rich a variety.***

24 NOVEMBER

# POTATOES, LEEKS AND SWISS CHARD IN A CREAM SAUCE

My favourite supper dish for this time of year, made with garden leeks and the Swiss chard that boldly goes on when other vegetables have long since bowed their heads.

4 large potatoes, peeled and sliced
4 leeks, washed and sliced into inch long pieces
1½ oz (40 g) butter
3-4 tablespoons chicken or vegetable stock
1 large handful Swiss chard
Sea salt and freshly ground black pepper
¼ pint (150 ml) cream

Melt the butter in a heavy pan and add the potatoes and leeks. Move gently around the pan, stirring in the stock and then allow to cook until the potatoes are just tender.

Wash and dry the Swiss chard, and then cut the white and green parts of the plant into strips. Add to the saucepan and season. Cover and cook for 5 minutes. Stir in the cream, heat through and eat.

*When the potato was first introduced to Russia, it was widely believed to be something evil and sexually tainted. Its name 'gulba' means 'going astray', a reference to the potato's alleged tainted ancestry.*

## 25 NOVEMBER
## THANKSGIVING
# SENATE BEAN SOUP

Thanksgiving falls on the fourth Thursday in November. This soup is so-called because it was served in the cafeteria in the United States Senate.

8 oz (225 g) potatoes
1 lb (450 g) dried white beans (haricot etc.), soaked overnight
A sprig of thyme
A bay leaf
$^{1}/_{4}$ pint (150 ml) warmed milk
2 stalks chopped celery
1 medium onion, finely chopped
3 tablespoons chopped parsley
1 clove garlic
Sea salt and freshly ground black pepper

Cook the beans with the thyme and bay leaf in enough water to cover until they are soft. Meanwhile, peel the potatoes, cook in a little salted water, and purée. Stir in the warmed milk.

Stir the purée into the beans, add all the other ingredients and cook on a very low heat for a further $^{3}/_{4}$ hour or so. You may need to add a little more water to make a soup-like consistency.

*"It may truly be said that it was the potato, which determined the atmosphere in which the subsequent relations between Americans, Irish and English, were to develop in the next hundred years. (i.e. after the Famine)."*

*From **The History and Social Influence of the Potato** by Redcliffe Salaman, 1949.*

26 NOVEMBER

# WINTER PIE

Potatoes appear here, both in the pie and in the pastry.

For the pastry:
4 oz (110 g) potatoes, peeled, cooked and puréed
2 oz (50 g) self-raising flour
3 oz (75 g) butter or margarine
2-3 tablespoons water

For the pie:
1 lb (450 g) potatoes, peeled and thinly sliced
6 oz (175 g) onions, thinly sliced
4 oz (110 g) Gruyère cheese, grated
2 cloves garlic, chopped
Sea salt and freshly ground black pepper
6 fl oz (175 ml) cream
Grated nutmeg
1 egg yolk

Make the pastry in the normal way by rubbing the fat into the flour and adding the potato purée. Bind with the water to make a smooth dough and put into the fridge for a half-hour.

Parboil or steam the potatoes for 5 minutes or until just tender. Blanch the onions for 4 minutes. Drain and arrange in a 9-inch pie dish with the potatoes, cheese, parsley, garlic and salt and pepper. Mix the nutmeg with the cream and pour over the whole.

Roll out the pastry and cover the pie. Brush with the beaten egg yolk. Bake at gas mark 6/400°F/200°C for 15 minutes and then turn down the oven to gas mark 4/350°F/180°C for a further 15-20 minutes until the pie is well browned.

*'Spuddy' was a slang term for someone who sold bad potatoes. It was also used to describe a short, stout person.*

## 27 NOVEMBER

# POTATO WINE

The ancient Peruvians brewed a beer from potatoes called *chicha* that is still consumed today, often at festival time. Potatoes, too, found their way into the illicit stills in Ireland to produce poteen and in Germany, Russia and Poland the vegetable was used in the production of schnapps and vodka. In Scandinavia it was the base for aquavit.

Potato wine must be kept for at least six months before using. A German recipe for potato wine, known as Poor Man's Rhine Wine is, it is claimed, if properly aged, hard to distinguish from a true Rhine wine. The following recipe was given to me by Katie McGuigan, mother of the boxer Barry. She is well skilled in the art of wine making and often uses potatoes in the process.

6 raw old potatoes, the size of an egg, peeled
2 oranges
3 lemons
8 oz (225 g) raisins
4 lb sugar
1 gallon water
$^{1}/_{2}$ oz (15 g) dried yeast or a piece of fresh yeast as big as a walnut

Slice the oranges and lemons thinly. Cut the potatoes into chunks and pull the raisins open. Put into a bucket with sugar. Pour over the water and stir well. Sprinkle the yeast on top and stir well. Cover with a clean cloth and leave for 10 days.

Strain and tip into a demijohn and if there is not enough liquid to fill the demijohn, top up with water. Fix in your bung and an airlock ( the airlock should have a little water in it). Stand the demijohn on a tray and place it in a fairly warm room (a kitchen is ideal). After a while the water in the airlock will emit bubbles at regular intervals which means the wine is working well. Keep in the demijohn until this ceases, then bottle or put into a cask and leave to mature.

*In* ***The Profitable Culture of Vegetables*** *(published 1911) the author Thos. Smith mentions available potato varieties that include the unlikely named Cigarette, Up-to-Date, Gladiator, Dalmeny Acme and Snowdrop. He also mentions an onion called the Potato Onion, which was planted on the longest day of the year and lifted on the shortest.*

## 28 NOVEMBER

# POTATO CAKES WITH BANANA FILLING

In Latin America, potato cakes are often served with fried bananas or plantains, and a very successful combination it is too. Here, the banana is used as a filling for the potato cake.

2 lb (900 g) potatoes
2 oz (50 g) butter
Sea salt and freshly ground black pepper
2 ripe bananas, sliced into inch long pieces
Lemon juice
A little flour
Oil or butter for frying

Peel and boil the potatoes. Drain and dry them well and then put through a sieve. Add the butter and the seasonings and mix thoroughly.

Sprinkle the banana slices with lemon juice, and then slightly flatten each piece of banana so that you can cover with a coating of the potato mixture to make a thickish cake. Dust with the flour and fry in the butter until brown on both sides.

*On November 28, 1858 a notice appeared in the* ***Missouri Democrat*** *appealing to farmers who had not paid their subscriptions. They were advised that the publisher had to eat like everyone else and suggested that delinquents "who have cabbage, potatoes or anything of that kind can pay their indebtedness that way."*

## 29 NOVEMBER

# SAWDUST POTATOES

This is a recipe from the Rhone region that is simple enough yet it gives boiled potatoes a little sophistication.

Potatoes, cleaned
Butter or oil

Stale breadcrumbs
Sea salt

Boil the potatoes in their skins and peel while still hot. Heat butter or oil in a frying pan, add the breadcrumbs and cook until they are golden. Sprinkle the potatoes with salt, then coat with the breadcrumbs.

*The Scottish poet William Wilkie (1721-72) achieved the nicknames 'Potato Poet' and 'Potato Wilkie' because of his keen interest in the cultivation of the potato.*

## 30 NOVEMBER
### ST. ANDREW'S DAY
# SKIRLIE-MIRLIE

This recipe was given to me by a Scottish friend, and the dish must indeed originate from there. A soup called Punchnep can be made in much the same way, by using puréed turnips and with more milk added. The verb 'to skirl' is to sound out in shrill, piercing tones, especially with a bagpipe. A similar dish, Orkney Clapshot, has the addition of chopped onion and chives and is traditionally served with haggis.

1 lb (450 g) potatoes
1 lb (450 g) swedes
2oz (50 g) butter
A little hot milk
Salt and freshly ground black pepper
A little chopped parsley

Cook the potatoes and the swedes separately in salted water. When tender, drain and purée both vegetables and fold together.

Melt the butter in a pan, add the potato and swede purée, stir in the warm milk and the seasonings. Sprinkle with the chopped parsley.

*In the spring of 1743, a Scottish landlord called Clanronald brought home some potato tubers from Northern Ireland after a visit to his relatives. He distributed these to his tenants in South Uist but they only agreed to plant them after a threat of imprisonment. The story goes that when they were harvested, the crops were deposited in sacks at his front door with a refusal to eat them.*

# PURÉE ALBERT NOEL

Albert Noel was a celebrated French chef. The ingredients for this purée originally included adding sugar to taste. I prefer to leave it out.

1 lb (450 g) potatoes, peeled and thickly sliced
1 pint (570 ml) milk
Sea salt
1 oz (25 g) butter
3 macaroons (or *amaretti*)

Cook the potatoes very gently in the milk until soft. Put through a sieve and add salt and butter and enough of the milk to make a smooth purée. Put into an ovenproof dish.

Pound the macaroons into crumbs and sprinkle over the purée. Put into a hot oven (gas mark 7/425°F/220°C) for 5 minutes.

*"To test flouriness in potatoes:- mix 11 parts water with 1 part salt, add the potatoes. Waxy ones will float, floury ones will sink."*

*Old Household Hint.*

## 2 DECEMBER

# POTATOES WITH CINNAMON AND PINE NUTS

Pine nuts are expensive and not always available, but these exquisite little nuts embellish many different dishes. The taste will intensify if they are quickly roasted, but be careful not to burn them.

2 lb (900 g) potatoes
1 teaspoon cinnamon
A little warmed milk
Sea salt and pepper
1 medium onion, sliced
2-3 oz (50-75 g) pine nuts

Peel, cook and purée the potatoes. Stir in the cinnamon, milk and seasonings. Meanwhile, fry the onion slices. Serve the potatoes in a warmed dish with the onion slices on top and the whole strewn with the pine nuts.

*"When I come to London there is always one thing on my mind...a plate of bangers and mash. It's still my passion."*

*The actress Elizabeth Taylor.*

## 3 DECEMBER

# POTATO SAUSAGES

For this rather ambitious but very worthwhile project you need the intestine of a pig in which to put your filling. A good butcher should oblige. He may even agree to fill the casings for you, the most difficult part of the exercise. My daughter Alice overcame this by making a funnel with a plastic tonic water bottle. She sliced off almost all the body of the bottle and then pushed the neck into the casing. The potato mixture was pushed down through the bottle opening into the intestine. The amounts given below make about 4 lb (1.8 kg) of sausages.

2¹/₄ lb (1 kg) potatoes, peeled and cut in little dice
12 oz (350 g) leeks, white part only, thinly sliced
1 large onion, diced
1 large carrot, diced
1 coffee cup melted pork fat
12 oz (350 g) belly of pork, cut into little pieces
5 fl oz (150 ml) dry white wine
Sea salt and freshly ground black pepper
*Bouquet garni*
4 oz (110 g) butter

In a large bowl, mix together the vegetables with the pork fat and the belly of pork. Season and add the wine. Allow the flavours to mingle for an hour or so.

Stuff the mixture into the pork casing, twist into sausage shapes and cut into individual sausages. Poach in salted water flavoured with the *bouquet garni* for about 40 minutes.

Drain and puncture with a needle in several places so the sausages do not burst. At this stage the sausages can be eaten. Alternatively, paint with melted butter and glaze in the oven at gas mark 6/400°F/200°C for about 15 minutes.

*Once believed to be the cause of leprosy, potatoes were burned in Burgundy by order of the Crown in order to "protect the citizenry from its base addiction and craving". It was reported that the scent of roasting potatoes proved irresistible and the tubers were snatched from the embers.*

4 DECEMBER

# POTATO AND HAZELNUT CAKE

This cake recipe comes from France. The cake would be served warm from the oven with coffee. I cook it in a well-greased 2 lb (900 g) loaf tin.

11 oz (310 g) potatoes,peeled, cooked and sieved
6 eggs, separated
7 oz (200 g) sugar
Grated peel of a lemon
A pinch of cinnamon
3 oz (75 g) ground hazelnuts (previously roasted and skins removed)

Beat the egg yolks into the sieved potato; add the sugar and the lemon peel, cinnamon and hazelnuts. Mix together. Whisk the egg whites until stiff and fold into the cake mixture.

Pour into the prepared tin and cook at gas mark 6/400°F/200°C for 35 minutes.

*"Though the potato is an excellent root, deserving to be brought into general use, yet it seems not likely that the use of it should ever be normal in the country."*

*From **The Case of the Labourers in Husbandry** by David Davies, 1795.*

## 5 DECEMBER

# POTATO SANDERS

This is based on a recipe of Mrs Beeton's that might be termed a curiosity rather than an irresistible dish. My husband likes to eat these with a spicy chutney or a little, sharp-tasting salad.

1 lb (450 g) potatoes, peeled and boiled
A little flour
Salt
A handful of breadcrumbs soaked in water
4 oz (110 g) mushrooms
1/2 onion chopped and soaked in boiling water
A handful of chopped herbs including parsley
1 egg yolk

Dry the boiled potatoes. Purée and, while they are still warm, work in sufficient flour to make a pliable dough. Roll it out and cut in squares.

Squeeze the bread dry, mix with the other ingredients except the egg and put a little of this mixture in each square. Roll up like a small sausage.

Brush with the beaten egg and bake at gas mark 6/400°F/200°C for about 20 minutes. Serve very hot.

*A 'hot potato' is a slang term for a situation that is difficult to handle. In the United Stated a 'cold potato' is a term that describes someone of few emotions.*

## 6 DECEMBER

# APPLE, SULTANA AND POTATO BAKE

I have adapted this from a recipe in Dorothy Hartley's *Food in England*, published in 1954.

1 lb (450 g) potatoes, peeled, cooked and puréed
1 oz (25 g) butter
1 teaspoon sugar
1/2 teaspoon ginger
4 oz (110 g) flour
4 medium cooking apples, peeled, cored and sliced
2 oz (50 g) sultanas
2-3 oz (50-75 g) brown sugar
1/2 teaspoon cinnamon
A knob of butter

While the potatoes are still warm, stir in the butter, sugar and ginger. Add the flour and with your hands make a soft dough. Divide into 2 halves and roll into circles. On 1 half put the apple slices and sultanas and then sprinkle with the sugar and the cinnamon.

Damp the edges of the base and cover with the remaining circle, pressing the edges well down together. Make a large X in the top and bake at gas mark 7/425°F/220°C for 15 minutes. When you take the pie out of the oven make a hole in the centre and put in a knob of butter before serving.

*A recipe first published in **The Perfect Cook**, 1656, marries potatoes with dates and grapes in chicken stock, seasoned with cinnamon and baked under shortcrust pastry.*

## 7 DECEMBER

# CHEESE PUFF POTATOES

The scrunch of the almost raw onion inside melting little clouds of cheese and potato is simple perfection.

1 lb (450 g) potatoes, peeled, cooked and puréed
4 oz (110 g) Gruyère cheese, grated
1 medium onion, diced
3 eggs, separated
4 fl oz (110 ml) milk
Sea salt and freshly ground black pepper
2 oz (50 g) plain flour

Stir the cheese, the onion, the egg yolks, the milk, seasoning and flour into the potato purée.

Beat the egg whites until stiff and fold into the potato mixture. Heat the oil in a wide frying pan and cook tablespoons of the mixture until barely golden. Eat at once.

*"Take away your mashed potatoes*
*Leave them in the desert to dry*
*Take away your mashed potatoes*
*You look like shepherd's pie."*
*From* ***Giving Potatoes*** *by Adrian Mitchell.*

## 8 DECEMBER

# POTATO CHESTNUTS

Chestnuts - not roasting by an open fire, but mashed potato masquerading as chestnuts. This is more of a game for children than a food, but the crisp and just-sweet little balls provide a treat during a long winter's evening.

8 oz (225 g) very floury potatoes, peeled, cooked and mashed
1 egg yolk, beaten
1 tablespoon honey

Once the potato mash is cool enough to handle - and it must be a very dry mash - roll into little chestnut-sized balls.

Combine the egg yolk and the honey and turn the balls in this so they are well coated. Put on a greased baking tray and cook in a hot oven, gas mark 7/425°F/220°C for about 10 minutes until well browned.

*In 1769, the parish priest of Saint-Roch in Paris decided to give his flock an economical potato soup. People were so suspicious of the vegetable that when the recipe was published in Dijon in 1772 it was euphemistically called 'Economy Rice Soup'.*

9 DECEMBER

# POTATO AND MUSSEL SOUP

Frozen mussels could be used for this soup but the result will be inferior. Use fresh mussels if possible.

1 lb (450 g) potatoes, peeled and cut into chunks
1 3/4 pint (1 litre) mussels
2 cloves garlic, chopped
1 tablespoon olive oil
1 oz (25 g) butter
Chopped parsley

Cook the potatoes, barely covered in salted water, until soft. Put through a sieve with the cooking water. Meanwhile, prepare the mussels by scrubbing, scraping and trimming. Cook the garlic in the oil for a few minutes. Add the mussels and cook, covered, over a high flame. As soon as the shells open (discard any that don't) remove from the pan. Scoop the mussels from the shells.

Sieve the cooking liquid from the mussels into the potato mixture. You may need to add a little water to achieve a thick soup consistency. Add the mussels, heat and at the last moment stir in the butter. Sprinkle with chopped parsley.

*When the potato was first introduced into Denmark in the 18th century, the Danes, unsure of this new vegetable, served it as a dessert, hot and salted in a napkin.*

10 DECEMBER

# BAKED POTATO WITH LOBSTER

The poet Roger McGough calls potatoes 'the soil's little lobsters'.

2 very large potatoes, cleaned
$^1/_4$ pint (150 ml) cream
2 oz (50 g) butter
Sea salt and freshly ground black pepper
2 just cooked lobsters
Rocket leaves

Bake the potatoes and when tender, cut in half and scoop out the flesh. Keep the shells warm. Mix the potato insides with the cream, butter and seasonings until you have a very smooth purée.

Divide the purée between the 4 shells and give each person half a potato, covered with slices of lobster flesh. Serve on a bed of rocket leaves, barely flavoured with a good oil, and surrounded with the claw meat.

*In the film **Close Encounters of the Third Kind** the hero solved a world-threatening problem whilst eating a plate of mashed potatoes.*

11 DECEMBER

# POTATO PANCAKE WITH FRUIT

Based on a recipe given to me by *An Bord Glas,* Ireland's Horticultural Development Board, this is more panbake than pancake. It goes well with chicken dishes.

1 lb (450 g) potatoes, peeled, cooked and puréed
2 oz (50 g) butter

1 egg yolk
4 oz (110 g) plain flour, sifted
1 teaspoon salt
10 fl oz (275 ml) fromage frais
1 lb (450 g) fruit - peaches, pears or apples

Rub the butter round a 9-inch flan tin. Stir the egg yolk into the potato purée and then add the flour, salt and finally the fromage frais.

Cut the fruit into thin slices and arrange on the base of the tin. Cover with the potato mixture and bake for 25 minutes at gas mark 5/375°F/190°C. The tin may then be inverted onto a serving plate so the fruit is served uppermost.

*Extravagant claims have been made down the years for the remedial benefits of potatoes. Warts, rheumatism, sore throats, infected wounds are just a few of the conditions that the vegetable is said to cure.*

12 DECEMBER

# POTATO PUNTS

Said to have been invented as a late-night antidote to alcohol at a New York restaurant called Simon's, these herbed potato balls were served in fried skins with a drink.

2 large potatoes
Vegetable oil
2 oz (50 g) butter
Dried rosemary
Sea salt and freshly ground black pepper

Prick the skins of the potatoes and lightly rub with oil. Bake in a hot oven until tender and then allow to cool. Cut the potatoes in half and scoop out the insides with a melon scoop.

Fry the skins in the oil until crisp, rub each half inside with 1/2 oz (15 g) butter per potato, sprinkle with rosemary and keep warm. Fry the little potato balls and serve at once in the shells, sprinkling a little salt and pepper on each.

*"This root, no matter how you prepare it, is tasteless and floury. It cannot pass for an agreeable food; but it supplies a food sufficiently abundant and sufficiently healthy for men who ask only to sustain themselves...The potato is blamed and with reason, for its windiness; but what is a question of wind to the virile organs of the peasant and workers...an Egyptian fruit whose cultivation may possibly have some value in the colonies."*

*From **L'Encyclopedie** by Diderot, 1746.*

13 DECEMBER

# SAUTÉED GINGER POTATOES

This would have to be in my top 10 favourite ways with the potato. Fresh ginger is essential.

2 lb (900 g) potatoes, peeled and thickly sliced
3 tablespoons olive oil
1 oz (25 g) butter
3 large cloves garlic, chopped
2 inch (5 cm ) fresh root ginger, peeled and chopped
3 teaspoons ground cumin
4 teaspoons caraway seeds
Sea salt and freshly ground black pepper
Chopped parsley

Steam or boil the potatoes until they are just tender. Heat the oil and butter together, stir in the garlic and ginger, cumin and the caraway seeds. Stir around for a few minutes.

Add the potatoes and move them around so they are generously coated. Sauté until browned and then sprinkle with salt and pepper and parsley.

*"The boiling of a potato has long been considered one of the tests by which the merits of a cook be decided. 'Can she cook a chop, and boil a potato?' is often the modest query of pater familias in England, and in nine cases out of ten you may wager your best hat that she can do neither."*

*From **Culinary Jottings of Madras** by 'Wyvern,' 1878.*

14 DECEMBER

# PETITES TIMBALES DE POMMES DE TERRE À LA HENRI HOCQUARD

I discovered this recipe in *The Gentle Art of Cookery*. The authors, Mrs C.F. Leyel and Miss Olga Hartley, claim it was brought home from the Sudan by the head cook on the French man-of-war, Justine. Few people have access to white currant jelly; a tart apple jelly would do instead.

12 oz (350 g) potatoes, cooked and puréed
3 fl oz (75 ml) cream
Sea salt
2 egg whites

For the sauce:
4 tablespoons redcurrant jelly
4 tablespoons white currant jelly
A liqueur glassful of maraschino

Stir the cream and salt into the potato purée. Add the egg whites beaten to a stiff froth. Divide between 8 well-buttered timbale moulds and cook at gas mark 6/400°F/200°C for 20 minutes.

Melt the fruit jellies together and add the maraschino. When the timbales are cooked turn them out and serve with the sauce poured over them.

*Castilian mercenaries fighting in Germany during the 30 Years' War began carrying potatoes as provisions for horses and, in dire circumstances, for themselves.*

## 15 DECEMBER

# POTATO AND CARAWAY BREAD

This will make 2 loaves and needs 2 'proving' periods.

5 oz (150 g) potatoes, baked and sieved
1 teaspoon dried yeast
2 tablespoons warm water
1 heaped tablespoon coarse salt
$^1/_2$ pint (275 ml) buttermilk
1 lb (450 g) strong flour
1 level teaspoon caraway seed

Stir the yeast in the warm water and leave for 10 minutes. Add the salt to the buttermilk and stir until dissolved. Blend in the hot sieved potato with a fork until it resembles coarse meal. Sift the flour and sprinkle over the caraway seeds and add potato and buttermilk mixture and yeast. Knead well. This can be done in a food processor.

Leave the dough to rise in a warm place, covered with a clean cloth, until doubled in size. Punch it down and knead again. Put the dough in 2 loaf tins, cover again and leave to rise for a second time.

Cook at gas mark 6/400°F/200°C for 40 minutes.

*The potato plant was called 'the lazy root' and 'the root of misery' by the Irish poet Dr Drennan (1754-1820).*

## 16 DECEMBER

## POSADAS (NATIVITY, MEXICO)

# MEXICAN POTATOES

Full-blooded food, a complete meal in itself, the ingredients of this can be varied according to what you have available, but the chilli peppers are integral.

2 lb (900 g) potatoes, peeled
6 slices bacon

4 hard boiled eggs, sliced
3 tablespoons olive oil, extra virgin
1 fat onion, chopped
3-4 tablespoons tomato purée
2 red chilli peppers
1 teaspoon cumin
Sea salt and freshly ground black pepper
4 oz (110 g) cheese

Cook the potatoes in lightly salted water until just tender. Slice them in half and lay cut-side down on an ovenproof dish. Have the bacon slices lightly grilled and lay on top, together with the eggs.

In a heavy pan, warm the olive oil and sauté the onion for a few minutes. Add the other ingredients, except the cheese and cook for about 10 minutes. Pour over the potatoes and cover with thin slices of cheese. Melt under the grill and eat.

*Although Mexico is rich in various species of wild tuber-bearing solanums, it was not until after the Spanish Conquest that potatoes were imported from Peru for cultivation.*

17 DECEMBER

# POTATOES WITH SMOKED BACON AND PRUNES

The smokiness of the bacon combined with the sweetness of the fruit produces a magical result. Apples, pears or apricots can be substituted for the prunes. This is lovely with a dish of chicken livers and leeks, both quickly fried in butter. The amount given below will feed 6 people.

2 lb (900 g) potatoes, peeled and sliced
2 oz (50 g) sugar
4 oz (110 g) prunes, stoned
12 oz (350 g) smoked bacon, diced
2 cloves garlic, chopped
2-2$^{1}/_{2}$ pints (1 -1.4 litres) good meat stock

Put the sugar in a heavy pan and leave it over a slow heat to caramelise - try not to stir until the last moment. Turn the dried fruit in this and remove from the heat.

Sauté the bacon and add to the dried fruit. Add the potatoes with the garlic and cover with the stock. Bring to the boil and then put into a casserole dish and cook, uncovered, in a moderate oven, gas mark 6/400°F/200°C for about 45 minutes or until the potatoes are cooked through and the sauce is a rich brown.

*"The brave Walter Raleigh*
*Queen Bess's own knight*
*Brought here from Virginia*
*The root of delight.*
*By him it was planted*
*At Youghal so gay;*
*An' sure Munster praties*
*Are famed to this day."*

***Popular Songs of Ireland*** *by Crofton Croker, 1886.*

18 DECEMBER

# POTATO BRIOCHE WITH GINGER

This would make a perfect breakfast for Christmas morning - or any other morning. Served with home-made jam or honey it makes an elegant and unusual start to a day. It will freeze well for a short time (2 weeks or so).

1$^1/_2$ lb (700 g) potatoes, peeled
1$^1/_2$ lb (700 g) plain flour
1 teaspoon ginger
2 sachets (approx. 50 g) active dry yeast,
4 oz (110 g) butter
2 oz (50 g) caster sugar
2 eggs
1 teaspoon salt
2 tablespoons water
Icing sugar

Boil the potatoes and put them through a sieve. Allow to cool. Sift the flour with the ginger and mix with the potato. (You can, at this stage, put the mixture into a food processor which takes away all the hard work). Sprinkle in the yeast, then rub in the butter.

Add the sugar, the eggs, the salt and the water and knead until a silky elasticity is achieved. Put in a clean bowl, cover with a clean cloth and leave until the mixture has doubled in size.

Punch down the mixture and knead again briefly. Put in a greased round cake tin, and leave to prove again until the dough reaches the top of the tin. Cook at gas mark 7/425°F/220°C for about 40 minutes (watching the top doesn't burn - you may need to turn down the heat after 20 minutes or so). Turn out and when still warm, sprinkle with icing sugar and eat.

*"She delicately moved the potato dish so as to cover the traces of a bygone egg, and her glance lingered on the flies that dragged their way across a melting mound of salt butter. 'I like local colour but I don't care for it on the tablecloth.' "*

*From* ***Some Experiences of an Irish R.M.*** *by Somerville and Ross, 1899.*

### 19 DECEMBER

# HOT GERMAN POTATO SALAD

Serve this with a few salad leaves dressed with a sharp vinaigrette.

1 1/2 lb (700 g) potatoes, cleaned and thickly sliced
1 small onion, diced
1 tablespoon sugar
1 tablespoon flour
1/4 pint (150 ml) water
1 tablespoon French or German mustard
1/4 pint (150 ml) white wine vinegar
1 egg
A little milk
Chopped parsley or chervil

Put the potatoes on to boil or steam and put the onion in a wide bowl. Make the dressing by mixing together the sugar and flour with 1 tablespoon of the water. Stir in the mustard and then the rest of the water and vinegar.

Bring to the boil and simmer for 5 minutes. Remove from the heat and stir in the egg. When the potatoes are cooked put them on top of the onions and pour over the sauce. Sprinkle with the chopped herbs and serve.

*"Mr. East gave a feast*
*Mr. North laid the cloth*
*Mr. West did his best*
*Mr. South burnt his mouth*
*While eating a cold potato."*

## 20 DECEMBER

# CRANBERRY PUDDING

The cranberry is said to have got its name from the cranes that feed off the berries. It seems a pity that cranberries make such a short appearance in the year, ending up as a sauce and little else. The following pudding is a novel way of presenting them. You can substitute cranberries with huckleberries, but you'll have to grow them yourself.

6 oz (175 g) potatoes, cleaned, cooked and puréed
1/2 oz (15 g) butter
1 lb (450 g) cranberries
7 oz (200 g) caster sugar
1/2 teaspoon ground cinnamon
3 eggs
1 tablespoon icing sugar

Spread the butter over the base of a 2-pint (1.1 litre) shallow, ovenproof dish. In a saucepan, gently heat the cranberries and 4 oz (110 g) of the caster sugar together for 5 minutes. Stir in the cinnamon and spoon into the prepared dish.

Separate the eggs and, in a bowl whisk the yolks with the remaining sugar until light and fluffy. Beat in the potato purée and continue beating for 1 minute.

In a clean bowl, whip the egg whites until they make soft peaks, then fold into the potato mixture. Pour over the cranberries and level the top.

Bake in the centre of the oven heated to gas mark 5/375°F/190°C for about 30 minutes until risen and a golden brown. Dust with the icing sugar and serve with cream or custard.

*The aphrodisiac qualities of the potato (once called The Apple of Love) were believed in the 19th century to account for the population explosion in Ireland.*

## 21 DECEMBER

# FRUIT SAVARIN

A savarin is a cake made with yeast that is soaked in syrup with rum or kirsch added. This elegant yeast ring takes a little time to make but the result, both visual and tastewise, is well worth the effort.

5 oz (150 g) potatoes, cleaned, cooked and sieved
3 teaspoons tepid water
2 teaspoons dried yeast
2 oz (50 g) butter
5 oz (150 g) plain flour
A pinch of salt
1 oz (25 g) caster sugar
3 eggs
2 oz (50 g) glacé cherries
2 oz (50 g) chopped mixed peel

Measure the water into a jug, add the dried yeast and mix to a smooth paste. Leave in a warm place for 10 minutes until risen and frothy. Melt the butter and cool.

Sift the flour and salt into a bowl and stir in the sugar. Add the yeast mixture and eggs and beat thoroughly. Beat in the butter and potato until smooth and elastic, then cover bowl with a clean cloth and leave to rise in a warm place until doubled in size. Lightly oil a 2 1/2 pint (1.4 litre) ring tin. Chop the glacé cherries and beat into the risen mixture with the mixed peel. Pour the mixture into the ring tin, then cover with oiled polythene and leave to double in size in a warm place. Set the oven at gas mark 7/425°F/220°C and bake for 30-40 minutes until golden brown. Cool on rack.

To make the syrup: Measure 2 oz (50 g) granulated sugar with 1/4 pint (150 ml) water and heat gently until dissolved. Simmer for 5 minutes. Remove from heat and stir in 3 tablespoons of rum. Stand the savarin on a plate and pour over syrup while warm.

To finish, rub 4 tablespoons apricot jam through a sieve into a pan, add 1 tablespoon water and heat. Brush the savarin with this and decorate with glacé fruits and angelica.

*'Smiling Murphies' was the name given to fat floury potatoes that burst their skins when they were cooked.*

## 22 DECEMBER
# MINCE PIES

The following recipe uses a large proportion of butter and makes wonderful mince pies.

2 1/2 oz (65 g) potatoes, cleaned, cooked and puréed
4 oz (110 g) self-raising flour
1/2 teaspoon salt
6 oz (175 g) butter
1 teaspoon cold water
Mincemeat for filling
Icing sugar

Sift the flour and salt into the potato and rub in the butter with your fingertips. Bind with the water, wrap in cling film and put in the fridge for an hour.

Roll out the pastry on a floured board and make the mince pies in the normal way. Cook for 12-15 minutes at gas mark 6/400°F/200°C. Dust with sifted icing sugar before serving.

*"I appreciate the potato only as a protection against famine, except for that I know of nothing more eminently tastleless".*

*From* ***La Physiologie de Goût, 1825*** *by Brillat-Savarin, 1825.*

## 23 DECEMBER

# APPLE AND POTATO PURÉE

The apples, in this recipe, are incorporated into the potato. Pears can be substituted for the apples. This purée makes a good accompaniment to duck, goose or a roast of pork. You can add a little sugar, but it is not necessary. I sometimes add a little lemon juice.

1 lb (450 g) potatoes, peeled and boiled
1 lb (450 g) apples
4 oz (110 g) butter
8 fl oz (225 ml) milk
Breadcrumbs

Cut the unpeeled apples into pieces, put into a pan with 2 oz (50 g) of the butter and cook very gently until the apples are soft. Put through a sieve. Meanwhile, boil the potatoes. Drain and stir into the cooked apples.

Warm the milk and stir in and add 1 oz (25 g) of the butter. Turn the breadcrumbs round in a pan with the remaining 1 oz (25 g) of butter until they are crisp. Strew over the purée and serve.

*"The potato is the true root of scarcity which promises to set Famine at defiance. The poorer sort of people dine and sup chiefly on potatoes, in the season of them. But those that are in a state of servitude (i.e. those who are fed in their employer's house) are commonly above eating potatoes."*

*From **The Statistical Account of Scotland**, 1797.*

## 24 DECEMBER
## CHRISTMAS EVE
# POTATO STUFFING FOR ROAST GOOSE

Potato makes a fine stuffing for poultry and meat as well as goose.

1 lb (450 g) potatoes, peeled
1 oz (25 g) butter
1 small onion, chopped
3 tablespoons chopped parsley
1/2 teaspoon chopped marjoram
Sea salt and freshly ground black pepper
Grated rind of a lemon
1 large Bramley apple, chopped
2 heaped tablespoons chopped celery
1 beaten egg

Boil or steam the potatoes and make a very dry purée. Add the butter and then all the other ingredients, leaving the beaten egg until last. Place the stuffing when cold into the goose and roast as normal.

*"Oh my corrugated lover*
*So creamy and so brown*
*Let us fly across to Lyons*
*And lay our tubers down."*
*From* ***Giving Potatoes*** *by Adrian Mitchell.*

## 25 DECEMBER
## CHRISTMAS DAY
# CHRISTMAS PUDDING

Lindsey Bareham, in her excellent *In Praise of the Potato*, gives this recipe which will make two 1 lb (450 g) or one 2 lb (900 g) puddings. These will, of course, have been made some time before Christmas Day.

4 oz (110 g) dry puréed potato
2 eggs
4 oz (110 g) shredded suet or melted butter
4 oz (110 g) flour
1 small carrot, grated
1 small apple, peeled and grated
1 lb (450 g) mixed dried fruit
1 tablespoon marmalade
4 oz (110 g) brown sugar
1 tablespoon golden syrup or black treacle
8 tablespoons ale, beer, stout, brandy or whisky
1 teaspoon each mixed spice, cinnamon, almond essence and lemon essence

Cream the eggs with the butter or mix with the suet, stir in the sifted flour and, when the mixture is smooth, the potatoes. Add all the other ingredients and continue mixing until the pudding seems well integrated. Butter two 1lb (450 g), or one 2 lb (900 g) pudding bowls, fill with the mixture, cover with foil and a pudding cloth and steam for a minimum of 6 hours and 2 more hours on Christmas Day.

*"One side of the potato-pits was white with frost -*
*How wonderful that was, how wonderful!*
*And when we put our ears to the paling-post*
*The music that came out was magical."*
*From* ***A Christmas Childhood*** *by Patrick Kavanagh.*

## 26 DECEMBER
## ST STEPHEN'S DAY (BOXING DAY)
# POTATO, HAM AND TURKEY CHOWDER

You can fiddle around with the ingredients according to how much turkey and ham you have left over.

1 lb (450 g) potatoes peeled and diced
1 pint (570 ml) turkey or chicken stock

1 onion, sliced
Sea salt and freshly ground black pepper
4 oz (110 g) frozen peas
4 oz (110 g) sweetcorn
1 pint (570 ml) milk
8 oz (225 g) cooked turkey, finely diced
8 oz (225 g) cooked ham, finely diced

Cook a third of the potatoes in the stock with the onion and when tender, add the seasonings. Purée in a food processor or put through a sieve.

Return to a clean pan and add the remaining vegetables and milk. Simmer until they are cooked. Add the cooked turkey and ham and heat for a further 5 minutes.

*"I applied my nails to divesting the potato of its coat, and my hostess urged the frequent use of the milk, saying 'It was provided on purpose for you and you must take it.' It must be remembered that a sup of sweet milk among the poor in Ireland, is as much a rarity as a slice of plum-pudding in a farmhouse in America."*

*From **The Bible in Ireland** by Asenath Nicholson, c. 1840.*

27 DECEMBER

# LEEK AND POTATO CAKES

This is a lovely way of cooking leeks and potatoes. Elegant in presentation, in taste perfection, with its crisp outside contrasting with the butter and leek filling. The goose fat is a fairly essential part of this dish but a substitute could be used with say, chicken fat. Nonetheless, to have these little cakes it is worth buying a goose.

1 lb (450 g) potatoes
3 leeks, cleaned and thinly sliced
2 oz (50 g) butter
Sea salt and freshly ground black pepper
Goose fat

Soften the leeks in butter. Season well. Peel the potatoes and grate them. Wash them well in a sieve and dry in a clean tea towel.

Heat the goose fat and using half the potato, press four flat little rounds of potato into the pan. Put a layer of leeks on each round, then cover with a further layer of potatoes. Cook over a fairly high heat until golden on each side of the cakes.

*"Her locks had been so frequently and so drastically brightened and curled that to caress them, one felt, would be rather like running one's fingers through julienne potatoes."*
*From* ***The Collected Dorothy Parker****.*

## 28 DECEMBER
# CANDIED POTATOES

I'm not sure when one would eat these potatoes - perhaps with cold meat or just on their own. This is a very old recipe and popular in the 19th century but it would not be to everybody's taste.

1 1/2 lb (700 g) potatoes, peeled and thinly sliced
3 oz (75 g) butter
Sea salt and freshly ground black pepper
4 fl oz (110 ml) Madeira or sweet sherry
1 oz (25 g) dark brown sugar

Melt the butter in a frying pan and brown the potatoes in this, turning them frequently. Put them in an ovenproof dish in layers, seasoning as you do so. Pour over the Madeira or sherry and cover with wet greaseproof paper. Bake at gas mark 4/350°F/180°C for 45 minutes. Uncover, sprinkle with the sugar and cook for another 15 minutes.

*A raw potato rubbed onto a frozen windscreen is said to de-ice it.*

## 29 DECEMBER
# POTATO GINGERBREAD

This cake will keep quite well but I suggest you eat it fresh, cut into little squares.

3 oz (75 g) peeled and grated raw potato
5 oz (150 g) wholemeal flour
1 level teaspoon baking powder
1 level teaspoon ground ginger
1 level teaspoon mixed spice
A pinch of salt
1 tablespoon chopped candied peel
2 oz (50 g) sultanas
2 oz (50 g) butter or margarine
4 tablespoons syrup, honey or treacle
1 egg
1 teaspoon bicarbonate of soda

Mix the flour, baking powder, ginger, spice and salt. Add the potato and dried fruit. Melt the butter or margarine and syrup and stir into the flour together with the beaten egg. Add the soda dissolved in 1 tablespoon water.

Pour into a prepared greased and lined cake tin (approx. 9x5 inch) and bake in a moderate oven, gas mark 4/350°F/180°C for 45 minutes.

*One of the first recorded encounters by Europeans with the potato was written during the 1530s by Juan de Castellanos. He wrote: "Plants with...scanty flowers of a dull purple colour and floury roots, of good flavour, a gift very acceptable to Indians and a dainty dish even for Spaniards."*

## 30 DECEMBER

# POTATOES À LA LANDAISE

The first time I ever cooked a goose, the large bowl of fat that resulted filled me with horror. How to get rid of it? To my shame I let it go cold, wrapped it in newspaper and threw it away. Now I'd rather have the fat than the goose. Here it is an integral part of this French farmhouse kitchen dish.

1½ lb (700 g) potatoes, cut in large dice
Goose fat

2 large onions
Sea salt and freshly ground black pepper
6 oz (175 g) ham
1 fat clove garlic, chopped
Chopped parsley

Warm the fat and brown the onions and the ham in this. Add the potatoes, season and cook with a lid on the pan, frequently stirring until the potatoes are soft.

Before serving, add the garlic and the parsley. Eat with a large slice of crusty bread with which you can clean the plate.

*"A diet that consists predominantly of rice leads to the use of opium, just as a diet which consists predominantly of potatoes leads to the use of liquor."*

*Nietzche, c. 1880.*

## 31 DECEMBER
## NEW YEAR'S EVE
# POTATO DIET

I make no claim for this diet. It comes from a Scandinavian health clinic and it is based on potato water only. It is said that not only do you loose weight but you have a beauty treatment, resulting in a soft, smooth and supple skin. If you are in good health, 24 hours on it would, at least, give your stomach a rest after the Yuletide binge.

Boil about 2 lb (900 g) well-scrubbed potatoes in approximately $2^1/_2$ pints (1.4 litres) of water. The actual duration of boiling should only be about 5-6 minutes, by which time all the natural goodness - Vitamin C and starch will have been extracted into the water.

The water is then allowed to cool and, before drinking it, finely chopped parsley or some other herb can be added for flavour. The $2^1/_2$ pints (1.4 litres) should be equalled out to last a day and nothing else consumed at all.

*"We praise all the flowers that we fancy*
*Sip the nectar of fruit ere they're peeled*
*Ignoring the common old tater,*
*When, in fact, he's King of the Field.*
*Let us show the old boy we esteem him*
*Sort of dig him up out of the mud;*
*Let us show him he shares our affections*
*And crown him with glory - King Spud."*

# INDEX